"The book titled *Psychoanalytic Perspectives on the Films of Ingmar Bergman: From Freud to Lacan and Beyond*, edited by Vanessa Sinclair, represents a particularly interesting contribution considering Ingmar Bergman's works. Through well-conducted Freudian-Lacanian analyses, the authors involved in the work presented new perspectives increasing the psychodynamic impact of Bergman's pieces. In particular, some specific themes as in the case of perversion, neurosis, psychosis, ethics, and sexuality, as well as literary references, are read through the above-mentioned lens in order to establish deep contacts with clinical and dynamic emergencies. As a valuable contribution, the book proposes relevant perspectives from high-level professionals, providing for a clear and considerable view of psychoanalytical impact and valour."

Emanuele Maria Merlo, PhD, Clinical Psychologist;
Contract Professor of Clinical Psychology for the Department
of Human and Pediatric Pathology "Gaetano Barresi" and the
Department of Cognitive Sciences, Education and Cultural Studies
of the University of Messina; Freudian-Lacanian psychoanalytic
approach; Clinical Advisor for Software Engineering Italia

"Ingmar Bergman is acknowledged as one of the world's greatest filmmakers. Vanessa Sinclair has assembled a wide-ranging and stimulating volume of essays by psychoanalysts, scholars and filmmakers that for the first time focuses on ways in which psychoanalysis from Freud to Lacan and beyond can help illuminate Bergman's films. Life, death, identity, sexual and family relationships come under fascinating psychoanalytical scrutiny in discussions of Bergman's dreamlike art. This is a volume that will be essential reading for anyone seriously interested both in Bergman's films and in cinema's potential for the exploration of creativity, denial and desire."

Peter William Evans, Emeritus Professor of Film,
Queen Mary University of London

Psychoanalytic Perspectives on the Films of Ingmar Bergman

Psychoanalytic Perspectives on the Films of Ingmar Bergman presents a contemporary Freudian-Lacanian assessment of this classic director. This collection is the first to bring together this unique psychological perspective on Bergman's work.

While Bergman and his films have been written about throughout the decades, until now there has not been a collection anthologizing Freudian-Lacanian perspectives on his work. Vanessa Sinclair brings together an international community of scholars and practicing psychoanalysts – some of whom are also filmmakers – to reflect on Bergman's films, life, and work in philosophical, historical, and cultural contexts. They assess individual films in depth, compare multiple films, and focus on Bergman's life and work in a cultural context. This book includes chapters on seminal films including *Persona* and *The Silence*.

Psychoanalytic Perspectives on the Films of Ingmar Bergman will be essential reading for academics and students of film studies, psychoanalytic theory, and Lacan, and of great interest to psychoanalysts and psychotherapists.

Vanessa Sinclair, PsyD is a psychoanalyst based in Vimmerby, Sweden. Dr. Sinclair is Senior Research Fellow at Global Centre for Advanced Studies (GCAS) – Dublin, founding member of Das Unbehagen: A Free Association for Psychoanalysis – New York, and the host of Rendering Unconscious Podcast.

Psychoanalytic Perspectives on the Films of Ingmar Bergman

From Freud to Lacan and Beyond

Edited by Vanessa Sinclair

Routledge
Taylor & Francis Group
LONDON AND NEW YORK

Cover image: Cover image copyright © AB Svensk Filmindustri (1966)
Photo: Sven Nykvist

First published 2023
by Routledge
4 Park Square, Milton Park, Abingdon, Oxon OX14 4RN

and by Routledge
605 Third Avenue, New York, NY 10158

Routledge is an imprint of the Taylor & Francis Group, an informa business

British Library Cataloguing-in-Publication Data
A catalogue record for this book is available from the British Library

ISBN: 9781032060064 (hbk)
ISBN: 9781032060071 (pbk)
ISBN: 9781003200246 (ebk)

DOI: 10.4324/9781003200246

Typeset in Times New Roman
by Deanta Global Publishing Services, Chennai, India

Dedicated to
Liv Ullmann

Contents

Notes on Contributors

Carl Abrahamsson is a Swedish author, publisher, and filmmaker. His books include *Codex Nordica* (2022), *Different People* (2021), *The Devil's Footprint* (2020), *Mother, Have a Safe Trip* (2016), and *The Fenris Wolf* series. His films include *My Silent Lips* (2019), *Lunacy* (2017), *Sub Umbra Alarum Luna* (2016), and the *An Art Apart* series. His publishing company is Trapart Books, Films, and Editions.

Walter A. Davis is Professor Emeritus, Ohio State University, USA. He is an actor and playwright, as well as a psychoanalyst and theoretician. His many books include *Art and Politics: Psychoanalysis, Ideology, Theatre* (2007), *Death's Dream Kingdom: The American Psyche Since 9-11* (2006), *Get the Guests: Psychoanalysis, Modern American Drama, and the Audience* (1993), and *Inwardness and Existence: Subjectivity in/and Hegel, Heidegger, Marx, and Freud* (1989).

Peter Jansson is a psychoanalyst and psychotherapist, who has his practice in Gothenburg, Sweden. He is also a philosopher and a writer. He has written a book about Swedish writer and poet, Karin Boye. He is also in the final phase of a larger book about Polish filmmaker Krzysztof Kieślowski, and in the future he will write a book about Italian painter Caravaggio.

Pablo Lerner is a psychologist from Gothenburg, Sweden, residing in Paris, France, offering psychoanalytic psychotherapies in private practice. He is the editor of the anthology *Freud och dödsdriften* (2021), and is currently working on a book entitled *Speculating on the Edge of Psychoanalysis: Rings and Voids*, which deals with the status of the void in Lacan's psychoanalysis and sheds new light on phenomena such as creation, poetry, solitude, grief, mysticism, clinical structures, and the poetic art of interpretation.

Elisabeth Punzi, PhD, is a licensed psychologist and lecturer at the Department of Psychology at Gothenburg University (GU), Sweden. She leads a project concerning heritage and health at the Centre for Critical Heritage Studies, GU, and teaches psychoanalytic theory, psychology of religion, and qualitative research methods, among other topics. Her research concerns clinical practice, critical psychology/psychiatry, and the importance of expressive arts for health and recovery, as well as Jewish identity, heritage, and congregational life.

Andrea Sabbadini is a Fellow of the British Psychoanalytical Society. He works in private practice in London, is an Honorary Senior Lecturer at UCL, a Consultant to the IPA in Culture Committee, and founder and former Director of the European Psychoanalytic Film Festival (EPFF). His books include *Boundaries and Bridges: Perspectives on Time and Space in Psychoanalysis* (2014) and *Moving Images: Psychoanalytic Reflections on Film* (2014). His edited books include *Even Paranoids Have Enemies* (1998), *The Couch and the Silver Screen* (2003), *Projected Shadows* (2007), and *Psychoanalytic Perspectives on Virtual Intimacy and Communication in Film* (2019), all published by Routledge.

Robert Samuels, PhD, is Lecturer in Advanced Writing at the University of California, Santa Barbara, USA. He holds doctorates in Psychoanalysis and English. He is the author of more than a dozen books, including *Viral Rhetoric: Psychoanalysis, Philosophy and Politics after Covid-19* (2021), *Generation X and the Rise of the Entertainment Subject* (2021), *Freud for the Twenty-First Century* (2019), *Psychoanalyzing the Politics of the New Brain Sciences* (2017), *Psychoanalyzing the Left and Right after Donald Trump* (2016), and *Why Public Higher Education Should Be Free* (2013).

Patrick Scanlon, PhD, focuses his writing, performance, and film on the composition of attention – that catalog of shapes and movements through which it gathers, disperses, and sustains. This research is concentrated most cogently in the book proposal *Fastened from the Start: Inquiry and the Poetics of Attention.* His films – *Surface Copernicus* and *Solar Somnium: Kepler from the Cusp* – refigure the astronomical and optical projects of the early modern astronomers to examine the more settled matters of attention's firmament. A work somewhat in kind is the essay "Lacan : Kepler : Freud : Copernicus" found in *Rendering Unconscious: Psychoanalytic Perspectives, Politics & Poetry* (2019) edited by Vanessa Sinclair. Most immediate is the project *Imaginal Figures: From Magic to Method*, for which the imaginal realm and its coterie of beings are explored according to their methodological status, rather than existentially. Scanlon received a PhD from Columbia University, USA, and MFA from the Jack Kerouac School at Naropa, USA. He currently lives in New York City.

Vanessa Sinclair, PsyD is a psychoanalyst based in Sweden, who sees analysands internationally. She is Senior Research Fellow at Global Centre for Advanced Studies (GCAS) and the host of Rendering Unconscious Podcast. Her books include *The Pathways of the Heart* (2021), *Outsider Inpatient: Reflections on Art as Therapy* (2021) with Elisabeth Punzi, *Scansion in Psychoanalysis and Art: The*

Cut in Creation (2020), *Rendering Unconscious: Psychoanalytic Perspectives, Politics & Poetry* (2019), *On Psychoanalysis and Violence: Contemporary Lacanian Perspectives* (2018) with Manya Steinkoler, *The Fenris Wolf*, vol. 9 (2017) with Carl Abrahamsson, and *Switching Mirrors* (2016).

Alireza Taheri, PhD, wrote his doctoral dissertation on Nietzsche, Freud, and Lacan at the University of Cambridge, UK, under the supervision of Professor John Forrester (dissertation examiners: Professors Raymond Geuss and Renata Salecl). Presently, he does psychoanalytic work in private practice in Toronto, Canada, where he is also actively involved in teaching Lacanian theory as part of the Toronto Psychoanalytic Society's extension program. He is a permanent faculty member of HamAva Psychoanalytic Institute in Tehran, Iran, where he teaches psychoanalytic theory and practice. He is also actively engaged in writing articles on philosophy and psychoanalysis and regularly participates in international conferences. He is the book review editor of *Psychoanalytic Discourse* (an independent international journal for the clinical, theoretical, and cultural discussion of psychoanalysis). He contributed a chapter to *On Psychoanalysis and Violence: Contemporary Lacanian Perspectives* (2018) edited by Vanessa Sinclair, PsyD, and Manya Steinkoler, PhD, and is currently working on a book project entitled *Specter of Madness: Reflections on the Paradoxes of Subjectivity and the Diremptions of Modernity*.

Wayne Wapeemukwa is a Métis and Canadian filmmaker and philosopher from Vancouver, Canada (un-ceded Coast Salish territories). His debut feature film as a writer and director, *Luk'Luk'I,* premiered at TIFF, winning Best First Feature, as well as the Directors Guild of Canada's Discovery Prize. He is currently in development for his sophomore feature, *Manhunt*, while completing a PhD in Philosophy at Pennsylvania State University, where he is writing a dissertation on Métis dispossession.

Mary Wild is the creator of the PROJECTIONS lecture series at Freud Museum London, applying psychoanalysis to film interpretation. She co-hosts Projections Podcast and contributes to the Evolution of Horror Podcast.

S. Alfonso Williams is currently a Respiratory Therapist in training and former library professional. He graduated from Case Western Reserve University, USA, in 2008 with a Bachelor's in Art History and Sociology. In addition to clinical medicine and anatomy and physiology, he has intense interests in philosophy, psychoanalysis, subjectivity, (bio)semiotics, bioethics, media ecology, ethology, and peripherally related fields. Williams also has a long history in the audio-visual and fine arts. His pursuits are always focused on emphasizing discovery, exploration, and experimentation.

Foreword

Cinema: The Pervert's Chamber

Mary Wild

If we accept Slavoj Žižek's premise to be true that "cinema is the ultimate pervert art, it doesn't give you what you desire – it tells you how to desire" (Fiennes, 2006) then we must assume that the pervert's "spell" hinges on achieving suspension of disbelief.

> Subversion in cinema starts when the theatre darkens and the screen lights up. For the cinema is a place of magic where psychological and environmental factors combine to create an openness to wonder and suggestion, an unlocking of the unconscious.
>
> (Vogel, 1974, p. 9)

That's what we sign up for, to align subjective sensory phenomena exclusively with the film material; everything else is silence and darkness, nothing else matters. We believe the reality of the story with which we are presented, even if it seems implausible. As Jean-Louis Baudry writes:

> No doubt the darkened room and the screen bordered with black like a letter of condolences already present privileged conditions of effectiveness – no exchange, no circulation, no communication with any outside. Projection and reflection take place in a closed space and those who remain there, whether they know it or not (but they do not), find themselves chained, captured, or captivated.
>
> (1975, p. 44)

The paradox of surrendering to the cinema is that somehow through that submission of being instructed how to desire, we are liberated within the fantasy space.

In the pervert's chamber we have entered into a contract. When we enter the sacred space of the cinema, a certain ritual is practiced that compels us to exchange our reality for the one we are shown on the screen. This ritual has a familiar frame – there is a beginning and an end to the experience – and within this framing we allow ourselves to be vulnerable. We submit to the story on the screen and accept the reality presented to us as the ruling ideology for a finite amount of time. Suspension of disbelief is the intentional avoidance of critical thinking or logic in examining something unreal or impossible in reality, such as a work of speculative fiction, in order to believe it for the sake of enjoyment. Aristotle first explored this notion with reference to the principles of live theater; the audience disregards the unreality of fiction in order to undergo catharsis.

The poet and aesthetic philosopher Samuel Taylor Coleridge introduced the term "suspension of disbelief" in 1817, proposing that if a writer could infuse "human interest and a semblance of truth" into a grandiose tale, the reader would suspend judgment concerning the implausibility of the narrative. Coleridge sought to revive the use of whimsical features in poetry and elaborated a concept to support how a contemporary, open-minded audience might continue to appreciate such styles of literature. The term resulted from a philosophical experiment that Coleridge conducted with William Wordsworth within the context of the creation and reading of poetry. It involved an attempt to explain supernatural characters so that these creatures of imagination constitute some semblance of truth (Ferri, 2007, pp. 6–7). Coleridge also referred to his concept as "poetic faith," citing a feeling comparable to the mystical, which stirs the mind.

Psychological critic Norman Holland has provided a neuroscientific explanation for suspension of disbelief. When we hear or watch any narrative, our brains enter entirely into perceiving mode, shutting down the systems for acting or planning to act, and with them our systems for evaluating reality. We have, in Coleridge's words, "poetic faith," and so find it difficult to detect inaccuracies. Initially we believe, then have to make a concerted effort to call things into question.

Only when we stop perceiving to reflect on what we have seen or heard, do we adjudicate its truth-value. If we are really immersed in the fictional aspect, then we are, as Immanuel Kant pointed out, "disinterested" (1790, pp. 204–210). We respond aesthetically, without purpose. We do not judge the truth of what we perceive, even though if we stop being transported for a moment to think about it, we know quite well that it is fiction (Holland, 2008).

The ritual that gives rise to suspension of disbelief in the cinema depends on our acceptance of the specific terms and conditions of the movie theater experience. There are rules and etiquette, after all: no talking, no texting, no ringtone, no kicking the seat in front of us, keeping snacking to a minimum (and as quietly as possible). Entering into an imaginary world onscreen requires a certain degree of respect for our environment, trust in the process, and willingness to surrender. This is especially pertinent when we consider the subject of this book, auteur director Ingmar Bergman, whose films are "profoundly personal meditations into the myriad struggles facing the psyche and the soul" (Ankeny, 2021). This level of sensitive artistry requires and deserves a spectator's unbroken attention; it is not feasible to access the boundless beauty of Bergman's cinema outside of the sacred contract of suspension of disbelief.

The COVID-19 pandemic's impact on spectatorship has been monumental; lockdown has caused a total dominance of "small screen" viewing, at times with no option of entering into the elevated "pervert's chamber" due to cinema closures. Streaming services, Instagram stories, and TikTok video-sharing were already ubiquitous pre-pandemic, but government "stay-at-home" orders ensured an overwhelming certainty of wall-to-wall small screen supremacy. It was amusing, in the early days of quarantine, to "binge" and not feel guilty about it – there was a novelty in being congratulated for keeping our distance and self-isolating. We were doing our civic duty, staying in to save lives. Watching Netflix on the couch for eight uninterrupted hours amounted to heroism in the Spring of 2020. But the bloom was off the rose after we lost count of how many days we had stayed indoors. The decision of watching yet another episode of *The Real Housewives of Orange County* was already made for us by the streaming service – and the answer, invariably, was, "Yes, play the next episode." Somewhere in the haze of the pandemic, "doom-scrolling" became an acceptable way of life. It was no longer shameful to waste several hours on the TikTok #ForYouPage; what else was there to do? Jacques Lacan's theory of *jouissance,* that too much of something that was once enjoyable eventually becomes "painful," was, yet again, proven to be correct. All of this inescapable content, constantly available, leads, unsurprisingly, to a less-than-ideal state of affairs.

This speaks to the difference between entering a designated space designed for viewing (i.e., the cinema) for an allotted amount of time (i.e., the length of a film) and the continuous presence of the small screen(s) in our home, as we stream a show, while working on our laptop, while scrolling Instagram on our phone. Our attention is divided, and we feel fragmented, as opposed to the experience of immersing ourselves fully in the pervert's chamber of the cinema. How can we achieve suspension of disbelief in an environment full of distractions? We can't expect to enter into a trance as a worshipful audience member when there are several screens competing relentlessly for our undivided attention. The reflective potential of the ever-shrinking screen upon which we might feel compelled to negotiate an idealized external image is compromised. The power of the *mirror stage* diminishes when detail is lost in the frame – opting to watch a feature film on an iPhone is like gazing into an unclean, foggy looking glass at an unreasonable distance. We cannot expect to achieve a satisfying sense of identification under sub-par viewing conditions.

If not taken away completely, this experience is diluted in an essential way. Without the boundaries of the chamber, without the frame of the space of the cinema – the darkened room with no other distractions – we are no longer completely immersed in the filmmaker's vision. Our senses are not honed, our emotions are not overwhelmed, and we are not able to be grasped by the clutches of the film in the same way when we are home. Although the cinema is a public space, we don't have the same privacy at home. Television monitors, tablets, and handsets are simply not as intimate; when it comes to screens, size matters. The surrealist director David Lynch once lambasted young people for watching films on mobile phones. Lynch, the Renaissance man of modern American filmmaking, unquestionably triumphs the finer arts of cinema, and does so by depicting uncanny eccentricities of reality. In a clip that surfaced as an extra from a special edition release of *Inland Empire* (2006), Lynch talks about spectators who opt to stream films on their smart phones. With barely concealed contempt, he states:

> If you're playing the movie on a telephone, you will never in a trillion years experience the film ... You'll think you have experienced it, but you'll be cheated. It's such a sadness, that you think you've seen a film, on your fucking telephone. Get real.

With cinemas shut down during the COVID-19 pandemic, we have had to make do with the limits of quarantine and watch films in David Lynch's nightmare scenario: on micro-screens. All the painstaking work of creating the glittering cinematic image, as delicate as a hummingbird in mid-flight, coming to no avail as we tune in and out, distracted by loved ones, pets, phone notifications, trending topics, IGTV, Facebook feuds, breaking news, Amazon deliveries, extended toilet breaks, our messy rooms, the changing of the light, and several other open browser tabs ... these things invariably interfere, and the spell is not just broken but shattered beyond repair. Some film buffs are so enamored by, and dependent on, the "sensory deprivation" only a movie theater can offer, that no other art-form is able to transport them as effectively as the cinema. Even going to see live theater is too off-putting and obnoxious, because there are live actors performing on the stage – what if one of them forgets their line, stutters, sneezes, pauses for too long, or trips? The irritation of an extraneous variable threatening to disrupt the longed-for outcome of total captivation is a risk some cinephiles are unwilling to take. A film – ephemeral, intangible, just flickering light on a big screen in the dark, never straying from the loving vision of the director, always perfect from start to finish, in glorious print and exquisite surround sound, mesmerizing, hypnotic, transcendent – that is the unparalleled superior experience cinephiles desire so passionately.

Admittedly, not all screens need to be enormous for magic to occur. The intention is not to dismiss the positive aspects of media technology and innovative methods of creating the moving image. Technology has allowed more people than ever to be able to make motion pictures. Sean Baker's *Tangerine* (2015), for example, was shot entirely on iPhone 5S. Platforms such as YouTube and TikTok have showcased emerging talent in comedy, music, and acting, launching the careers of exciting names in performance arts. Generation Z, in particular, has become accustomed to consuming content on mobile devices regularly, multitasking happily.

But without the boundary-setting ritual and finite running time of the cinematic experience, ushering us in with velvet curtains pulling back and releasing us with end credits rolling, those of us seeking a more profound spectatorship are merely on a viewing hamster wheel with no end in sight, while never fully inhabiting any fantasy world. The small screen experience during the pandemic has been an all-you-can-eat buffet of sensory pandemonium, in which we checked our autonomy (and dignity) at the door, but for the life of us, we cannot even remember what we watched!

Bibliography

Ankeny, J. "Ingmar Bergman: Biography, movie highlights and photos." *AllMovie*. Retrieved November 4, 2021. https://www.allmovie.com/artist/ingmar-bergman -p81548

Baker, S. (Dir.) (2015). *Tangerine*. USA.

Baudry, J-L. (1975). "Ideological effects of the basic cinematographic apparatus." *Film Quarterly*, Vol. 28, No. 2 (Winter, 1974-1975), pp.39–47.

Coleridge, S.T. (1817). "Biographia literaria." In I.A. Richards (Ed.). (1950). *The Portable Coleridge*. New York: The Viking Press.

Ferri, A.J. (2007). *Willing Suspension of Disbelief: Poetic Faith in Film*. Lanham: Lexington Books. pp.6–7.

Fiennes, S. (Dir.) (2006). *The Pervert's Guide to Cinema*. UK.

Holland, N. (2008). "Spiderman? Sure! The neuroscience of disbelief." *Interdisciplinary Science Reviews*, Vol. 33, No. 4, pp.312–320.

Kant, I. (1790). *Critique of the Power of Judgment (Kritik der Urteilskraft)*. Edited and Translated by Paul Guyer and Eric Matthews (2000). Cambridge: Cambridge University Press.

Lacan, J. (2006). "The mirror stage as formative of the I function as revealed in psychoanalytic experience." *Écrits*. Translated by Bruce Fink. New York: W.W. Norton & Co. pp.75–81.

Lynch, D. (Dir.) (2006). *Inland Empire*. USA.

Vogel, A. (1974). *Film as a Subversive Art*. New York: Random House.

Introduction

Vanessa Sinclair

Psychoanalysis and cinema have developed alongside one another since the inception of both fields and have certainly influenced each other throughout the years. The phenomenon of the moving image was first developed in the late 19th century. In 1895 – the same year Sigmund Freud published *Studies on Hysteria* with Josef Breuer – the Lumière brothers presented the first projected moving pictures to a paying audience in Paris, using the Cinématographe, a device of their own making consisting of a camera, projector, and film printer. Over the turn of the century, Freud continued developing his theories, and in the early 20th century, the field of psychoanalysis – and the burgeoning film industry – really began to establish itself with the founding of psychoanalytic societies – and cinemas[1] – across Europe and North America. By the time Carl Gustav Jung gave his resignation as the first president of the International Psychoanalytical Association (IPA) in 1914, the international film industry was well under way.

Early on in his career, Freud studied with Jean-Martin Charcot at the Salpêtrière Hospital in France. Utilizing cutting-edge technologies of the time, Charcot focused on documenting the symptoms of hysteric patients using freeze-frame photography to capture every nuance of their expressions, movements, and behavior.

> Hysterical symptoms were reproduced at the Salpêtrière in a number of ways – as staged re-enactments, sketches, wax and plaster casts, and photographs. Art became a method to immobilize the tumultuous fits of his patients and order the savage thrashing into a sequence of static images.
>
> (Hustvedt, 2011, p. 22)

Charcot's live demonstrations became popular outings for Parisians. Medical students, artists, actors, socialites, and tourists flooded the Salpêtrière to witness the "madness" of the hysterics – the theatrics enthralling the audience, who flocked from near and far.

With his development of psychoanalysis, Freud harnessed a method for capturing elusive traces of the unconscious suggested by repetition, dreams, fantasies, slips of the tongue, bungled actions, puns, and jokes. The experience of being in

DOI: 10.4324/9781003200246-1

psychoanalysis often creates a sort of distance from oneself. This "observing ego" as it came to be known, allows a person to observe one's mind as thoughts arise, as if a spectator. Even the way Freud describes free association is cinematic:

> What you tell me must differ in one respect from an ordinary conversation … in this case you must proceed differently. You will notice that as you relate things various thoughts will occur to you which you would like to put aside … You must never give into these criticisms, but must say it in spite of them – indeed, you must say it precisely *because* you feel an aversion to do so. Later on you will find out and learn to understand the reason for this injunction, which is really the only one you have to follow. So say whatever goes through your mind. Act as though, for instance, you were a traveller sitting next to the window of a railway carriage and describing to someone inside the carriage the changing views which you see outside.
>
> (1913, pp. 134–135)

This could very well be re-envisioned as an analysand describing the scenes one witnesses as they cross the inner screen of the mind.

Observing our experiences in this way allows us to glean a fresh understanding of ourselves and the world around us. British object relations psychoanalyst Donald W. Winnicott championed the idea of the *transitional space*: the space of play, experimentation, sublimation, artistic creation, and psychoanalysis. The sphere of the cinema also provides this type of space. A place for us to explore aspects of ourselves that may otherwise feel inaccessible. A space for us to try on various personalities and personae, and to emerge with something new.

Lacan's early theory of the *mirror stage* is often referenced in film studies as a way of understanding the experience of the audience immersed in the chamber of the cinema:

> The arrangement of the different elements – projector, darkened hall, screen – in addition from reproducing in a striking way the *mis-en-scène* of Plato's cave … reconstructs the situation necessary to the release of the 'mirror stage' discovered by Lacan.
>
> (Baudry, 1975, p. 45)

Therefore, I will take a few moments here to reflect upon Lacan's conceptualization of the *mirror stage* – the originary process of identity formation. According to Lacan, during the period between the ages of approximately six to eighteen months, the infant looks into a mirror and sees her own image reflected back to her. This image she sees in the mirror appears to be whole, and the underlying assumption is that appearing whole equates with feeling whole, too, or experiencing wholeness. As the child's experience of herself in her own body feels fragmented, she then identifies with the wholeness that she imagines the image in the mirror experiences. Once the child has introjected this imagined sense of wholeness, she then begins to equate this with her "self." This forms the original template or underlying structure of the ego – the conscious aspect of the self with which we identify. This process continues on throughout life. As we continually come into contact with others, we identify with, introject, and integrate various aspects of them, constantly adding to, eliminating, working, and reworking our internalized ego or sense of self. In this way, identity may be seen as in an ongoing process of creation that we work on and play with throughout our lives.

The mirror in this case need not be a literal mirror. We may also be reflected in the gaze of others, whether they be close, intimate relationships, or people we idealize but have never met, or more generally the gaze of society at large. The mirror may also be a screen – whether the big screen of the cinema, the small screen of the television, or the even smaller interactive screens of computers and phones. The screen provides a place for us to explore aspects of our identities, as we try on various personas and explore parts of ourselves that may otherwise feel out of reach in the public social sphere. Understanding this proves useful when examining the myriad of ways we engage with our media viewing.

The experience of viewing a film plays not only with identification in this way, but also with the positioning between characters. As Freud relates in "'A Child Is Being Beaten': A Contribution to the Study of the Origin of Sexual Perversions" (1919), there are power dynamics involved in every interpersonal relation. Akin to the sexual relation, someone is always on top. This positioning may not be overt or intentional, but it is present. There is an element of dominance and submission, whether the participants are aware of it or not. Many people have ingrained unconscious interpersonal dynamics, entering into the same relationship patterns over and over again. While others are versatile, switching position depending on the situation and/or to whom they are in relation. Through the act of viewing a film, we are able to temporarily identify with each and every person (and position) presented to us on the screen. We move from being dominant to submissive to dominant again, as we imagine ourselves as and in relation to various characters. At the same time, we are acting as witness to that which is presented. In the position of the witness, we may thereby distance ourselves from the actions being committed, feeling a sense of safety and perhaps superiority in simply being a detached observer. In this way, we are simultaneously inside and outside the scenario being presented. Todd McGowan notes that "Being absent as perceived and present as perceiver allows the spectator to escape the sense of lack that we endure simply by existing as subjects in the world" (2007, p. 2). Yet we are still voyeur and exhibitionist.

As Mary Wild relays in her work,[2] films are projective surfaces. Not only are films projected onto screens, but audience members project their own internal worlds onto the film as well. In this way, film may be seen as acting in a similar manner to the classic projective tests facilitated by psychoanalysts, i.e., the Rorschach Inkblot Test and Thematic Apperception Test. When a filmmaker is a true artist, their vision and own unconscious processes are projected and worked through via the medium of film.

It is for all these reasons (and more) that a psychoanalytic lens proves useful when considering the art of film, hence why film theory is a discourse in which psychoanalysis maintains a strong foothold. Viewing such dynamics at play within the psychoanalytic session and/or cinema aids our understanding of our own unconscious processes, identifications, dreams, fantasies, and artistic creations, as well as social dynamics in the world around us, of which we are a part.

While the Hollywood film industry is mainly run by businessmen, there are nevertheless some filmmakers who are true artists and are able to squeeze through. They are usually referred to as *auteurs*, and their films reflect a personal style or signature that tends to be immediately recognizable, similar to that of a painter or visual artist. Ingmar Bergman is one such filmmaker. His style is immediately recognizable, aided by star cinematographer Sven Nykvist. Thereby his films are ripe for taking on the projections of the audience (and critics).

The film industry is often criticized – and rightly so – as too often writing women as one-dimensional support characters to leading men. Many women actors lament having to play such reductive, stereotyped roles over and over again; Marilyn Monroe being a prime example of how women become pigeon-holed. Contrary to this industry standard, throughout his career Ingmar Bergman wrote intense, psychologically complex women characters, often in relation to one another rather than in relation to men. Take *Persona* (1966) for example, which will be much discussed from varying perspectives throughout this book, as well as *Autumn Sonata* (1978), which I will write a bit about, as it is not otherwise explored in this collection.

Sweden's two most famous Bergmans came together to create the critically acclaimed film *Autumn Sonata* (1978). This marked Ingrid Bergman's first and only film with Ingmar, and came at the tail end of her career. Ingrid was suffering from cancer during filming, and the weight of this can be felt in her incredible performance. The relationship between Ingrid Bergman's character, Charlotte, and her daughters, Eva (played by Liv Ullmann) and Helena (played by Lena Nyman), is complex, intense, and palpable. As an internationally renowned concert pianist, Charlotte chose to travel for her career, leaving her now-resentful daughter Eva and chronically ill, seemingly hysterically-paralyzed daughter Helena in the care of their father for the majority of their childhood. Their father has since passed away, and Eva removed her sister Helena from the inpatient care facility in which their mother had placed her, to care for her at home where she lives with her pastor husband. Eva's husband is present in the film, mainly as a narrator to provide context, but his attention, too, is focused on his wife and the mysteries of what he perceives to be her complex internal world.

The dynamics between Bergman's characters are always rich, no matter what the interpersonal relations are. When Bergman writes relationships between men and women, they are always complex – often complicated – and his characters stand on equal footing. Even if the woman seems subservient to the man, as with Alma and Johan in *Hour of the Wolf* (1968) for example, her complexity, inner world, and screen presence are no less vital and compelling. When children are present in Bergman's films, they often have rich, imaginative inner worlds as well. Rather than Hollywood films, which historically have centered on one particular point of view (namely that of the white, cis-het US American male), Bergman's characters display a complexity and dynamism, not only regarding their own internal struggles but also in their relation to and impact upon one another.

Bergman's genius lays not only in the exquisite scripts, direction, cast, and cinematography, but in the uncanny way he is able to draw in the audience, bringing the dynamic depths of the unconscious to light, inviting projections and associations. His films confront sexuality, neurosis, war, death, and the taboo with unparalleled intimacy and understanding, delving into realms most tend to avoid.

As progressive as our era is, it's surprising to discover how many people still have such conservative and moralistic reactions to Bergman's work. To me, in his films Bergman, like no other, captures the essence of what it is to be human. His masterful depictions of the intricacies of human psychology are unmatched. His films are like dreams – streams of free associations in the most psychoanalytic sense. The way his scenes flow from one to another, characters moving from excitement and delight to love and lust, pride and inspiration to confusion and terror, anxiety and envy to jealousy and shame, defeat and resignation to regret and remorse, then a sparkle in the eye as a glimmer of hope returns again ... or perhaps not. Bergman seamlessly puts the full range of human emotions, insights, and follies on display. Through his films, he lays bare what many of us work so hard to repress, deny, or cover up. Power dynamics, sensuality, sexual tension, ambivalence, and resentment are pervasive in interpersonal relations, as well as in Bergman's films.

Bergman consistently whets our appetites by presenting a restrained yet potent dialogue, matched with images that amplify or contradict the psychological depth of the drama, as he subtly pushes his actors to genuinely take on the personae of the characters. How we deal with this overwhelming effect is usually a retraction to subjectivity, engaging our own projections and transferences. Our preferred frames of reference become the binoculars and/or microscopes that allow for analysis of the film in question. We seek to express our own interpretation of the film (or *any* artwork worth its salt) because it has moved us to such a degree that we feel the need to ventilate and share the experience with others.

This subjectivity ultimately relies upon artistic ambiguity in order to function. Had Bergman favored more prefabricated, overtly clear or clever explanations – whether in the films themselves or in related post facto interviews – the films would have to a great extent lost their capacity to attract. Although Bergman's films are often rich in both form and content, the overall attitude is one of restraint; a discipline that often merges with his "economic" aesthetics, thereby creating an impression that transcends concepts like "form" or "content" in favor of a totality that mesmerizes and attracts.

Hence one and the same film will appeal differently to different people. This has certainly been one of the most enjoyable aspects of editing this anthology: the more the strictly subjective lenses capture and express, the greater the value of the artwork. It is as if Bergman's own *Laterna Magica* keeps on spinning, casting spells that fascinate viewers of each new generation. These cinematic spells are timeless expressions of the human condition – existing outside trends, discourses, and even the larger Zeitgeists of the times – yet resonating throughout. The greatest artworks, as well as artists, are positioned outside the limitations of critical temporality by way of integrity, intelligence, and drive.

Bergman's strength lies not in intellectual constructions, nor in theoretical insights into the human condition or psychology, but rather in his drive to create. As with all great art, Bergman's films – perhaps especially those that deal with distinctly psychoanalytical issues or topics – are ambiguous enough to not only allow, but actively encourage, the projections and interpretative faculties of the viewer. In fact, I found this to be the case so much so when reading the contributions to this collection, for example, that at times I wondered if we'd seen the same film! In the end, what we write about Bergman says more about us than it does about him.

Swedish author and filmmaker Carl Abrahamsson opens the collection with his reflections on Bergman's masterpiece *Hour of the Wolf* (1968), situating the film with regard to what was happening in Bergman's life personally, in culture and politics more generally, and in relation to other films created during his "decade of deep introspection" as Abrahamsson calls it, most notably *Persona* (1966) and *Shame* (1968). Abrahamsson contemplates recurring themes in Bergman's work having to do with the dynamism and reciprocity of interpersonal relations, identity, and consciousness, and how this can veer into neurosis or psychosis, reflected in the repeated statements of Alma (the leading female role, played by Liv Ullmann), "Isn't it true that couples who spend so much time together begin to resemble one another ... they think alike and even look alike. Why is that?"

Walter Benjamin's *optical unconscious* is explored in Métis and Canadian filmmaker and philosopher Wayne Wapeemukwa's contribution. First developed while defending Sergei Eisenstein's *Battleship Potemkin* (1925), Benjamin's concept undergoes a transformation as his focus moves from the cinematic to the photographic. Wapeemukwa illustrates this transition by bringing to light the opening sequence of Bergman's *Persona* (1966) as a sequence of images comprised of discarded cutaways from his previous films. In this case, Bergman's cinematic optical unconscious is quite literally comprised of "the other scene of the *cutaway* ... those images which have been excised, that is, *repressed.*" By doing so Bergman jars his audience into self-consciousness, rather than suspension of disbelief. Perhaps this is why so many find his films difficult to watch; they are *too* real, *too* resonant, reflecting the most repressed dynamics of our unconscious minds.

From the cinematic optical unconscious to the ethical unconscious, California-based professor Robert Samuels reveals important insights gleaned by viewing Bergman's films through the lenses of Freud and Shakespeare. Analyzing the plot of *Fanny and Alexander* (1982) via an exploration of themes from *Hamlet*,

Samuels delves into the theories of Freud, Lacan, and Descartes to reveal what Lacan calls "the ethical core of the subject."[3] Expanding upon Freud's insight that "the conscience is unconscious,"[4] Samuels explores the function of ghosts in these productions, revisiting theories of consciousness and psychosis, ego, and identity formation, as well as discussing the function of comedy and the arts, sublimation and metafiction within politics and culture at large.

In "Island Earth: Bergman, Brahe, and the Many Suns," New York-based scholar and filmmaker Patrick Scanlon places Bergman alongside the 16th century astronomer Tycho Brahe. Although separated by several centuries and the terms of their respective disciplines, Bergman and Brahe are nonetheless a suitable pair. Beyond their island life – both figures cultivated their distinct styles and advanced their fields while living and working on islands off the coast of Sweden – they share a unique devotion to light in its solar, lunar, celestial, and mechanical forms. In this sense, light does not constitute an object or aim of their art and inquiry – some utility that allows the work to proceed – its status is more methodological in nature, if not initiatic, and as such generates innovations that exceed the bounds of the personal. Fortunately, Bergman and Brahe are rather explicit about their first encounters with this special dispensation of light, and provide a somewhat continuous commentary on its effects, which always show something of the originary scene. In "Island Earth" Scanlon thus privileges the autobiographical, and while conscious of the great depth of technical knowledge produced by Bergman and Brahe, the focus remains on those more ordinary and phenomenological experiences, however mystical their conceits. From Brahe's camera obscura to Bergman's magic lantern, Scanlon shows there are many ways to illumine the many suns.

Swedish psychoanalyst Peter Jansson reflects on existential issues involving individuals as subjects and their relation to the world, culture, and society by exploring *The Silence* (1963), "Bergman's masterpiece about the world." In contrast to a traditional film analysis, where the filmmaking is interpreted and analyzed, Jansson illustrates how a theory takes shape *in* the cinematic world of Bergman. From that perspective, what can *The Silence* teach us about the world and life? What picture of society and culture emerges from the film in a psychoanalytic sense? What ideas and fantasies dwell inside the narrative, the representations of human beings and the world they inhabit, their bodies, desires, loneliness, silence, spirituality …? The theories of Jacques Lacan, the existentialist philosophers, and Krzysztof Kieślowski – Polish film director and script writer who has written in depth about *The Silence* – serve as a guiding light to that which conceals itself behind, evading language and image in the film. In this sense, Jansson's project is situated in *the real* – what has not been expressed in words and evades all symbolization – the space beyond the silence, the void concealed by the visible. In this way, Jansson shows how *The Silence* depicts a world that is falling apart – where God is dead – and how people, in darkness, emptiness, and despair, try to give meaning to this world.

We then turn from *The Silence* (1963) to *Cries and Whispers* (1972) as Andrea Sabbadini, London-based psychoanalyst and founder of the European

Psychoanalytic Film Festival, examines another of Bergman's masterpieces. Three sisters interact with one another at a dramatic juncture in their lives – that of Agnes's illness and nearing death – on which Bergman focuses his camera, transformed into a magnifying lens for the observation of the human soul, both in its suffering and intense sensuality. As it is almost impossible for the sisters to overcome their extreme form of sibling rivalry – rooted in their unresolved oedipal conflicts – painful issues of greed, jealousy, cruelty, and guilt emerge in their relationships. Bergman's cinematic scrutiny can be seen as a documentaristic (if also dreamlike and lyrical) equivalent of our own psychoanalytic work of uncovering the uncomfortable truths buried inside our patients' unconscious.

As a scholar with a history in the audio-visual and fine arts, S. Alfonso Williams reflects upon Bergman's classic *The Seventh Seal* (1957) through the lenses of French theoreticians, Jean Baudrillard, Gilles Deleuze, and Jacques Lacan. Williams utilizes Baudrillard's concept of seduction to explore the aspect Chance plays – as well as touching upon the theme of Time – throughout the film. He then applies notions gleaned from Deleuze's work on repetition and difference to Bergman's treatment of Time. Finally, Death is addressed through Lacan's perspectives on the hysterical and obsessive subjects, in this case, both present in the protagonist of the knight. As Williams poignantly states, "Death is pure difference, and does not make chance encounters. Not even for the knight whose random, rhizomatic encounters seem accidental." As Death and the knight are forced into a situation neither may exit, what implications arise from this complex?

Considering the philosophic import of Bergman's work, Toronto-based Lacanian scholar and clinician Alireza Taheri reflects on Bergman's ideas regarding the autophagic nature of art, maintaining that this refers to the concept's tendency to devour itself until it veers to its opposite. Taheri examines *The Silence* (1963) and *Persona* (1966), two films which stage vicious dialectical reversals wherein every opposition the "lower" term triumphs over the "higher" element whose truth it represents. For instance, in the opposition of truth and lies, everything veers towards the dominance of lies. Taheri considers the following oppositions in this paper: adult and child, masculine and feminine, power and impotence, semblance and the real, truth and lie, beauty and ugliness, innocence and guilt, identity and fragmentation, Eden and the fall, light and darkness, reality and fiction, good and evil, love and hate, faith and atheism, sense and nonsense. For Taheri, Bergman's films stage a space of insanity where the "lower" terms triumph madly over the semblances provided by the "higher" terms. Taheri finally asks, does Bergman provide an alternative that eschews both the madness of triumphing "lower" terms and a solution hinging on the falsity of semblance? Can one find respite from the spiraling descent of the concept without relying on deception?

Swedish psychologist Elisabeth Punzi turns our focus to *Fanny & Alexander* (1982), specifically looking at the character Isak Jacobi, a Jewish antique dealer, banker, and magician, who has a central place in the film, as well as in the life and development of the title character Alexander. Jacobi is understood through the lens of *Moses and Monotheism* (1939), in which Freud examines anti-Semitism, characteristics of the Jewish people, and the myth of the male hero. In *Fanny & Alexander*, as well as in *Moses and Monotheism*, father figures have central positions, and the male hero must both defeat and identify with them. Through the present analysis it is possible to see that Bergman in *Fanny & Alexander*, just like Freud in *Moses and Monotheism*, examines biological kinship, religion, heritage, and family ties, reflecting on what it means to be loved and cared for.

Professor Emeritus Walter A. Davis explores the intricate details of Bergman's cinematic masterpiece *Persona* (1966) from his position, not only as a psychoanalyst but also as an actor and playwright, bringing our attention to intimate details, such as the intricate ways Bergman utilizes language and frames scenes, matched by his exquisite ability to pull such depth from his actors. As Liv Ullmann once stated, "He moved his camera so close to my face that most of the time I thought I was acting only for him."[5] Davis envisions *Persona* as akin to a five act play, guiding us through each movement like the conductor of an orchestra.

Closing the collection we have "Beyond Silence: On the Absence of God in the Films of Ingmar Bergman," by Pablo Lerner, a Swedish psychologist residing in Paris. In this chapter, Lerner analyzes *The Seventh Seal* (1957), *Through a Mirror Darkly* (1961), and *Winter Light* (1963) in order to arrive at a psychoanalytic interpretation of the staging of the absence of God in Bergman's films. It is argued that Bergman oscillates between representing this absence, on the one hand, as the silence of God, meaning the abandonment of God-the-Father and the non-articulation of the Word in the field of language, and, on the other hand, as lovelessness, understood as the non-rebirth of Christ in man as love according to St John's equation of love and God. Lastly, it is argued that there is yet another "hidden" form of absence of the divine in his films, namely, the absence of that which pertains to polytheism, drawing on the fact that nothing corresponding to the phenomenology of awe takes place.

Notes

1 "A Very Short History of Cinema" Accessed January 10, 2022: www.scienceandmedia museum.org.uk/objects-and-stories/very-short-history-of-cinema
2 See Mary Wild's Projections series at the Freud Museum, London, as well as Projections Podcast.
3 Lacan, J. (1998). *The Four Fundamental Concepts of Psycho-analysis*. Vol. 11. New York: W.W. Norton & Company.
4 Freud, S. (1958). "A note on the unconscious in psycho-analysis." *The Standard Edition of the Complete Psychological Works of Sigmund Freud, Volume XII (1911–1913): The Case of Schreber, Papers on Technique and Other Works*. London: Hogarth Press, pp. 255–266.
5 Wright Wexman, V. & Ullmann, L. "An Interview with Liv Ullmann." *Cinema Journal*, Vol. 20, No. 1, Special Issue on Film Acting (Autumn, 1980). Austin: University of Texas Press. pp. 68–78.

Bibliography

Baudry, J.-L. (1975). "Ideological effects of the basic cinematographic apparatus." *Film Quarterly*, Vol. 28, No. 2 (Winter, 1974–1975), pp. 39–47.

Bergman, I. (2007). *The Magic Lantern: An Autobiography*. Chicago, IL: University of Chicago Press.

Freud, S. (1913). "On beginning the treatment (further recommendations on the technique of psycho-analysis I)." In *SE XII*. London: Hogarth Press, pp. 121–144.

Freud, S. (1919). "'A child is being beaten': A contribution to the study of the origin of sexual perversions." In *SE XVII*. London: Hogarth Press, pp. 175–204.

Freud, S., and Breuer, J. (1895). "Studies on hysteria." In *The Complete Standard Edition of the Psychological Works of Sigmund Freud (SE) II*. London: Hogarth Press, pp. 1–335.

Hustvedt, A. (2011). *Medical Muses: Hysteria in Nineteenth Century Paris*. New York: W.W. Norton & Company.

Lacan, J. (2006). "The mirror stage as formative of the I function as revealed in psychoanalytic experience." In *Écrits: The First Complete Edition in English*, translated by Bruce Fink. New York: W.W. Norton & Co, pp. 75–81.

Leader, D. (2000). "Beating fantasies and sexuality." In *Sexuation*, edited by Renata Salecl. Durham, NC: Duke University Press.

Loewenberg, P., and Thompson, N. (2011). *100 Years of the IPA: The Centenary History of the International Psychoanalytical Association, 1910–2010, Evolution and Change*. London: Karnac.

McGowan, T. (2007). *The Real Gaze: Film Theory After Lacan*. Albany: State University of New York Press.

Sinclair, V. (2020). *Scansion in Psychoanalysis and Art: The Cut in Creation*. London: Routledge.

Vogel, A. (1974). *Film as a Subversive Art*. New York: Random House.

Winnicott, D. W. (2005). *Playing and Reality*. London: Routledge.

Chapter 1

The People Eaters Are Having a Great Feast

Some Reflections on Ingmar Bergman's *Hour of the Wolf*

Carl Abrahamsson

In a body of work as rich and dynamic as Ingmar Bergman's, it can sometimes be hard to stay focused on his overwhelmingly precise psychological insights – although always appealing. One of the key reasons for this is his unwillingness to intellectually explain and rather just show the psychic processes in a beautifully executed cinematic language. This affects the viewer considerably more than any attempts at explanation. We are drawn in, into other people's problems and neuroses, and although there might not be a complete resonance (let's hope not!) at least there will be emotions strong enough to evoke an overall sympathy and fascination.

The reason why all of this works so well is not only because of his masterful treatment of the medium itself and its creative parts. It also has to do with an attractive psychological insight, pure and simple, that seems decidedly more intuitive than scholarly. Whether we're watching a Bergman drama, a romance, a comedy, or perhaps almost a horror film, there's always more than meets the eye and ear. Bergman's scripts and audiovisual interpretations attract by psychological prurience as much as by the strictly cinematically sensual.

One of Bergman's strongest interpretations of the artistic condition/neurosis or dilemma is *Vargtimmen* (*Hour of the Wolf*, 1968). It is a brutal and terrifying display of a painter's gradual breakdown from neurosis into psychosis. It has elements of the psychological horror film, in some ways echoing the then young star Roman Polanski's much lauded *Repulsion* (1965). However, the overheated neurosis isn't sexual in Bergman's case but rather deals with the artist's seemingly insurmountable outsider-ship. In this case, the painter Johan Borg (Max von Sydow) is haunted by his insomnia and nightmares to the degree that they spill over into hallucinations and distortions in waking life. His devoted wife, Alma (Liv Ullmann), looks after him but is increasingly terrified herself.

The couple arrive at an island to spend the summer; him painting and her taking care of the household. It doesn't take long before they are visited by members of a noble family that live in a castle nearby, the von Merkens, and their entourage of relatives and associates. Johan is noticeably disturbed by their presence, and yet the couple accepts an invitation to dinner. Tossed into the decadent and superficial shenanigans of this *haute bourgeoisie*, Johan and Alma realize that they are

DOI: 10.4324/9781003200246-2

there to be provoked and, to some degree, scrutinized. References are made to a former lover of Johan's, Veronica Vogler, which upsets the timid and humble Alma. Johan becomes inebriated and keeps his eyes closed as Lindhorst, a friend of the family, mysteriously shows a puppet theater performance of a segment from Mozart's "The Magic Flute" (with a real miniature human as the "puppet"). At the insistence of the assembled group, a drunk Johan tells them, almost as if in defense: "I only call myself an artist for the lack of a better term ... Art has very little importance in the world of humans."

The artist tries to confess and be honest to his wife, as she has already read his diary (encouraged to do so by the grand matriarch of the castle). She realizes that he is sinking deeper and deeper into his fear of the "Hour of the Wolf" – the hour just before the sun rises, when (allegedly) most people die. It is in this dark, emotional twilight that Johan's boundaries are increasingly blurred, and the creatures of his nightmares (the "people eaters") morph into the characters of the castle – and/or vice versa.

Several times in the film, Alma mentions that when couples have been together for a long enough time, they take on each other's traits and features. This seems to be something she initially finds romantic, but at the end, when Johan has mysteriously disappeared after his full-on madness, she doesn't sound quite as convinced. That there is a crossover or gray area we notice already in the film's beginning when the frail matron from the castle tells Alma where to find Johan's sketchbooks and diary – something she couldn't really "know." If the old lady is in fact a ghost or a "demon" of sorts, then Alma is obviously susceptible to her influence, too.

Where Johan happily sketches Alma on an early summer's day, he soon finds it harder and harder to formulate, sketch, and paint in a desired way. Images of the "people eaters" instead fill the pages, and these he shows to his wife in some attempt at exorcism or at least shared angst. Johan desperately tries to tell Alma about what he feels and remembers, but this only increases her own dread. Confessions of being punished and beaten by his father and then asking his mother's forgiveness ... Confessions of the horror of being locked into a cupboard, being told that there is a small man in there that eats children's toes ... While going through some financial details, Alma references Johan's son, but in such a way that suggests it is not her child. In fact, Alma is pregnant in the film. It is also revealed that Johan's relationship with the married Veronica Vogler lasted for five years and ended with a "scandal." Perhaps Vogler is actually the mother of the son to which Alma refers?

One day Johan comes home with what Alma believes is a snakebite, but which isn't. As he tells her the story, we drift into a dream/nightmare sequence where Johan is down by the cliffs, fishing. Together with him is a small boy. We can't hear what they say – the soundtrack only consists of terrifying music – but there is an argument and a fight that leads to the boy biting and scratching the artist. This leads to Johan beating the boy to death, subsequently ensuring his dead body is submerged in the sea. The only scene-specific sounds heard are guttural grunts from the boy when they fight. The scenes are over-exposed, in a higher contrast, which amplifies the eeriness of the goings-on.

As the couple drift apart in their claustrophobic cottage, an invitation to actually meet Veronica Vogler is handed to Johan. The messenger, curator Heerbrand, also gives Johan a gun, to "protect them from the small fowl of the island." Johan uses this gun to shoot at his wife, and then rushes to the castle. Here we enter full on psychosis. Another castle guest, impresario Kreisler, performs music to a spellbound collection of "people eaters." In order to hear better, the ghostly matriarch removes her face (which is glued on to her skull) and then pops her eyes into glasses of sherry. Baron von Merkens confesses his jealousy, as he too has been involved with Veronica Vogler; to the extent of walking up the wall and onto the ceiling upside down, justifying this magical act with his jealousy. The Lindhorst character convinces Johan to add a bit of make-up, silk pajamas, and a nice robe for his upcoming tryst. "You are yourself yet not yourself – the ideal prerequisite for a love rendezvous," he says, while Johan apparently accepts everything. As he leaves Johan by the door to Vogler, he flaps his now visible bird wings and exclaims, "You see what you want to see!"

Vogler is laid out naked on a table, as a corpse on a slab. Johan touches her, she wakes up and they embrace, being watched by the entire group in a static "tableau vivant" that evokes the genuinely bizarre horror of a Hieronymus Bosch painting, complete with the Baroness lifting up her dress and masturbating.

In his smudged makeup Johan now addresses the congregation of "people eaters," and says: "I thank you for that the limit has been transcended. The mirror is broken. But what do the shards reflect? Can you tell me?" We can then see him continue talking but there's no sound to be heard. No one listens, no one understands.

It's a painful moment of utter resignation, and in some ways, the end of the film – specifically from Johan's perspective. But a segment follows that again is displayed in the dream-like over-exposure. Johan is lost in nature close by: dark thickets, shrubs, gnarly branches. Alma looks for him. The detached Baron appears from time to time. Johan is physically attacked by the curator Heerbrand as well as by Lindhorst, the "bird man." The dead boy resurfaces in the water.

The final scene of the film is Alma talking straight to the camera, again mentioning that perhaps couples start looking and behaving like each other after a long enough time. Then … The End.

The aestheticized fluidity between fact and fiction, dream and nightmare, neurosis and psychosis, is, I would argue, Bergman's most powerful tool, and perhaps especially during his decade of deep introspection (ca. 1960–1970). What seems intuitive may of course in actual fact be contrived and constructed, but the opposite is equally true: what seems so well crafted and constructed may have been created on an intuitive whim.

We can never escape the fact that Ingmar Bergman was a genuine artist. Meaning: whatever was created of artistic merit inherently carries a large part of its creator. As the mid-1960s constituted somewhat of a life crisis for Bergman, it's not surprising that there is extra fluidity in the films of that period:

> A production stretches its tentacle roots a long way down through time and dreams. I like to imagine the roots as dwelling in the special room of the soul, where they live maturing comfortably like mighty cheeses. Some, reluctantly or quite enthusiastically and quite often, come into view; others do not emerge at all. They see no necessity to take part in this perpetual production.[1]

Some themes were obviously maturing comfortably, "like cheeses," during this period. For instance, Bergman worked for a long time on a story about a twenty-eight-year-old nanny called Alma:

> It's about mercy or grace, that's what I had in mind if it can be done. I had been thinking about the defenseless. And how the bad conscience always wants to punish. And how the defenseless always provoke cruelty. And how guilt must always seek its absolution.[2]

These quite "Bergmanesque" themes crystallized into a manuscript written while hospitalized in 1965: "Människoätarna" ("The People Eaters"). This, in turn, morphed into treatments and subsequent manuscripts for *Persona* (1966) and *Hour of the Wolf* (1968). To say that there is kinship between these two films is an understatement.

The redeeming and subjugated Alma (played by Bibi Andersson in *Persona* and by Liv Ullmann in *Hour of the Wolf*) has to deal with her respective neurotic artists: inpatient and celebrated actress Elisabeth Vogler (played by Liv Ullmann in *Persona*) and husband Johan Berg (played by von Sydow in *Hour of the Wolf*). By negating herself, Alma makes herself susceptible to outer manipulation but also her own complete effacing. To some degree she is aware of it, but nevertheless allows herself to be entangled inside the illnesses of Vogler and Borg, respectively. Their being artists undoubtedly casts a spell on the considerably less individuated Alma, but the problem is that they don't share of themselves at all, as in a relationship symbiosis – on the contrary, they simply devour aspects of her in an epiphytic or parasitic sense (another kind of reference to the "people eaters").

The crisis obviously reflects Bergman's own. He had made a critical and financial "flop" with the comedy *All These Women* (1964) and was stressed out about having just been hired as main director at Stockholm's most prestigious theater, Dramaten, and the workload and responsibility that entailed. In his stages of gradual exhaustion, it's not at all surprising to find him questioning meaning, work, himself, as well as the artistic process. Nor is it surprising that the disappointment of the failure with *All These Women* would allow for thematic spillovers into the more genuine and pressing "people eater" project, as if trying to purify genuine themes that had real artistic meaning, but had not yet found their proper expression; a creative compensation of sorts. In an entry in his work diary, from June 30, 1964, Bergman states:

To mature to the degree that you can make a serious work of art that is really worth taking seriously. If all of this merely becomes a game produced through sanctimonious self- mirroring and with a lot of unmotivated pompousness on one side and met by a temporary interest on the other, then it's meaningless. It can be meaningless no matter what. But if I can't reach someone or something with this work it is shit. All these formulations, all this misfitted hoopla. So helplessly risky for the artist. Then perhaps one could tell the story about Alma and the artist. It's almost like a ghost story.[3]

And that's essentially what *Hour of the Wolf* turned out to be: an uncanny ghost story that has strong similarities with the horror film genre. Whereas *Persona* is an almost Zeitgeistishly avant-garde and self-conscious film about how two women try to express their need of each other – for good and bad – the drama of Alma and Johan Borg is like a psychologically stripped version of a 19th century Gothic tale of terror.

Looking at Bergman at this time, and how basically one story was turned into two, we can see how his own troubled mind feverishly created, constructed, conflated, and connected a whole lot of relevant associations that were "au courant" in his life. This also gives ample insight into his own very intuitive creative process, in which the boundaries between fact and fiction were not always clear – possibly not even to himself.

Between 1959 and 1969, Ingmar Bergman was married to Estonian-Swedish concert pianist Käbi Laretei. In 1962, they had a son, Daniel Bergman. In his autobiography there are long sections about Laretei and their relationship, and perhaps of special importance here is her studying with a piano teacher in Stuttgart called Andrea Vogler-Corelli. At times, Bergman was present, too, and he must have been very impressed as he quotes lengthily ad verbatim from decades old conversations between Laretei and Vogler-Corelli.

The name Vogler we recognize not only from *Hour of the Wolf* (the paramour Veronica Vogler) and *Persona* (the actress Elisabeth Vogler), but also from *The Magician* (1958, Albert Emanuel Vogler and the wife Manda Vogler – played by Ingrid Thulin who also plays Veronica Vogler in *Hour of the Wolf*). Andrea Vogler seems to have made an impression in this regard also.

But who was she? In *The Magic Lantern*, Bergman claims she was the wife of violin Maestro Jonathan Vogler, who had been a frequent guest at the musical soirées of Mathilda von Merkens at the family castle outside of Stuttgart. The many stories Andrea told Bergman about these soirées initially became the fodder for the *All These Women* film/fiasco. And they obviously lingered on in Bergman's mind.

Jonathan Vogler was, however, merely a pseudonym for the violin Maestro Max Strub, who is the basis of the character of the cellist Felix in *All These Women*. His wife's name was Maria-Luisa Strub-Moresco, and this woman was indeed the piano teacher of Käbi Laretei's, and someone who Bergman actually met.

The fact that Bergman changed a few names in his autobiography is not really remarkable. But there are other oddities in this particular drama. There was no such person as Mathilda von Merkens. Very likely the declining noble family is simply an amalgamation of similar families both Bergman and Maria-Luisa had met and talked about. Bergman remembers a photograph "Andrea" had shown him from one of the soirées at the von Merkens' and which obviously impressed him:

> The stucco is flaking off the wall, a windowpane has been replaced with a square of wood, a Cupid has lost its head. The picture radiates a good dinner, perspiring heat, lechery and gentle decay. After these gentlemen have belched, farted and had their laced coffee, they presumably gather in Mathilde von Merkens' huge salon, with its smell of mould, and there they make music. They are, like the angels, perfect.[4]

In a way, this sounds like the very stylized "tableau vivant" I mentioned earlier, at the very moment when Johan Borg goes into full psychosis. But these are no angels, much rather like Boschean demons. Present in this tableau is the Kapell-Meister Kreisler, who also originates in Bergman's recollection of Andrea's recollection.

There seems to exist an obsession of sorts with not only the name Vogler but also specifically Andrea/Maria-Luisa as a source perhaps not only of information but also of amorous attention. Bergman liberally quotes Andrea talking to Käbi, but the messages seem more pertinent to him as a theater and film director: "I listened to Andrea and thought about theatre, about myself and actors, our sloppiness, our ignorance, the damned common stuff we produce in exchange for payment."[5]

I suspect that Bergman was enamored with this woman and projected himself onto her, and also her onto himself. Hence the dynamic between the dominant, manipulative, and volatile Vogler, and the almost non-existing Alma figure. As Käbi and Maria-Luisa were close friends, it is also as if Bergman watches them as being Alma and Vogler, respectively – one submissive, one dominant. Again, the fluidity of Bergman's creative mind certainly allows for a great number of combinations and compensations.

Their relationship simply goes beyond mere information and inspiration. If one really wanted to speculate, one could perhaps see Bergman's crisis as one having to do with increased work pressure in tandem with a failing marriage to Laretei right there in the mid to late 1960s. Perhaps the young son in the film that haunts Johan Borg is even a specter of Bergman's own son Daniel, as a guilt-tripping reminder of paternal obligation failures?

In *The Magic Lantern*, Bergman lets us know that Käbi had problems sleeping at night, and this soon plagued him, too:

> My sleeping mechanism fell apart and my insomnia, or poor sleep, became chronic. I am still all right as long as I sleep for four or five hours. I am often

drawn up in a spiral out of deep slumber, an irresistible force which makes me wonder where it hides itself. Is it diffuse feelings of guilt or an inextinguishable need to control reality? I don't know. The only key thing is to make the night endurable with books, music, biscuits and mineral water. Worst are the 'hours of the wolf' in the small hours between three and five. That is when the demons come: mortification, loathing, fear and rage. There is no point in trying to suppress them, for that makes it worse. When my eyes tire of reading, there is music. I close my eyes and listen with concentration and give the demons free rein: come on then, I know you, I know how you function, you just carry on until you tire of it. After a while the bottom falls out of them and they become foolish, then disappear, and I sleep for a few hours.[6]

This could just as well be Johan Borg talking to Alma late at night, as he's nervously lighting match after match to stay awake, while Alma sadly watches the troubled artist deteriorate. Writing in his work diary about the Wolf film (then in production), Bergman seems quite mortified himself:

Without any property I wanted to step out of the cold splendor of the deranged words. Never more will I find the red ball of play. Cut off and gone. The snow falls over the mountain of old age. A man on a desolate road gapes, tearless: damn it, was that how the fake looked? The perspective crooked and poorly drawn. Can the eye no longer be reached by a light from the sources of fire. The shadow falls black and sober on the worn weave of the backdrop.[7]

Years later, however, Bergman seemed to have cheered up, and could look at these dark films with renewed fire and light:

I have previously been quick to devalue 'Hour of the Wolf,' probably because it has touched upon repressed aspects of myself. 'Persona' contains an intense light, a continual focus. 'Hour of the Wolf' takes place in a twilight. It also uses elements that were new to me – the romantic irony, ghost films – and that it plays with. I still think it's funny when the Baron without any problems walks on the ceiling and says 'Don't mind this, it's just because I'm jealous.' I am also a little happy when the old lady takes off her face and says that she hears the music better that way. Then she puts her eye in the sherry glass.[8]

Here Bergman was no longer in the process of exorcizing his own ghosts and demons, and could allow for an appreciation of his own dark sense of humor. Perhaps a safety measure or defense mechanism, or perhaps just a well needed level of abstraction from an expression that I'm sure must have been painful to (re)watch.

Another level of abstraction is also the final "justification" or "incentive" for the film. In the standard version of the film it is explained by text that the film is based on a story that was told Bergman by a woman in Germany, who had also sent him her husband's diary. Basically the same story: they went to an island, the artist–husband became mad. While shooting the actual film, Bergman also shot a prologue and epilogue of a meta nature, in which Bergman tells the background story about the diary, etc. to attentive actors Max von Sydow and Liv Ullmann, who are ready to be filmed in the studio.[9] In many ways, this could be seen as a whitewashing or distancing from the very real neurosis and possible psychosis that Bergman lived through while writing this masterpiece. As if saying, "look closely and admire this fiction, but let's not look too closely at me as its creator."

In *Hour of the Wolf*, Ingmar Bergman compensates for perceived weaknesses inside himself by externalizing his inner processes – both "real"/emotional and constructed/intellectual. It's essentially a control function in which he himself can attempt to regulate that which is essentially not possible to fully regulate. Bergman hides behind his artistic mastery and apparent honesty, thereby creating another level of actual defense. That is, the film itself is not enough: he needs to contextualize it for us. Not necessarily in the pathologically post-modern way that we are so accustomed to today, but definitely enough to realize the personal importance (and thereby the related vulnerability) of this particular phase of his personal and creative life.

Hence also the exquisite dream-like qualities of both *Persona* and *Hour of the Wolf*. It is a fluid form most suitable for displaying deep and often painful content – more so than a mere clinical recollection and evaluation of psychotic episodes.

> Since the meaning of most dreams is *not* in accord with the tendencies of the conscious mind but shows peculiar deviations, we must assume that the unconscious, the matrix of dreams, has an independent function. This is what I call the autonomy of the unconscious. The dream not only fails to obey our will but very often stands in flagrant opposition to our conscious intentions.[10]

Artistic expression for Bergman, in films like *Persona* and *Hour of the Wolf*, becomes an attempt at controlling his own dreams, or at least bridging the gap of opposition that Carl Jung refers to; perhaps simply because at times they are "too close to home." It can of course be argued that these kinds of soul-searching analyses and creative expressions can definitely be cathartic (perhaps even "exorcising" in Bergman's own language) – to a great extent, thanks to the public exposure of the finished works and their integration into another level of semi-public discourse; from the personal, over the creatively abstracted, and on to the intellectually abstracted.

In hindsight, Ingmar Bergman seems to have walked this tightrope quite successfully, at least in comparison with his various alter egos (whether named Vogler, Borg, or the various Almas). This seems even clearer when looking at what actually followed in terms of output. *Shame* (1968) also features von Sydow and Ullmann as a couple, living remotely on an island under tense circumstances (with marital problems, as well as an actual civil war going on around them). But in this film, which must have been shot almost back to back with *Hour of the Wolf*, there is almost no introspection whatsoever.

The married couple, Eva and Jan Rosenberg, are former philharmonic musicians who now grow vegetables and berries on a rural farm. They are preoccupied with each other and their work. Both swing between rational evaluations and emotional moments, and at times these are in synch between them. But it's always the outer circumstances that dictate; never the inner.

The soldiers of both sides of the civil war try to figure out where the Rosenbergs stand; where their allegiances lie. But in actual fact, the Rosenbergs are not interested in either side. They essentially want to be left alone, live and work, and perhaps some day play music again. But they are constantly forced, again and again, to respond to the violence of a divided reality.

The name Rosenberg is of course interesting in this regard. The American communists Ethel and Julius Rosenberg were executed in 1953 for espionage during the second world war. And then there's Alfred Rosenberg, one of the main National Socialist theorists and strategists. The obvious juxtaposition of these extremes is brilliant, in the sense that it makes us uneasy as to exactly what (or who – if anyone) Bergman might be referring.

By this time, Bergman was emerging from his soul-searching period as an artist, and had found a new voice and outlook that better catered to constructive creativity. I suspect the renewed vigor was in part a reaction against the violent madness of the (mainly) French students and intellectuals in 1968, who attempted to integrate an astonishingly naive political discourse in fields that belong to artists and creative people. Bergman seems here to stress the necessity of the artist to stay pure; to stay out of these reactive and detrimental trends and fads, and at any cost.

Jan Rosenberg is forced by partisans (some of which he knows) to kill their friend, the Mayor, in what is essentially a fit of jealousy (Eva had recently had sex with the Mayor for money). The personal dilemma or issue here becomes extra violent and exaggerated by the influence of primitive allegiances that require some form of brutal loyalty. These themes were seemingly often on Bergman's mind at this time, as they were in the general Zeitgeist:

> Sometimes I have a feeling that this is the realm of death. Death and killing is such a natural part of our existence. Death has also attacked our finer instincts and insights. Humanity. Compassion. Understanding. Tenderness. Closeness. Warmth. Loyalty. There is a panic around us. Some have discovered it but it goes on all the time and it's gone far. I have a sense of a twilight realm that exists around me. It whispers and moves and there are always things going on in the twilight. Sighs, screams, curses, cries for mercy. Obscenities, broken commitments. A continuous stream of movement, heavy and bloody, that wallows and crawls and elevates itself and sinks and is disgusting like a huge corpse whose sighs stink of death and decomposition.[11]

This is reminiscent of a powerful scene at the end of *Shame*, in which a small boat carrying the Rosenbergs and a few others away from the island gets stuck in a mass of floating corpses at sea. Jan tries to stave them off in horror to keep their vessel undisturbed, but no one can close their eyes to the terror and sadness around them. Eva is equally traumatized by these outer circumstances, to the degree that in the very last scene of the film she admits that she has forgotten what she had just dreamed. Even this weirdly haunting scene contains central themes of Bergman at this time:

> The only mission of art today is to, with the modest possibilities of art, remind people that they despite everything still are human beings. A real dream play, a fresco of tones and timbres and efforts and failures, everything should coalesce in one consciousness. If only I could. My boat is so small and the ocean so big.[12]

Yet Bergman's boat was steady and successful in its navigations, and perhaps especially after the crisis of the late 1960s had dissolved itself in new clarities and visions. *Persona* and *Hour of the Wolf* are indicative of this process of dissolving, in which the artist, like the proverbial physician, "heals himself." Whatever Bergman may have felt was ailing in terms of his own weaknesses, his sublime, aestheticized projections (and let's not forget his intuitive psychology) obviously worked wonders not only for his career but also for himself as a human being and an artist. It was a brave and successful attempt at displaying his own (perceived) inadequacies and allowing them to be transformed into a cinematic poetry few have been able to surpass.

> Although in the great majority of cases compensation aims at establishing a normal psychological balance and thus appears as a kind of self-regulation of the psychic system, one must not forget that under certain circumstances and in certain cases (for instance, in latent psychoses) compensation may lead to a fatal outcome owing to the preponderance of destructive tendencies. The result is suicide or some other abnormal action, apparently preordained in the life-pattern of certain hereditarily tainted individuals.[13]

Ingmar Bergman came out on the other side of the gnarly thickets where Johan Borg was lost and disappeared, now filled with a new focus on how couples handle *external* pressure. This was to be a theme that defined most of his 1970s production, and one certainly not less interesting than that of the 1960s soul-searching introspection.

Notes

1 Bergman, I. (2007). *The Magic Lantern*. Chicago: The University of Chicago Press, p. 227.
2 Bergman, I. (2018). *Arbetsboken 1955–1974*, entry of June 28th 1964. Stockholm: Norstedts, p. 164 (Translation mine).

3 Bergman, I. (2018). *Arbetsboken 1955–1974*, entry of June 30th 1964. Stockholm: Norstedts, p. 170 (Translation mine).
4 Bergman, I. (2007). *The Magic Lantern*. Chicago: The University of Chicago Press, p. 221.
5 Ibid., p. 225.
6 Ibid., pp. 226–227.
7 Bergman, I. (2018). *Arbetsboken 1955–1974*, entry of June 30th 1964. Stockholm: Norstedts, p. 205 (Translation mine) (December 2, 1966).
8 Ingmar Bergman quoted in the booklet "1960–1973" of the DVD box set Ingmar Bergman, SF Studios/Studio S, Sweden, 2018.
9 These sequences are usually available on current DVD releases of the film, as for instance the box set Ingmar Bergman, SF Studios/Studio S, Sweden, 2018.
10 Jung, C. G. (1974). *Dreams*. Princeton: Princeton University Press, p. 73.
11 Bergman, I. (2018). *Arbetsboken 1955–1974*, entry of June 30th 1964. Stockholm: Norstedts, p. 248 (Translation mine) (July 11, 1968).
12 Ibid., p. 233 (April 5, 1968).
13 Jung, C. G. (1974). *Dreams*. Princeton: Princeton University Press, p. 74.

Bibliography

Jung, C. G. (1974). *Dreams*. Princeton, NJ: Princeton University Press.

Chapter 2

The Cinematic Optical Unconscious of Bergman's *Persona*

Wayne Wapeemukwa

Penis spider Christ's stigmata sheep for slaughter its eye arc lamp lighting cartoon the title:

PERSONA.

What undergirds these disparate elements?[1] From between the interstitial broken-ness of these frames, emerges an underlying – thoroughly cinematic – optical unconscious.

It is (falsely) assumed that the "optical unconscious" first emerges in Walter Benjamin's 1931 "Little History of Photography." There, Benjamin casts it as exclusively *photographic*.[2] As Miriam Hansen repeatedly reminds us (1999, 2005), this error supplants Benjamin's original *cinematic* formulations. In a 1927 critical appraisal, Benjamin describes Sergei Eisenstein's film *Battleship Potemkin* (1925) as a "prism" opening up "*a new region of consciousness*" (1977, p. 751, emphasis original). Can this "new consciousness" be witnessed elsewhere? On Bergman's centennial, I look to the interstices of *Persona* (1966) in order to alloy the optical unconscious with cinema.

"Any account which leaves out or dismisses as incidental how *Persona* begins and ends," cautions Susan Sontag, "hasn't been talking about the film that Bergman made" (1970, p. 138). Immediately, a kaleidoscope of readings erupt from consid-ering the opening montage: David L. Vierling sees it as a "statement of integra-tion" (1974, p. 51); John Jones spies a cryptic yet "identifiable relation" (1977, p. 86) between it and the film that follows; Andrew Tracy (2015) flails, opining that the montage is "designedly, unreadable";[3] Bergman himself describes it as a "poem in images" (Björkman et al., 1973, p. 198). Indeed, John Simon (1972) makes the only notable insight: the opening montage is comprised of *discarded cutaways* from Bergman's previous films. The significance of this observation can only be grasped from the (repressed) vantage of the optical unconscious, the other scene of the *cutaway*. This montage is a sequence of *censored images*; a sil-ver-nitrate mirror into Bergman's unconscious via *juxtaposed repression*. It is no mistake, then, that Bergman self-narrates in voice-over after the montage's titular punctuation. "The film's self-consciousness appears to originate from within,"

DOI: 10.4324/9781003200246-3

Bruce F. Kawin presciently observes: "the film becomes first person – speaks itself" (1978, pp. 113–114). *Persona* is self-conscious.

Indeed, *Persona* only realizes the optical *unconscious* through this self-consciousness. "Kinematography" – the working title of *Persona* – bluntly signals the motility of cinema, i.e., how motion is imaginarily derived from a synthesis of static frames.[4] Synthesis is created where it did not formerly exist. Thus, only by way of synthetic–imaginative complicity does the spectator render cinema possible. "When I show a film I am guilty of deceit. I use an apparatus which is constructed to take advantage of a certain human weakness" (Bergman, 1960, p. 15).[5] By "absenting images before they can be assimilated into some acceptable psychological or intellectual order," Lloyd I. Michaels rejoins, "we are searching for something that isn't there" (1978, p. 74). Effectively, the optical unconscious of *Persona* cannot be derived from its observable – that is, *conscious* – battery of images: its unconscious must be constructed from those images which have been excised, that is, *repressed*.

Recall Bergman's inclusion of the film's own production within *Persona*. Following Alma and Elisabet's final confrontation is a split-second cut of a film director (Bergman himself) descending on a crane operated by a cinematographer (Sven Nykvist). Bergman not only includes himself in *Persona* via narrative track but also in the very production of the film-itself-within-the-film. Reality is produced in cinema not through the subtraction of artifice but, paradoxically, through its amplification: the more meticulous the frame, the more artificial the editing, the more rehearsed the actors, the more detailed the production design – all the more "real" the film looks. Benjamin explains:

> In the studio the mechanical equipment has penetrated so deeply into reality that its pure aspect, freed from the foreign substance of equipment, is the result of a special procedure, namely, shooting from a particular camera set-up and linking the shot with other similar ones. The equipment-free aspect here has become the height of artifice.
>
> (1969, p. 233)[6]

Bergman exposes this cinematic ontological paradox – the achievement of natural reality by way of amplifying mechanical artifice – through including the film production of *Persona* within its own narrative. "Movies seem more natural than reality," Stanley Cavell writes, "not because they are escapes into fantasy, but because they are reliefs from private fantasy and its responsibilities; from the fact that the world is already drawn by fantasy" (1979, p. 102). Bergman's inclusion of the-film-production-within-the film-itself entices the film spectator's consciousness to consider how reality only appears as natural when artificially – that is, unconsciously – predetermined.

Eisenstein prefigures Bergman's cinematic optical unconscious. As aforementioned, Benjamin first develops the optical unconscious while defending Eisenstein's *Battleship Potemkin* (Hansen, 2005). The concept then undergoes a pivotal theoretical transformation between 1927 and 1931, turning from a *quali-tative* into a *quantitative* concept. This pivot coincides with eschewing a cine-matic context for one photographic. The optical – photographic – unconscious of 1931 *quantitatively* relates the mechanical apparatus of the camera to the eye through the ability of the camera to register unnoticed aspects of reality. In other words, the camera magnifies what the eye glazes over. Conversely, the optical – cinematic – unconscious of 1927 instantiates a *qualitative* difference between the eye and camera.[7] In a letter to Oscar A. H. Schmitz from 1927, Benjamin describes film as a "prism" opening up "*a new region of consciousness*" (1977, p. 751, emphasis original).[8] Bergman accesses this "new region of consciousness" through re-inserting that which is repressed: instead of abandoning cutaways to the bin, Bergman joins them to his opening moments; instead of suspending the disbelief of his audience, Bergman jars them into self-consciousness; instead of effacing the presence of machinery, Bergman inserts it into the most climactic moment of his film. Much like the little boy gazing at and boxed away from Elisabet's face at the beginning of *Persona*, Bergman's audience also occupies a new cinematic consciousness.

As a stand in for this new consciousness we might ask who this boy is.[9] Since we first see him outside a screen, Kawin identifies him as the film audience. "Whether character or artist, he belongs to a frame that is somehow opposite both to the fictional world and to the theater audience, as if the theater screen were somehow three-sided" (1978, p. 118). The boy wields a super-positional con-sciousness between those outside (the audience) and inside (Alma and Elisabet).[10] The boy – unlike Elisabet – has one foot in reality and one in *Persona*.[11] Within this interstitial realm resides the cinematic optical unconscious. The boy super-positions reality and fiction.

Bergman alludes to this super-position in his statement for winning the Erasmus Prize in 1965. There, he proclaimed that "people today can reject the theatre, since they live in the midst of a drama which is constantly exploding in local tragedy" (1972, p. 14). Local tragedy engulfs Elisabet three times: (1) first when she backs away in horror from television newsreels of the Vietnam War, (2) next when she gazes upon a photo of a little boy – similar in appearance to the entrapped boy of *Persona* – at the Warsaw Ghetto, (3) and finally when she witnesses Alma's desire.[12] Thus, Bergman inter-textualizes *Persona* between theater, television, and photography, all the while super-positioning reality and fiction.[13] In this respect, Kawin sees *Persona* as an inheritor of Dziga Vertov's hybrid film *Man With A Movie Camera* (1928). Following Kawin, I also view *Persona* within the genre of hybrid cinema. Instead of looking to predecessors like Vertov, however, I orient *Persona* as progenitor to Michael Haneke's *Funny Games* (1997/2007). Observing Haneke's reality–fiction super-position sheds light on Bergman's inceptive hybridity.

In one of the most horrifying scenes in *Funny Games*, Ann/Anna is paralyzed in her living room following the murder of her little boy (perhaps a nod to the boy of *Persona*). She sobs. Blood trickles down a television loudly playing a

Nascar race (which, it must be reminded, was the most popular televised sport in the United States at the time). After agonizing minutes, she painfully rises, hops, then turns it off. She – unlike us – has had enough entertainment.[14] Associating his violent cinematic entertainment *with* Nascar, Haneke critically visualizes the quintessentially American pastime of schadenfreude.[15] (*Exactly how the audience is perceptually complicit in cinema by way of its motional synthesis, so too is it ethically complicit in on-screen violence.*) Gruesomely perpetuating the violence that American filmgoers lust for, Haneke "gives back to violence that which it is: pain, a violation of others."[16] A subversion of the commodification of violence.[17] So, much like Alma's vampiric offering to Elisabet near the final moments of *Persona*, Haneke also offers audiences the blood for which they thirst.

Where Haneke's critique of cinematic violence mostly targets television, Bergman focuses on photography. Sontag describes Bergman's photographic references as "images of total violence, of unredeemed cruelty." Such images "occur in *Persona* as images of what cannot be imaginatively encompassed or digested, rather than as occasion for right political and moral thoughts" (1970, p. 141). Unable to sleep, Elisabet flicks the television on (that ubiquitous gesture of boredom). Newsreel footage of equal banality plays: another monk self-immolating in protest of the Vietnam War. Where others are inoculated to this suffering, Elisabet backs away in horror covering her mouth.[18] Uncaring for her suffering, Bergman repeatedly cuts between the television and her close-up as if to suggest – as Haneke does – that *neither Elisabet nor we can help but watch.* What will become Elisabet's symptom and retroactive rationale for psychotherapy is her inability to ignore such violence. Empathy is her symptom.

This is no ordinary neurosis. Elisabet perceives the horror of the Warsaw Ghetto with almost photographic clarity. In point of fact, the descriptors in which the doctor couches Elisabet's affliction denote photographic jargon: her urge "to be exposed" and "seen through" despite "every gesture a lie" (Bergman, 1972, p. 41).[19] Akin to the television sequence, Bergman intercuts close-ups of Elisabet's splintering face with dissected shards of the Warsaw Ghetto photo. Vierling intuits these fragmentary close-ups as conveying Elisabet's inability to synthesize the horror of the photo (1974, p. 48).[20] *But could this fragmentation not equally signify a true comprehension of macabre horror? Is Elisabet not reacting the way one should when faced with such horror?*[21] Could these fragments not be construed as elements of the *optical unconscious*, unnoticed to the naked eye of all except Elisabet? Elisabet's access to the optical unconscious of the photo indicates an over-proximity with reality (contra the doctor's prognosis of constitutional inauthenticity). Elisabet suffers not from *a lack of reality* – but from a world *all too real.*[22] When comparing our generalized inoculation to violence with Elisabet's almost photographic sensitivity to it, Elisabet indeed appears as pathological – *but only to the extent that she behaves as we ought to.*

Alma also suffers. She gleefully drives to the post office in the scene following her vampiric rendezvous with Elisabet. In a moment of snoopiness passed off as patronizing surveillance, she opens Elisabet's private correspondence. Horror strikes. She realizes that it is not she who is watching but Elisabet who is watching her. Alma's position as spectatorial subject inverts: her status descends from subject to object. Bergman up-mixes dripping water to emphasize Alma's schizoid revelation. Liquidity underlays Alma's aphanisis, eroding rigid boundaries.[23] The doctor becomes patient; the rational ego undermined by libidinous excess. Alma's optics are reversed.

Alma's imaginary entrapment crystallizes during a later moment in the film which is overdetermined both by her performative debut and Elisabet's emotional nadir. There, Elisabet balks in horror (exactly as she did in front of the Vietnam War newsreel and Warsaw Ghetto photo) at a vision of Alma romancing with her husband, Mr. Vogler. Elisabet's reaction is certainly unexpected, given her self-acknowledged apathy towards her family, but her horror is not a result of her husband and Alma's promiscuity; rather, her horror derives from the fact that *Alma is realizing her desire.* Of note is a contrast in image quality between Alma with Mr. Vogler and Elisabet: while her medium close-up is of a similar quality to the rest of the film, the embrace of Alma and Mr. Vogler degrades – as if back-screen projected. On screen for Elisabet to gaze, Alma realizes both of her desires: *to be a wife and actress.* The horrific thing of her unconscious desire made manifest.

So, too, does *Persona* render visible the underscored cinematic dimensions of the optical unconscious. Casting this concept in photographic light not only effaces the "sensory-somatic immediacy, anonymous collectivity, and unpredictability" of the cinema (Hansen, 1999, p. 341), but also obscures the way in which cinema realizes unconscious dimensions of desire. Whereas the optical unconscious of photography arises from a quantitative distinction between the camera and eye, the optical unconscious of cinema arises from their qualitative incongruity. *The eye cannot see desire – the cinema can.* Looking to the interstitial frames between the opening montage of *Persona*, its hybridization of violence and reality, as well as the super-positional consciousness of Elisabet and the little boy, the cinematic optical unconscious brings to light understudied dimensions in Benjamin's thought and Bergman's *Persona*. On Bergman's centennial let us grant *Persona* its due: a foundational moment in the history of cinema by way of a cinematic optical unconscious.

Notes

1 I am deeply indebted to the incisive feedback I received on this draft from my mentor Mariana Ortega. I would also like to thank the continued presence of Carl Hofbauer in my life and cinema.

2 Benjamin writes that the photographic apparatus registers aspects of reality which are invisible and unnoticed to the naked eye: "It is, after all, a different nature that speaks to the camera than to the human eye; different in particular in the sense that an unconsciously permeated space takes the place of the space that man has interwoven with consciousness" (2015, p. 111).

3 Cf., Tracy's close but not quite review of *Persona* in www.reverseshot.org/symposiums/entry/2039/persona_space.

4 "When we experience a film," Bergman remarks, "we consciously prime ourselves for illusion. Putting aside will and intellect, we make way for it in our *imagination*" (1960, p. 51, emphasis mine).

5 Bergman's mendacity also arises from his sexual proximity to the film. While preparing the script for *The Silence* (1963), Bergman confided in Vilgot Sjöman that he would translate a dream he had of two men into a story about two women. A masculinized *Persona* would be "too close to himself," Sjöman reports (p. 190). Femininity provides enough of a distance from Bergman to himself so that he may self-disclose. In this vein Gwendolyn Audrey Foster (2000) views *Persona* as a "queertopia," projecting "meaning on Bergman who, in effect, becomes the spectator" (p. 132). Bergman's reflection is a woman; he is his own imaginary transgender spectator.

6 Here I apply Benjamin's comments to the context of film but, as Miriam Hansen notes, Benjamin's comments also target the ever increasing inclusion of machinery into the social life of the proletariat. As Hansen explains: "The complex and highly artificial manner in which film creates an illusion of reality, Benjamin argues, gives it a particular status in the technical mediation of contemporary life" (1987, p. 203).

7 Connecting the optical unconscious with Benjamin's 1927 thoughts on cinema also explains the conceptual changes between its 1931 version in "A Little History on Photography" and its famous reappearance in the 1936 "Work of Art" essay. Consider §16 from this late work: "with the close-up, space expands; with slow motion, movement is extended. Clearly it is another nature which speaks to the camera as compared to the eye." A phenomenological difference between the eye and camera is marked; a difference effaced in the concept's 1931 version. This insight is crucial for Shawn Michelle Smith's (2013) recent uptake. In her otherwise striking manuscript, *At the Edge of Sight*, Smith overlooks the origins of Benjamin's optical unconscious. By her lights, the optical unconscious merely illuminates sights formerly unseen: to "make visible what usually evades perception" (p. 4). As I argue, this misreading arises from casting the optical unconscious in mere photographic, as opposed to cinematic, terms.

8 It is no accident that Benjamin first formulates the optical unconscious upon viewing the first systematic deployment of Eisensteinian intellectual montage. Eisenstein connects the elevation of consciousness with montage in language not unlike Benjamin's 1927 elaborations. Intellectual montage, Eisenstein tells us, illuminates "an immense collection of so-called *subsensory phenomena, i.e.,* those that act on us not only *without being noticed in the field of consciousness*" (p. 178, emphasis mine). Could we then consider Bergman's opening montage of *Persona* as a development upon Eisenstein's intellectual montage?

9 Multiple candidates emerge: Alma's aborted child, Elisabet's abandoned son, or, in Bergman's own words, the director himself. Self-identifying as the boy, Bergman describes him as someone "not allowed to be dead" (Björkman et al., p. 199). Does the meaning of the boy extend beyond Bergman's self-identification to other, unforeseen, personas?

10 Mistakenly, I argue, Kawin ascribes Elisabet the same super-positional consciousness as the boy. Kawin compares the boy's ability to break the fourth wall with Elisabet's (apparent) cognizance of her audience (p. 118). The parallel breaks when we consider Mr. Vogler's intrusive presence. Elisabet hallucinates Alma and Mr. Vogler embracing. Elisabet looks to our direction but does not make eye-contact: her gaze absently peering off our eye-line. Elisabet never makes eye contact with the audience the way in which the little boy can.

11 Take, for example, Alma's soliloquy in the film's opening act: "I'll marry Karl-Henrik and we'll have a couple of kids that I'll bring up. That's all decided, it's in me somewhere. I don't have to work things out at all, how they're going to be. That makes you

feel safe." The moment seeps with theatricality though performed by the doctor (as opposed to the thespian patient). From its inceptive moments, *Persona* already obscures who is watched and watching. P. Adams Sitney (1986) acutely notices how Alma turns to the camera as though it were a mirror. Perhaps, then, Alma is *unaware* of the fourth wall *the same way* in which Elisabet is.

12 A scene I return to at the end of my remarks.

13 "On one level," Sitney writes, "the distinction between documentary and fictive images corresponds to the discrimination between narrative and poetic modes of representation." At the "boundaries of cinematography, television, and photograph" (p. 126).

14 Tarja Laine writes: "the audience functions as an accomplice to the torture of the Schobers [Farbers, in the US version], who cannot move between the diegesis and non-diegesis in the ways the torturers can" (p. 57). Both *Persona* and *Funny Games*, then, play with migrating between diegetic and nondiegetic realities in similar ways.

15 Cf., Jeffries, Stuart: "Master Manipulator," *The Guardian*, March 31, 2008, Arts Section, p. 23.

16 qtd. in Adam Minns, "*Funny Games*," www.filmfestivals.com/cannes97/cfilmd17 .htm

17 Susan Sontag shares a similar concern: "our failure is one of imagination, of *empathy*," she writes (2003, p. 8). Sontag continues: "We have failed to hold the reality of violence in mind because of the steady flow of accessional ("entertaining") violence in films and mass media" (2003, p. 8). Bergman himself exhibits this modern lack of empathy when he admits that he is "unable to grasp large catastrophes … they leave my heart untouched. At most I can read about such atrocities with a kind of greed – a pornography of horror" (1994, p. 59).

18 Why would she cover her mouth if her psychic affliction is an inability to speak? Perhaps the question is ill-framed. Maybe this violence is the *cause* of her speechlessness, i.e, no words can describe horror. But can images?

19 Kawin compares "Elisabet's search for 'being'" to "a photograph's attempt to become unfiltered, undefined light" (p. 120).

20 "Again," Vierling writes, "just as the photograph meant nothing except as a totality, *Persona* exists as a thematic meditation upon the very idea of synthesis" (p. 49). This narrative meditation also reflects a formal meditation. Vierling continues: "film itself is fusion, the bringing together of static separate images and, by importing temporality to them, causing them to synthesize into a motion picture" (pp. 49–50). Simon (1972) goes as far as to run *Persona* through a movieola, seeing it as a series of images (rather than a cohesive film).

21 An incisive point I owe to my mentor, Mariana Ortega.

22 "It appears that [Elisabet's] demand for truth leads her, out of disgust with her falseness, to drop her artistic roles and other role she has been playing," rejoins Jones. She "seems to be in a life more real and brutal than the world of artistic roles and defences" (p. 78).

23 In "Liquid Intelligence," Jeff Wall (1989) articulates that photography commences not with technological reproduction but liquid chemical bathing. Writing during the proliferation of digital photography, Wall speculates that photography's liquidity has been systematically overshadowed. Suppressing liquidity buttresses the mass perception of photography as dry, optical, and rational (as opposed to moist, sensorial, and suprarational. While the "dry intelligence" of optics and camera machinery freezes imagery, it is the "liquid intelligence" of chemical development that "achieves a historical self-reflection, a memory of the path [photography] has traversed" (p. 209). Photography switches the dry for the liquid, the rational for the alchemical. Bergman, I assert, sonically interpolates this photographic eschewal by underscoring Alma's psychotic break with dripping water.

Bibliography

Adorno, T. W. (1997). *Aesthetic Theory.* Translated and Edited by Robert Hullot-Kentor. London and New York: Continuum.

Barr, A. P. (1987). "The Unraveling of Character in Bergman's *Persona.*" *Literature/Film Quarterly*, Vol. 15, No. 2, pp. 123–136. Salisbury: Salisbury University.

Benjamin, W. (1969). "The Work of Art in the Age of Mechanical Reproduction." In*Illuminations*, edited by Hannah Arendt and translated by Harry Zohn. New York: Schocken Book.

Benjamin, W. (1977). "Erwiderung an Oskar A. H. Schmitz." *Gesammelte Schriften*, Vol. 2, pp. 751–755. Frankfurt: Suhrkamp Verlag.

Benjamin, W. (2010). "The Work of Art in the Age of Its Technological Reproducibility" [First Version]. In *Grey Room, No. 39, Walter Benjamin's Media Tactics: Optics, Perception, and the Work of Art (Spring 2010)*, translated by Michael W. Jennings. Cambridge: MIT Press, pp. 11–38.

Benjamin, W. (2015). "A Short History of Photography." In*On Photography, Walter Benjamin*, translated and edited by Esther Leslie. London: Reaktion Books, pp. 123–136.

Bergman, I. (1960). *Ingmar Bergman: A Guide to References and Resources*. New York: Simon & Shuster.

Bergman, I. (1972). *Bergman: Persona and Shame*. Translated by Keith Bradfield. New York: Grossman.

Bergman, I. (1994). *Images*. New York: Arcade.

Björkman, S., Manns, T., and Sima, J. (1973). *Bergman on Bergman*. Translated by Paul Britten Austin. New York: Simon & Shuster.

Cavell, S. (1979). *The World Viewed*. Cambridge: Harvard University Press.

Eisenstein, S. (1987). *Nonindifferent Nature: Film and the Structure of Things*. Translated by Herbert Marshall. Cambridge: Cambridge University Press.

Foster, G. A. (2000). "Feminist Theory and the Performance of Lesbian Desire in *Persona.*" In *Ingmar Bergman's Persona*, edited by Lloyd Michaels. Cambridge: Cambridge University Press.

Hansen, M. B. (1987). "Benjamin, Cinema and Experience: The Blue Flower in the Land of Technology." *New German Critique*, No. 40, Special Issue on *Weimar Film Theory* (Winter 1987). Durham, NC: Duke University Press, pp. 179–224.

Hansen, M. B. (1999). "Benjamin and Cinema: Not a One-Way Street." *Critical Inquiry*, Vol. 25, No. 2, pp. 306–343. In 'Angelus Novus': Perspectives on Walter Benjamin *(Winter 1999)*. Durham, NC: Duke University Press.

Hansen, M. B. (2005). "'Of Lightning Rods, Prisms, and Forgotten Scissors': Potemkin and German Film Theory." *New German Critique*, No. 95, Special Issue *for David Bathrick* (Spring–Summer 2005). Durham, NC: Duke University Press, pp. 162–179.

Jones, C. J. (1977). "Bergman's *Persona* and the Artistic Dilemma of the Modern Narrative." *Literature/Film Quarterly*, Vol. 5, No. 1 (Winter 1977), pp.75–88. Salisbury: Salisbury University.

Kawin, B. F. (1978). *Mindscreen: Bergman, Godard, and First-Person Film*. Princeton, NJ: Princeton University Press.

Lacan, J. (2006). *Écrits*. Translated by Bruce Fink in Collaboration With Héloïse Fink and Russell Grigg. New York: W. W. Norton & Company.

Laine, T. (2010). "Haneke's "Funny" Games With the Audience (Revisited)." In *On Michael Haneke*, edited by Brian Price and John David Rhodes. Detroit: Wayne State University Press.

Metz, C. (1975). "The Imaginary Signifier." In *Screen*, translated by Ben Brewster, Vol. 16, No. 2 (Summer 1975). Oxford: Oxford University Press, pp. 14–76.

Michaels, L. I. (1978). "The Imaginary Signifier in Bergman's *Persona*." *Film Criticism*, Vol. 2, No. 2/3, *Special Double Issue on Film Theory* (Winter/Spring 1978). Meadville: Allegheny College, pp. 72–77.

Samuels, C. (1972). *Encountering Directors*. New York: G.P. Putnam's Sons/Capricorn.

Simon, J. (1972). *Ingmar Bergman Directs*. New York: Harcourt Brace Jovanovich.

Sitney, P. A. (1986). "Kinematography and the Analytic Text: A Reading of *Persona*." *October*, Vol. 38 (Autumn 1986), pp. 112–130. Cambridge: MIT Press.

Sjöman, V. (1978). *L 136: Diary With Ingmar Bergman*. Translated by Alan Blair. Ann Arbor: Karoma.

Smith, S. M. (2013). *At the Edge of Sight: Photography and the Unseen*. Durham, NC: Duke University Press.

Sontag, S. (1967). "Persona." *Sight and Sound*, Vol. 36, No. 4 (Autumn), pp. 186–191.

Sontag, S. (1970). "Bergman's *Persona*." In *Styles of Radical Will*. New York: Delta, pp. 123–145.

Sontag, S. (2003). *Regarding the Pain of Others*. New York: Farrar, Straus and Giroux.

Tracy, A. (2015). "Persona." *Reverse Shot*, April 8, 2015.

Vierling, D. L. (1974). "Bergman's *Persona*: The Metaphysics of Meta-Cinema." *Diacritics*, Vol. 4, No. 2 (Summer 1974), pp. 48–51. Baltimore: Johns Hopkins University Press.

Wall, J. (1989). "Photography and Liquid Intelligence." In *Jeff Wall: The Complete Edition*, edited by Thierry de Duve. New York: Phaidon, pp. 209–210.

Chapter 3

Fanny and Alexander, Hamlet, and the Ethical Unconscious

Robert Samuels

Throughout Bergman's *Fanny and Alexander* (1982), there are allusions to Shakespeare's *Hamlet*, but what do these references tells us about the relations among film, psychoanalysis, and life itself? It will be my argument that Bergman's work reveals an important insight derived from a combination of Freud and Shakespeare, which concerns the ethical status of the unconscious. In fact, as Lacan surprisingly argues in his *Four Fundamental Concepts of Psychoanalysis*, the unconscious represents the ethical core of the subject.[1]

The Ethical Unconscious

Within the plot of the film, the father of Fanny and Alexander dies while he is preparing to play Hamlet's father's ghost in a theatrical production at the family's theater. Moreover, throughout the movie, Alexander continues to see his dead father, who often just looks at him with a face of discontent. In fact, the young boy cannot comprehend why his father does not just go away forever, and like Hamlet himself, he appears conflicted over seeing the presence of his already dead father. To begin to understand this appearance of Hamlet's ghost in the film, we can look at the most famous speech in theater history, which is Hamlet's "To be or not to be" soliloquy:

> To be, or not to be, that is the question:
> Whether 'tis nobler in the mind to suffer
> The slings and arrows of outrageous fortune,
> Or to take arms against a sea of troubles
> And by opposing end them. To die—to sleep ...[2]

The first part of the speech asks if it is better to live or commit suicide when one faces a traumatic event. However, the key move is to equate dying with sleeping, so that the dream state becomes equivalent with purgatory.[3] Here, premodern religion is being internalized by the early modern subject as the ethical dimension moves from the afterlife to the present life. Importantly, this displacement of purgatory as the space for moral judgment is located in the unconscious.

DOI: 10.4324/9781003200246-4

Hamlet implies that the reason why he does not want to end his life is that he knows he cannot escape the consequences of his actions because his sin will be remembered in his dreams:

> To sleep, perchance to dream—ay, there's the rub:
> For in that sleep of death what dreams may come,
> When we have shuffled off this mortal coil,
> Must give us pause—there's the respect
> That makes calamity of so long life.

It is therefore the fear of what will happen in his dreams that prevents Hamlet from ending his own life. Of course, this makes no sense since if he was dead, he would no longer dream, but what I believe Shakespeare is pointing to is the broader point that what makes us ethical subjects is the fact that we cannot escape the return of the truth in our unconscious dreams. In other words, the conscience is unconscious.[4]

Instead of simply talking about committing suicide or killing his uncle, it should be clear that Hamlet is indicating a much broader range of acts:

> For who would bear the whips and scorns of time,
> Th'oppressor's wrong, the proud man's contumely,
> The pangs of dispriz'd love, the law's delay,
> The insolence of office, and the spurns
> That patient merit of th'unworthy takes,
> When he himself might his quietus make
> With a bare bodkin? Who would fardels bear,
> To grunt and sweat under a weary life,
> But that the dread of something after death,
> The undiscove'd country, from whose bourn
> No traveller returns, puzzles the will,
> And makes us rather bear those ills we have
> Than fly to others that we know not of?
> Thus conscience does make cowards of us all,
> And thus the native hue of resolution
> Is sicklied o'er with the pale cast of thought,
> And enterprises of great pitch and moment
> With this regard their currents turn awry
> And lose the name of action.

It should be clear that the undiscovered land that houses our conscience must be the unconscious as a new form of purgatory. What then puzzles the will of Hamlet are the thoughts that he cannot escape when he goes to sleep.

Shakespeare is clearly representing in this play something beyond the inability of one man to follow his father's quest for revenge. By anticipating Freud, this early modern playwright realizes that the only thing that stops us from suicide and other destructive acts is that we know that we cannot escape our own unconscious thoughts and memories. As Freud insisted, memories can never be completely effaced, and so they return in an uncontrollable manner, like the presence of Alexander's dead father.[5]

The Play's the Thing

In discussing Hamlet's ghost in relation to Freud's example of an anxiety dream, Lacan makes the following interesting observation: "What he is burning with, if not that with which we see emerging at other points designated by the Freudian topology, namely the weight of the sins of the father, born by the ghost in the myth of Hamlet, which Freud couples with the myth of Oedipus."[6] Lacan here indicates that Hamlet is not only guilty of his own sins, but he is also being judged by the sins of his father. While Hamlet tends to idealize his dead father, the father himself tells his son that he was "cut off in the blossoms of his sins."[7]

It is probably just a coincidence, but Freud's dream of the burning child is very similar to the murder of the evil stepfather's sister in *Fanny and Alexander*, who is also burned in her bed when a lamp is tipped over. In the film, this event is partially blamed on Alexander who tries to will it telepathically into action. As we see in many scenes, Alexander's desires often transform reality, just as the artist seeks to create a magical world; however, what Bergman stresses is the continuity between real life and theater. Just as Shakespeare proclaimed that we are all actors on a stage, Bergman films the first half of his movie to stress the theatrical nature of everyday life: virtually every room is framed by theater curtains, and there are constant references to people playing their roles and saying scripted things.[8]

This blending of theater and reality returns to *Hamlet*, since this play is itself framed as a play within a play. Not only does Hamlet put on a play that repeats vital aspects of his father's murder, but once Hamlet starts giving the actors stage directions, he becomes a double for Shakespeare himself.[9] As the writer and direc tor of his own theater production, Hamlet as Shakespeare comments on the ethical function of theater itself:

> For murder, though it have no tongue, will speak
> With most miraculous organ. I'll have these players
> Play something like the murder of my father
> Before mine uncle. I'll observe his looks.
> …
> More relative than this. The play's the thing
> Wherein I'll catch the conscience of the king.

Shakespeare posits here that theater has the ability to access the conscience of the audience through its symbolic repetition of sin. From this perspective, art can trigger the ethical unconscious by using indirect symbolic representations.

As metafictions, both *Hamlet* and *Fanny and Alexander* create a doubled, ironic discourse where the depiction of events is coupled with an awareness of the difference between reality and fiction.[10] In the case of the film, Alexander's father's speech about theater reveals this self-reflexive nature of the movie:

> I love this little world inside the thick walls of this playhouse. And I'm fond of the people who work in this little world. Outside is the big world, and sometimes the little world succeeds for a moment in reflecting the big world, so that we understand it better. Or is it perhaps that we give the people who come here the chance of forgetting for a while ... the harsh world outside.[11]

From this perspective, theater does at times help us to understand reality, but it can also serve to allow us to escape from reality. This doubled nature of cultural productions points to the complex and overdetermined nature of artistic creation: art may mirror nature; however, there is always an escape hatch that allows us to not take artistic productions too seriously.

From a psychoanalytic perspective, irony and metafiction can be best understood through Freud's theory of humor where he argues that the joke teller gives the audience pleasure, and in return, they promise not to criticize the speaker.[12] Here we see how culture can function to suspend the social conscience as one is able to transgress laws and norms without fear of consequence. However, Freud also posits that since we can never fully erase the memories of our thoughts and feelings, whatever we try to repress or deny continues to return in the form of an unconscious symptom.

The Child of Theater

A crucial aspect of the film is that it is shaped by the reconstructed memories of an imaginative child. From this perspective, we see how reality and fiction are combined as the recollection of the past is full of supernatural representations. Moreover, we learn from psychoanalysis that our understanding of our own family histories is often shaped by fantasy, and so on the level of our unconscious, it is unclear what is fact and what is fiction.[13] Bergman himself notes in reference to his own art, the close relationship between childhood fantasy and sublimation:

> The prerogative of childhood is to move unhindered between magic and oatmeal porridge, between boundless terror and explosive joy ... It was difficult to differentiate what was fantasy and what was considered real. If I made an effort, I was perhaps able to make reality stay real. But, for instance there were the ghosts and spectres. What should I do with them? ... Then came the cinematograph.[14]

From Bergman's perspective, the artist is able to use the unconscious by transforming fantasy into a shared cultural experience, which itself transgresses the reality principle. The problematic nature of artistic creation thus matches the contradictions of the unconscious; on one level, art and other unconscious formations give us access to truth, but this truth is presented in a disguised form.[15]

Like Hamlet, the central issues facing Alexander concern the relation between the death of the father and the anxiety of the son. Not only is this young boy haunted by the ghost of his father, but he is also threatened by the power of his own thoughts and their ability to shape reality. Since he believes that he has caused a death by wishing for someone to die, we can see how his Oedipal desire to be with his mother and kill off his stepfather resembles Hamlet's conflicted relation to his parents and uncle.[16] Due to the Freudian notion that on the level of the unconscious, there is no distinction made between intention and reality, one is prone to what Freud called in *Totem and Taboo*, the "omnipotence of thoughts."[17]

The Ghost of Consciousness

For Freud, we find in animistic cultures, psychotic delusions, and infantile hallucinations, the same confusion between internal representations and the perception of the external world. In fact, Freud posits that when an infant is faced with an unmet need, the first response is to hallucinate the object of satisfaction.[18] Freud adds that what happens in this structure is that the memory of an earlier scene of fulfillment is activated and treated as if it was the perception of an external reality. Human thought is then defined by psychoanalysis as founded on the psychotic equivalence between internal mental representations and the perception of reality. On the level of pure thought, symbols are treated as things, and things are treated as symbols. Moreover, as Descartes insists, since when we are thinking we never know if we are awake or dreaming, consciousness is prone to the psychotic suspension of reality testing.[19] For Freud and Descartes, then, thinking is itself a problem that leads to the power of imagination and the escape from the reality principle.

We can employ this theory of consciousness to understand the use of ghosts in *Hamlet* and *Fanny and Alexander*. On the most basic level, a ghost is a projection and hallucination caused by treating a memory as if it is a direct perception of reality.[20] According to Lacan, what is rejected in the symbolic returns in the real, and so hallucinations and delusions are centered on the confusion of foreclosed symbolic memories and the perception of external reality.[21] For example, as Freud discovered, when paranoid subjects are hearing voices or are certain that they are being observed, what is really happening is that they are perceiving their own internal conscience as if it is coming from the Other.[22] Freud states that this form of psychosis represents the truth, since we are constantly observing ourselves from the perspective of the social order embodied by other people. The difference between psychotics and non-psychotics is that the psychotic subject actually perceives the super-ego in the form of another person, idea, or thing. A ghost is then an externalized super-ego that watches over the subject and externalizes the internal censor and critic.

For Freud, the first stage of civilization is defined by the belief in spirits (animism), and one of the causes for this thought–system is the refusal to accept death or the distinction between humans and other beings and things.[23] In an animistic culture, social norms and values are perceived to be natural, and nature itself is experienced through the mediation of unintentional social symbols and meanings.

A ghost then is seen as part of nature, but in reality, it is created through the subjective experience of cultural values. With Alexander and Hamlet, we can say that the subject experiences his guilt through the form of an external perception of the hallucinated ghost.

It is vital to stress that Freud's essential insight is that consciousness itself is psychotic, and what allows us to break from this initial state is the reality principle through the process of separating thoughts from perceptions.[24] For example, Freud hypothesizes that the baby will hallucinate the satisfaction of its desire until it becomes frustrated by the lack of the object in reality.[25] Once the loss of the object is accepted, then the memory of a previous satisfaction can be dis-invested. In a structure of mourning, one has to acknowledge both the loss of the object and the past scene of fulfillment.[26] From this perspective, psychosis and animism are caused by a lack of mourning and the dominance of hallucination.

Moreover, what Freud finds in paranoia, dreams, and "primitive" cultures is the same foreclosure and projection of the conscience. In all of the states, one feels as if one is being observed, and everything is full of meaning, and yet one is not in control of what is being seen or thought. Here thought comes from the Other as the ego is suspended and reality testing is removed. If Hamlet and Alexander see ghosts, it must be because they have rejected aspects of their own super-ego, and so they experience their guilt and shame as if they are embodied by an external perception.

Beyond Consciousness

This radical definition of consciousness as psychosis by both Freud and Descartes pushes us to ask how we escape our own psychotic perceptions, and for Freud, the first response is through the formation of the unconscious with the process of repression.[27] If the neurotic represses the conscience and consciousness, it is because the formation of the ego is essentially a defense mechanism.[28] Unlike the dream or the hallucination, the subject of reflexive consciousness sees and understands from the individual's point of view. What we often call subjectivity relies on the imaginary belief in intentionality and the controlling of thoughts. As Lacan insists, in a dream we have no control over what we are shown, but in our waking state of self-consciousness, we believe that we are in charge of our thoughts and feelings.[29] Paradoxically, this creation of imaginary ego intentionality is derived from our ability to identify with external representations. As Freud posits, since the ego is not there in the beginning, it has to be produced, and Lacan uses his theory of the mirror stage to show how this formation occurs when the child first recognizes itself in a mirrored reflection.[30] The key to this explanation is to see the mirrored image as only a metaphor for the larger processes of identifying with a similar object in the world. Thus, one sees another child around the same age, and then this external image helps to build an internal virtual body map.[31] Ironically, the child starts to perceive itself as a separate being with intention and a point of view by copying the movements and representations of a mirrored other. Individuality is then born out of alienation and conformity.

In terms of watching a movie, like *Fanny and Alexander*, this theory of the imaginary ego helps us to understand how we can become interested in a fictional character. On one level, we identify with these characters and feel what they feel, but at the same time, this conforming identification helps to re-enforce our own sense of individuality. Since we learn about ourselves through imitation, self-knowledge is founded on identification. Thus, as Lacan argues, the ego is an other for the Other.[32] In fact, when Hamlet puts on a play so that he can catch the conscience of the king, he implies that by using a fiction to imitate the scene of the original crime, he can access the repressed guilt of his audience. From Shakespeare's perspective, art functions by using the symbolic repetition of repressed content to make the repressed consciousness of the audience conscious. In this structure, the unconscious of the creator communicates with the unconscious of the audience, and so both are unaware of what is really happening.[33]

Art and Unconscious Communication

This idea of unconscious communication sheds light on the psychoanalytic conception of sublimation: true art occurs when the artist freely expresses repressed fantasies so that they can be experienced by the repressed desires and fears of the audience.[34] Moreover, the way that art circumvents internal and external censorship is by representing its truths in an indirect, disguised form. Thus, art turns to symbolism so that it can both express and repress its desired content, and all of this happens in an uncontrolled and unaware way.

In the case of *Fanny and Alexander*, the external censor and super-ego is represented primarily by the strict, religious stepfather.[35] As the one who wants to control what Alexander says and does, this symbol of cultural normativity becomes the target of the boy's fear and rage. Unlike his father's ghost, the real presence of the castrating stepfather forces Alexander to turn to the reality principle to determine the difference between the products of his own imagination and the reality of things he cannot change through thoughts and memories.

Ironic Metafiction

To further elaborate on the psychoanalytic theory of art and sublimation, I want to address the role of irony in the film and in *Hamlet*. As I mentioned above, we can consider both artistic creations to be metafictions because they present a self-reflexive awareness of the conditions of their own production.[36] In the case of *Hamlet*, by having the main character put on a play to catch the conscience of his audience, Shakespeare creates an ironic doubling since the creator and the audience are both represented within the plot and outside of the story.[37] Since Hamlet acts as a theater director, he takes on the role of Shakespeare, and so everything Hamlet says to his actors can be related to what Shakespeare thinks about acting and direction.[38] Likewise, because he puts on his play with the intention of creating a reaction in his audience, which is represented by his stepfather/uncle, we as the audience are both watching the play, while being represented as a character in the play. One of the main effects of this doubling structure is that everything has to be interpreted on two very different levels: one level concerns the inner logic of the plot, and the other level concerns how theater itself is imagined to work.

From a psychoanalytic perspective, this doubling effect not only relates to the process of imaginary identification, where one is both a separate individual and an imitation of another person, but doubling also creates the ironic ability to both say and unsay the same thing.[39] In other terms, when one is using irony, one cannot be held responsible for what one says because one is taking a distance to one's own words.[40] Moreover, by highlighting one's awareness of what one is doing, it is hard to critique one for being unaware. Likewise, irony trades in the complicity of the awareness of the audience, and this complicity is founded on the idea that knowingness trumps guilt and shame. In fact, Freud argued that the representations of the cultural production give the audience pleasure, and in exchange, the audience promises to not hold the producer responsible for what is said and done.[41] Ironic art and humor thus circumvent the social super-ego and so, on a political level, we can say that metafiction has the effect of removing responsibility from the audience and the artist. Like the court jester, the artist cannot be attacked because it is only a character or a story or a joke.

In the case of *Fanny and Alexander*, the use of metafiction is signaled by the constant visual and verbal references to theater. People are represented as playing roles in real life as actors are affected by real events. Moreover, it is clear that Alexander represents aspects of Bergman himself and his own biography, and so this character is both a portrait of the artist as a young man and a fictional representation with no direct relation to the artist.[42] Furthermore, to the consternation of many critics, events occur in the film that have no logical explanation.[43] For instance, in the scene where Fanny and Alexander escape in a chest, the two characters are shown to be in two different locations at the same time. So it is not only Alexander who sees ghosts and moving statues, but we as the audience, also see things that cannot happen in reality.[44]

Self-reflexive, irony, like the kind we see in *Hamlet* and *Fanny and Alexander*, forces us to ponder the effect of fictional art from a psychoanalytic perspective. On a fundamental level, what we encounter in both of these artistic creations is that the conscience and consciousness are repressed into the unconscious through a process of doubling and splitting. People are able to escape their guilt and shame because they create an inner distance to their own words and actions. This denial of responsibility, in turn, allows us to satisfy the pleasure principle, which represents the human desire to avoid all inner and outer tension. As an escape from freedom and responsibility, the enjoyment of fiction and art can therefore pose a series of personal and social problems. In fact Freud makes the following argument about pleasure in *Civilization and its Discontents*:

The service rendered by intoxicating media in the struggle for happiness and in keeping misery at a distance is so highly prized as a benefit that individuals and people alike have given them an established place in the economics of the libido. We owe to such media not merely the immediate yield of pleasure, but also a greatly desired degree of independence from the external world.[45]

Although Freud is talking about the use of drugs here to provide pleasure through escape, we can also apply the same logic to the consumption of media like films and plays. In fact, it is in Freud's theory of jokes that we discover the most fundamental psychoanalytic conception of cultural media in relation to the unconscious and the pleasure principle.[46]

Culture Is a Joke

Even though Freud's work on humor focuses on only one form of popular culture, it can be read as a more general approach to the psychoanalysis of culture, subjectivity, and society. Freud's first surprising point is that jokes, as a form of play, help to lead to contemplation and offer a non-demanding relationship with objects:

the aesthetic attitude towards an object is characterized by the condition that we expect nothing from this object – especially no gratification of our serious needs – but that we content ourselves with the pleasure of contemplating the same. In contrast to labor the aesthetic attitude is playful.[47]

From this perspective, jokes and other forms of entertainment can constitute non-exploitative relationships because the joke teller does not expect anything from other people other than their laughter. Furthermore, humor can also lead to disinterested analysis and critical thought because it is not focused on direct satisfaction and self-interest.[48]

As a potential form of critical thinking, jokes also allow us to think about the relationship between different things that we do not normally connect together: "wit as the skill to combine with surprising quickness many ideas, which through inner content and connections are foreign to one another."[49] Humor and other forms of popular culture then can help us to think new thoughts, which enables us to see how different aspects of the world are actually related. In fact, as Freud summarizes past theories of humor, he sees comedy as a central aspect of the modern enlightenment:

For the criteria and attributes of wit mentioned by these authors, such as – activity, the relation of the content of wit to our thoughts, the character of the playful judgment, the union of dissimilarities, contrasting ideas, "sense in nonsense," the succession of confusion and clearness, the sudden emergence of the hidden, and the peculiar brevity of wit, seem to us, at first glance, so very pertinent and so easily demonstrable by examples that we cannot succumb to the danger of underestimating the value of such ideas.[50]

For Freud, humor represents an advanced level of thinking, but the problem is that people do not know how to take it seriously.[51]

One of Freud's main points is that since societies have to control our sexual and violent impulses in order to maintain some level of order, it is also necessary to allow for indirect ways of expressing these repressed urges:

> Owing to the repression brought about by civilization many primary pleasures are now disapproved by the censor and lost. But the human psyche finds renunciation very difficult; hence we discover that tendency-wit furnishes us with a means to make the renunciation retrogressive and thus to regain what has been lost.[52]

From both a subjective and social perspective, the ability of humor and other forms of popular culture to provide a safe and acceptable venue for the expression of repressed impulses can be understood as a positive thing.[53] In other words, entertainment plays a role in keeping people happy and content, which could have both positive and negative results. On the positive side, since we need some level of social organization, it is important to provide individuals with a space for expressing what they normally cannot express. However, this social safety-valve can also play a negative role since it may motivate people not to pursue positive social change.[54]

As Steven Pinker[55] has documented, our cultures have become increasingly less violent, and for Freud, one reason for this progress is the way jokes provide a relatively peaceful form of aggression: "Violent hostility, no longer tolerated by law, has been replaced by verbal invectives."[56] Humor and different modes of entertainment thus replace direct violence with indirect symbolic aggression, and this transformation represents a possible positive side to popular culture and everyday humor. Instead of killing each other directly, we may be using jokes as a way of releasing our pent-up aggression in a relatively safe and peaceful way.[57]

Freud also sees humor as a potential political weapon against unjust authorities and other exploitative social elites:

> The prevention of abuse or insulting retorts through outer circumstances is so often the case that tendency-wit is used with special preference as a weapon of attack or criticism of superiors who claim to be an authority. Wit then serves as a resistance against such authority and as an escape from its pressure. In this factor, too, lies the charm of caricature, at which we laugh even if it is badly done simply because we consider its resistance to authority a great merit.[58]

Mockery and other forms of popular culture can play a positive role in undermining authorities and lowering the status of oppressive elites. As a mode of resistance for disempowered people, humor and other forms of culture serve as alternative forms of social protest.[59]

Freud also insists that popular culture as a type of humorous entertainment helps us to challenge rigid dogma and unjust social hierarchies:

The object of attack by wit may equally well be institutions, persons, in so far as they may act as agents of these, moral or religious precepts, or even philosophies of life which enjoy so much respect that they can be challenged in no other way than under the guise of a witticism, and one that is veiled by a façade at that.[60]

Since humor hides its social criticism under the façade of being just meaningless entertainment, it has the ability to say what one normally is not allowed to say.[61] For instance, monarchs often would have a court jester who got away with speaking the truth because no one took him seriously.[62] Although this lack of seriousness could undermine his message, it also worked to allow the truth to come to the surface.[63]

It is interesting that Freud is at his most political when he is discussing the way humor serves as compensation for an unjust social order:

One can plainly tell what these witticisms whisper, namely, that the wishes and desires of man have a right to make themselves perceptible next to our pretentious and inconsiderate morality. And in our times it has been said in emphatic and striking terms that this morality is merely the selfish precept of the few rich and mighty who can gratify their desires at any time without deferment. As long as the art of healing has not succeeded in safeguarding our lives, and as long as the social organizations do not do more towards making conditions more agreeable, just so long cannot the voice within us which is striving against the demands of morality, be stifled. Every honest person finally makes this admission – at least to himself. The decision in this conflict is possible only through the roundabout way of a new understanding.[64]

Since people with power determine the morality affecting the disempowered, the people without power should be able to release their immoral impulses in an indirect manner.[65] Of course, a problem with this formulation is that the people in power often allow indirect forms of freedom for the masses in order to redirect their protests and maintain social order.[66] However, as Freud insists, everyone needs a way to blow off steam, and so the culture of entertainment can improve mental and social health.

The Role of Interpretation

As we see in the above discussion of Freud's theory of humor, popular culture can be considered to be ambivalent, ambiguous, and overdetermined. On one level, jokes, movies, and plays can function to release aggressive and sexual tendencies in a safe and contained way, but on another level, these forms of popular culture disguise what they are doing by representing desires and fears in an indirect, symbolic mode. In the case of *Fanny and Alexander*, the truth of the unconscious nature of the conscience is both revealed and concealed. It is then the role of interpretation to make the unconscious conscious by explaining both the content and form of creative expression.

Notes

1 Lacan, J. (1998). *The Four Fundamental Concepts of Psycho-analysis*. Vol. 11. New York: W.W. Norton & Company.
2 Shakespeare, W. (1905). *Hamlet*. New York: E.P. Dutton & Co.
3 Greenblatt, S. (2013). *Hamlet in Purgatory: Expanded Edition*. Vol. 103. Princeton: Princeton University Press.
4 Freud, S. (1958). "A note on the unconscious in psycho-analysis." *The Standard Edition of the Complete Psychological Works of Sigmund Freud, Volume XII (1911–1913): The Case of Schreber, Papers on Technique and Other Works*. London: Hogarth Press, pp. 255–266.
5 Freud, S. (1961). "A note upon the 'Mystic Writing-Pa'." *The Standard Edition of the Complete Psychological Works of Sigmund Freud, Volume XIX (1923–1925): The Ego and the Id and Other Works*. London: Hogarth Press, pp. 225–232.
6 Lacan, J. (1998). *The Four Fundamental Concepts of Psycho-analysis*. Vol. 11. New York: W.W. Norton & Company, p. 34.
7 Freeman, J. (2003). "This side of purgatory: Ghostly fathers and the recusant legacy in Hamlet." In *Shakespeare and the Culture of Christianity in Early Modern England*. Edited by Dennis Taylor and David Beauregard. New York: Fordham University Press, pp. 222–259.
8 Bundtzen, L.K. "Bergman's *Fanny and Alexander*: Family romance or artistic allegory?" *Criticism*, 29.1 (1987): 89–117.
9 Waugh, P. (2013). *Metafiction*. London: Routledge.
10 Hutcheon, L. (2014). *Narcissistic Narrative: The Metafictional Paradox*. Waterloo: Wilfrid Laurier University Press.
11 Bergman, I., et al. (1982). *Fanny and Alexander*. New York: Pantheon books.
12 Freud, S. (1960). *Jokes and their Relation to the Unconscious*. New York: W.W. Norton & Company.
13 Freud, S. (1955). "'A child is being beaten': A contribution to the study of the origin of sexual perversions." *The Standard Edition of the Complete Psychological Works of Sigmund Freud, Volume XVII (1917–1919): An Infantile Neurosis and Other Works*. London: Hogarth Press, pp.175–204.
14 Diamond, D. "Attachment disorganization and creativity in *Fanny and Alexander*." *Psychoanalytic Inquiry: A Topical Journal for Mental Health Professionals*, 27.4 (2007): 474–480.
15 Freud, S. (2020). *The Interpretation of Dreams*. Toronto: McClelland & Stewart.
16 Jones, E. "The Oedipus-complex as an explanation of Hamlet's mystery: a study in motive." *The American Journal of Psychology* (1910): 72–113.
17 Freud, S. (2019). *Totem and Taboo: Resemblances between the Psychic Lives of Savages and Neurotics*. Glasgow: Good Press.
18 Freud, S. (1966). "Project for a scientific psychology (1950 [1895])." *The Standard Edition of the Complete Psychological Works of Sigmund Freud, Volume I (1886–1899): Pre-Psycho-Analytic Publications and Unpublished Drafts*. London: Hogarth Press, pp. 281–391.
19 Descartes, R. & Cress, D.A. (1998). *Discourse on Method*. Indianapolis: Hackett Publishing.
20 Freud, S. (2003). *The Uncanny*. London: Penguin.
21 Lacan, J. (1993). "The seminar of Jacques Lacan, Book 3: The psychoses 1955–1956." *Translation of the seminar that Lacan delivered to the Société Française de Psychoanalyse over the course of the academic year 1955–1956*. Edited by Jacques-Alain Miller and Translated by Russell Grigg. New York: W.W. Norton & Company.
22 Freud, S. "Certain neurotic mechanisms in jealousy, paranoia and homosexuality." *International Journal of Psycho-Analysis*, 4 (1923): 1–10.

23 Freud, S. (1913) "Animism, magic and the omnipotence of thoughts." *Totem and Taboo*. London: Hogarth Press, pp. 75–99.

24 Freud, S. (1958). "Formulations on the two principles of mental functioning." *The Standard Edition of the Complete Psychological Works of Sigmund Freud, Volume XII (1911–1913): The Case of Schreber, Papers on Technique and Other Works*. London: Hogarth Press, pp. 213–226.

25 Perelberg, R. J. "Negative hallucinations, dreams and hallucinations: The framing structure and its representation in the analytic setting." *The International Journal of Psychoanalysis*, 97.6 (2016): 1575–1590.

26 Freud, S. (1951). "Negation." *Organization and pathology of thought: Selected sources*. New York: Columbia University Press, pp. 338–348.

27 Freud, S. (1957). "Repression." *The Standard Edition of the Complete Psychological Works of Sigmund Freud, Volume XIV (1914-1916): On the History of the Psycho-Analytic Movement, Papers on Metapsychology and Other Works*. London: Hogarth Press, pp. 141–158.

28 Lacan, J. "Some reflections on the ego." *International Journal of Psycho-Analysis*, 34 (1953): 11–17.

29 Lacan, J. (1998). *The Four Fundamental Concepts of Psycho-analysis*. Vol. 11. New York: W.W. Norton & Company.

30 Lacan, J. (1949). "The mirror stage as formative of the function of the I as revealed in psychoanalytic experience." *Cultural Theory and Popular Culture: A Reader*, pp. 287–292.

31 Gallop, J. "Lacan's 'mirror stage': Where to begin." *SubStance*, 11 (1982): 118–128.

32 Lacan, J., Sheridan, A. & Bowie, M. (2020). "Aggressivity in psychoanalysis." *Écrits: A selection*. London: Routledge, pp. 9–32.

33 Freud, S. (1959). "Creative writers and day-dreaming." *The Standard Edition of the Complete Psychological Works of Sigmund Freud, Volume IX (1906–1908): Jensen's 'Gradiva' and Other Works*. London: Hogarth Press, pp. 141–154.

34 Laplanche, J. (1980). *La sublimation*. Paris: Presses universitaires de France.

35 Ping-hua, H.E. "Power of *The Magic Lantern*: On the Theme of Ingmar Bergman's Scenario." *Journal of Sichuan Teachers College (Social Science)*, 4 (2004): 18.

36 Landa, J. A. G. (2014). "Notes on Metafiction." *SSRN Electronic Journal*.

37 Waugh, P. (2013). *Metafiction*. London: Routledge.

38 Neumann, B. & Nünning, A. "Metanarration and metafiction." *Handbook of Narratology* (2015): 204–211.

39 Tanaka, R. "The concept of irony: Theory and practice." *Journal of literary semantics*, 2.1 (1973): 43–56.

40 Magill, R. J. (2009). *Chic Ironic Bitterness*. Ann Arbor: University of Michigan Press.

41 Samuels, R. (2020). "Catharsis: The politics of enjoyment." *Žižek and the Rhetorical Unconscious*. London: Palgrave Macmillan, pp.7–31.

42 Haverty, L. "Strindbergman: The problem of filming autobiography in Bergman's *Fanny and Alexander*." *Literature/Film Quarterly*, 16.3 (1988): 174.

43 Bundtzen, L. K. "Bergman's *Fanny and Alexander*: Family romance or artistic allegory?." *Criticism*, 29.1 (1987): 89–117.

44 Quart, B. & Quart, L. "*Fanny and Alexander* by Ingmar Bergman." *Film Quarterly*, 37:1 (1983): 22–27.

45 Freud, S. (2015). *Civilization and its Discontents*. Peterborough: Broadview Press, p. 25.

46 Freud, S. (1960). *Jokes and their Relation to the Unconscious*. New York: W.W. Norton & Company.

47 Freud, S. (1960). *Jokes and their Relation to the Unconscious*. New York: W.W. Norton & Company, p. 7.

48 Cohen, T. (2008). *Jokes: Philosophical Thoughts on Joking Matters*. Chicago: University of Chicago Press.

49 Freud, S. (1960). *Jokes and their Relation to the Unconscious*. New York: W.W. Norton & Company, p. 8.
50 Freud, S. (1960). *Jokes and their Relation to the Unconscious*. New York: W.W. Norton & Company, p. 11.
51 McGowan, T. (2017). *Only a Joke Can Save Us: A Theory of Comedy*. Evanston: Northwestern University Press.
52 Freud, S. (1960). *Jokes and their Relation to the Unconscious*. New York: W.W. Norton & Company, p. 120.
53 Coser, Rose Laub. "Some social functions of laughter: A study of humor in a hospital setting." *Human relations*, 12.2 (1959): 171–182.
54 Potter, E. T. (2004). *Containment or Subversion? Early Enlightenment Comedy and the Alternatives to the Ideology of Marriage* (Dissertation). The University of North Carolina at Chapel Hill.
55 Pinker, S. (2012). *The Better Angels of Our Nature: Why Violence Has Declined*. New York: Penguin Group USA.
56 Freud, S. (1960). *Jokes and Their Relation to the Unconscious*. New York: W.W. Norton & Company, p. 122.
57 Polimeni, J. & Reiss, J. P. "The first joke: Exploring the evolutionary origins of humor." *Evolutionary psychology*, 4.1 (2006): 347–366.
58 Freud, S. (1960). *Jokes and Their Relation to the Unconscious*. New York: W.W. Norton & Company, p. 125.
59 Bruner, M.L. "Carnivalesque protest and the humorless state." *Text and Performance Quarterly*, 25.2 (2005): 136–155.
60 Freud, S. (1960). *Jokes and Their Relation to the Unconscious*. New York: W.W. Norton & Company, p. 129.
61 Boler, M. & Etienne, T. (2008). "The Daily Show and Crossfire: Satire and sincerity as truth to power." *Faculty of Engineering and Information Sciences – Papers: Part A*, pp. 383–403.
62 Otto, B. K. (2001). *Fools are Everywhere: The Court Jester around the World*. Chicago: University of Chicago Press.
63 Morreall, J. (2005). "Humour and the Conduct of Politics." *Beyond a Joke*. London: Palgrave Macmillan, pp. 63–78.
64 Freud, S. (1960). *Jokes and Their Relation to the Unconscious*. New York: W.W. Norton & Company, p. 131.
65 Bakhtin, M. M. & Bakhtin, M. (1984). *Rabelais and his world*. Vol. 341. Bloomington: Indiana University Press.
66 Fiske, J. (2010). *Understanding Popular Culture*. London: Routledge.

Chapter 4

Island Earth

Bergman, Brahe, and the Many Suns

Patrick Scanlon

for Lary Seven – Minister of Audiology

Part I. Kinship: Solar Dust

The sun makes of the earth an island. To be on the water, in the sea, of the ocean is to experience space, if not more acutely, the heft of being out to space … stuck to a rock … propelled through the ether. Movement is nonetheless nil, while the chaotic surroundings signal that our vision is but a trick of the light. Whether or not the gravity of this galactic situation is incorporated by our momentary bouts at cognition, the fact persists: we are severely island bound in what remains an infinite expanse, floating that other ocean – cold, black, bottomless sky. Perception is precarious for both the filmmaker and the astronomer, and in this sense, who better to illustrate the bond of siblinghood than these two: spawn of sun and moon, shadowed by their analogs, day–night and light–darkness?

More keenly still, is the measure of these celestial bodies distilled through clouds and scattered according to volatility and density. And, with a slight change in either, the things of the world are put to rest, or roused into depth and breadth, dimension by dimension. This process occurs for everyone, not simply those who have, in the optic field, become kin. The sun, for which Georges Bataille's *Accursed Share* sets as the primordial model of economy, determines worth to the degree that it renders existence. Bataille writes:

> Overcast weather, when the sun is filtered by the clouds and the play of light goes dim, appears to 'reduce things to what they are.' The error is obvious: What is before me is never anything less than the universe; the universe is not a thing and I am not at all mistaken when I see its brilliance in the sun. But if the sun is hidden I more clearly see the barn, the field, the hedgerow. I no longer see the splendor of the light that played over the barn; rather I see this barn or this hedgerow like a screen between the universe and me.[1]

DOI: 10.4324/9781003200246-5

The essay that follows makes of the sun's hiding, a drama in which seeking coincides with seeing, and from the difference that leaks, one is compelled to compound this error, or to clarify it. Of course, in dividing these compulsions too cleanly, one runs the risk of reducing persons and pursuits to the contours of a hedgerow. Besides, the artist and the scientist, and specifically, the filmmaker and astronomer, have always found in the obvious some excess or lack to exploit. The confusions within these disciplines are consonant, and their coincidence can just as well make the whole of perception crisp if angled appropriately. Toward this end, Island Earth will employ the speculative to project the pursuits of one ocular figure through the patina of another. Closeness of purpose or profession is not the aim here – nor is it likeness per se, or the familial in general. Rather, the question concerns what might materialize through these shards of distinction whose odd cut sacrifices the symmetry in reflection for the progeny in refraction. The possibility here is that select motifs, some of which are familiar to enthusiasts of film and astronomy alike, might be cast anew; that facts can flash over whatever façades prop up our knowledge of an artist's world, or screen the complexity out of an astronomer's research, means that novel encounters with their work can always emerge.

No doubt the differences between filmmaker Ingmar Bergman and 16th-century astronomer Tycho Brahe are significant enough to have assured their complete and categorical separation. There are several compelling reasons for them to share the space of an essay, however. The great disparity of time, some 400 years, which also maintains certain divisions regarding their respective methods, is nonetheless recouped if the terms lineage and transmission mean anything for us. Whether as lines, or from the chain of loops which transmission implies, etymologically speaking, we are obliged here to consider initiation, that most esoteric of events for which the light of revelation is experienced in literal *and* symbolic ways. What often holds together those of a lineage – undoubtedly more interesting and messy than the direction of a single line – is some special thing, some rare encounter for which to mark, to pledge, to swear, to sacrifice. In the lives of Bergman and Brahe this thing is the sun.

This is not any sun, however; it's a Scandinavian sun, an island sun, and given these two, our solar orbit is made more evident than is usual. The term Scandinavian is not perfect given the intervening centuries and changes of crown and state, though it works, supported by the reality that both men matured in their professional endeavors on islands off the coast of Sweden. During Brahe's time, the Island of Hven (Hveen, Ven) to the south-west, was the property of the Danes, and while it now is under the flag of Sweden, since 1658, it is forever marked by the innovations of the Danish astronomer, most of which are specifically the product of his island life. Much has been said about Bergman and the Island Fårö, where he not only made some of his most lauded films, but took up residence and in a way that exceeded the simple conditions of place and shelter. Both figures lived and worked at their island compounds that were constructed with the intention to educate and further the general scope of their fields.

Understandably, Brahe's elaborate and ingenious observatories – Uraniborg or the Castle of Urania, dedicated to the Muse of Astronomy, and Stjerneborg, or "Star Castle," an improvement on Uraniborg in that its instruments were buried in the basement to improve their stability – have been abandoned in terms of function, though efforts continue to restore something of their prominence. According to his daughter Linn Ullmann, Bergman's estate is currently "a place for artists, scholars, and journalists needing somewhere to work."[2] This function is accurate though, as it was written from Ullmann's "initial project outline," it does not present the formality of his intention, which operates through a foundation and application process for residencies.

What is it about their island situations in particular, and perhaps island life in general that contributed to their exceptional catalog of works, as well as to their unique approaches which, rather than simply adding to the content of astronomy and film, transformed their respective methodologies? Somewhat beyond these coincidences of biography and professional acumen, to be explored further below, there is the manner in which the sun organizes their vision in such a way that ordinary moments become haloed, and special moments bloom beyond the garden in which they were sown. Even without much knowledge of astronomy, it is easy to concede that our star is an appropriate focus for the astronomer and yet we will see that Brahe's methods for studying its existence are unrivaled.

While disciplined observation is standard for Brahe's ilk, the constancy of his devotion was rare. J.L.E. Dreyer, in his eminent biography, *Tycho Brahe: A Picture of Scientific Life and Work in the Sixteenth Century*, notes that "On Brahe's birthday, "14th December he commenced a series of observations on the sun, which were steadily continued for over twenty years" (1963, p. 94). In service of what he understood to be the major problem of astronomy, Brahe would fashion new instruments for tracking celestial bodies, and constantly improve old ones in favor of an accuracy that was at that time absent. The ingenuity he employed regarding the architecture of his observatories is translated into his model of the universe, an odd geo-heliocentric system: he accepted Copernicus' notion that the earth revolved around the sun, but retained the prominence of the former, setting the other planets in orbit around the earth.

For Bergman, as fans of his films can recall, the sun is referenced in the titles of his work, or is implied by the time of day and the season, to say nothing of how it informs the plots and cinematography, both of which often make of these solar effects an essential character. A brief list gives us *Summer Interlude* (1951); *Summer with Monica* (1953); *Smiles of a Summer Night* (1955); *The Virgin Spring* (1960); *Winter Light* (1963); *Autumn Sonata* (1978); and *Hour of the Wolf* (1968). This last piece signifies that special period between night and day (dusk and dawn), what has been designated in French as "L'heure entre chien et loup," that time after sunset when one cannot tell, from a certain distance and in such hazy light, the difference between a dog and a wolf. This enchanting time reflects more than a confusion of perception; it is also the preferred time for prayer, meditation, ritual and incantation for a variety of preternatural paths. One might also include the possibility of that special dispensation of dreams and nightmares, as well as the exploitation of these ambiguities for occult aims, all of which feature in Bergman's oeuvre.

The pertinent scenes for our essay come from Bergman's interviews and biography, which bring his attention closer to that of the astronomer. And, although the purpose of noting the sun's position and movement remains different for each figure, there is something singular that unites them. Bergman doesn't maintain as strict a schedule as does Brahe, though there are countless references from his childhood that intimate his devotion to this solar body, and to what the sun, in turn, indicates. He states in an interview (*Playboy*, 1964):

> When I wake up during the winter – I always get up at six, ever since I was a child – I look at the wall opposite my window. November, December, there is no light at all. Then, in January, comes a tiny thread of light. Every morning I watch that line of light getting a little bigger. This is what sustains me through the black and terrible winter: seeing that line of light growing as we get closer to spring.[3]

Tracing the sun of Bergman and Brahe, or rather some of their sun, will no doubt cast what is solar more broadly to include its genres of brilliance. There is that which is *from* the sun, the very material way that it comes through the window and sticks to the wall above Bergman's head, or conditions the instruments made in Brahe's basement. Bergman writes in his autobiography, *The Magic Lantern* (2007):

> As a child, I had often stood in the dark dining room at home, peeping into the salon through the half-open sliding doors. The sun lit up furniture and objects, glittered in the chandelier and cast moving shadows on to the carpet. Everything was green, as in an aquarium. Inside, people moved, disappeared, reappeared, stood quite still and spoke in low voices. The flowers in the window glowed, the clocks ticked and struck, a magical room.
>
> (p.37)

This description, one among many that features the sun in a way that transcends its utility, shows that its appearance corresponds to a ritual, or a rite, and thus it implies a scene, with sound, objects, time, dimensionality …

There are also those phenomena that are *of* the sun, which operate in kind – film projectors, the moon, streetlights, and at times one's gaze. Each of these shine as a little sun would; they flare like cousins of the sun, for all light occurs under the auspices of the sun. In recalling the spooky pleasures of his nursery when the blinds were drawn, Bergman states,

> No little men or animals, or heads or faces, but *something for which no words existed*. In the fleeting darkness they crept out of the curtains and moved toward the green lampshade or to the table where the drinking water stood. They … disappeared only if it became really dark or quite light, or when sleep came.[4]

The study of illumination has been for the greater part of history devoted to the sun: the diffusion of its rays, the way its spreads, as much as the many ways it can be cut, by clouds, trees, a window pane, punctuating the very time and space that coordinate the living.

As much as Bergman's films are informed by his theatrical origins, and there-fore by the necessity of developing characters, he makes clear, in a moment of sage reflection, what will be missed when filmmaking ceases:

> Sometimes I probably do mourn the fact that I no longer make films. This is natural and it passes. Most of all I miss working with Sven Nykvist, perhaps because we are both utterly captivated by the problems of light, the gentle, dangerous, dreamlike, living, dead, clear, misty, hot, violent, bare, sudden, dark, springlike, falling, straight, slanting, sensual, subdued, limited, poison-ous, calming, pale light. Light.[5]

Here Bergman sounds like a physicist, a painter, or to speak in the parlance of the 16th century, a natural philosopher, if not a mystic. Perhaps the ease with which he can be associated with these professions, and certainly the list could be longer – demonstrates his remarkable sensitivity to light's many qualities, which is to infer that light itself was an object of his study, and not just a medium to improve vision, or assist in storytelling. His strange lists cannot be found in any manual on light, nor do they represent only an intimate and personal set of encounters. Rather, its diverse names, which function as faculties – Bergman's misty, poison-ous, sudden, and dark – emerge in relation to light's problems. We might posit for a brief moment, the correspondence between Bergman's great care for light and his presentation of its assorted rays decorating the human condition. What is nota-ble, even as speculation, is that Bergman's illustrious career is propelled through collaborating with light's riddles.

His concern with what might be called a phenomenology of light – an interest begun during his childhood that persisted somewhat candidly despite the advance of optical technology – aligns Bergman with the early astronomers who worked before and during the advent of the telescope. In fact, it was the problems of light that led to the development of not only the first cameras, but of the notion of a cam-era itself. Essential to this evolution was the need to measure the diameter of the sun and moon during an eclipse, an event that was dangerous to witness directly. Brahe's question around the distortion of cosmic bodies during this special occa-sion was exactly the issue that attracted his most important student, Johannes Kepler. An eclipse may seem entirely in the purview of an astronomer, or an occultist, but ultimately in its simplest form, the bewilderment involves a peculiar relationship between the proximity of a light source, and its prominence. We can safely infer that for Brahe and Bergman, the point from which radiance radiates, especially the celestial sort, can signify worth, or something fervid and foreboding.

Another problem at play in this pivotal time for astronomy (and one studied of the coast of Sweden no less), concerned the way that light was apt to round itself when projected through an opening that is not round. The "principles of propagation of light" were studied by Brahe (and Kepler) as they concerned the "problem of pinhole images." It's important to clarify within this archaic language that a pinhole sort of assumes a "camera," and specifically, a camera obscura, or what is known as the camera obscura effect. Coined by Kepler in 1604, the term *camera obscura* was first theorized by the 11th century Arab figure Alhazen, although it has been in operation for millennia, whether functioning naturally through a crack in a wall that mysteriously projected the outside world within, or through some version of this fabricated "dark chamber." This phenomenon has advanced through countless designs, which eventually were to include the insertion of a lens into the pinnule to refine and invert the already inverted image.

While not linked perfectly, the camera obscura can be considered a precursor to the magic lantern, a term that titles Bergman's autobiography, *The Magic Lantern*.[6] In addition to the device, this title also bears reference to the 1903 film by one of the field's principle innovators, George Méliès, to whom Bergman considered himself an heir. This inheritance from Méliès persists in terms of film's maturation, and the subject matter of his work, which is, in large part, based on the former, on the internal mechanisms of the instruments. Méliès was an illusionist as well as a filmmaker, a dual position to which most filmmakers are privy. Bergman was, more than most, not simply aware of this, but found it to be a motivating factor in his work. He comments, "Méliès was always there without having to think about it. He was a magician by profession" (2007, p. 73). The titles of some fifteen hundred films of Méliès, most of which have been lost, bear out the entangled relationship between the magic and technics of the film process.[7]

Similar themes are available in Bergman's oeuvre – magic, enchantment, illusions, dreams, delusions, and devils – though my focus is on what is perhaps his earliest encounter with film, that scene that may have allowed Méliès to be installed, and to persist indelibly: "from the first and therefore always there." Consider his statement on how the enigmatic outcomes of film are embedded in the austere physicality of the device. The impossible knowledge, mystifying atmosphere, and bizarre perspective do not result only from philosophical speculation, but manifest within the eye itself, or the analog eye fashioned from metal and glass. With a beautiful mix of mystery, mechanics, and mortality, Bergman points us to his initiatic moment, connecting the most marvelous of filmic effects to the darkness of the family's wardrobe:

> No form of art goes beyond ordinary consciousness as film does, straight to our emotions, deep into the twilight room of the soul. A little twitch in our optic nerve, a shock effect: twenty-four illuminated frames a second, darkness in between, the optic nerve incapable of registering darkness. At the editing table, when I run the strip of film through, frame by frame, I still feel that dizzy sense of magic of my childhood: in the darkness of the wardrobe, I slowly wind on one frame after another, see the almost imperceptible changes, wind faster – a movement.
>
> (2007, pp. 73–74)

Part II. Initiation: Lunar Vale

The only image inside Bergman's theater at his compound on Fårö was the tapestry, *The Magic Flute on Fårö*, by Anita Grede. Given his famed visual discipline, the loneliness of this piece might suggest that it was not something to regard casually. In the essay "The three o'clock rite: Ingmar Bergman's Home Cinema" (2014), his daughter Lena Bergman designates the tapestry as an official guide presiding over the strict ceremony to which her father was committed: a daily film screening at three o'clock (two o'clock on Saturdays).[8] Pressed somewhere between ritual and institution, Bergman would arrive at the converted barn and watch one of the films in his collection. Though the tapestry is in part a depiction of his 1975 film *The Magic Flute*, its privileged status connects us to Brahe and the tools of astronomy. Lena Bergman's description below makes this relation plain:

> In his essay collection Ballaciner, J.M.G. Le Clézio describes the moon, lit by the sun, as being the prototypical film projector – and the darkness of night might be a first camera obscura lit by other worlds. Light and darkness are the prerequisites for film, and guess what – on the tapestry a moon is floating in a pale, mysterious light. We also behold the Queen of the Night, white-breasted and dressed in black, brandishing her knife. Here in this cinema, the Queen of the Night reigns – but over there is the wise Sarastro, who has made a pact with the sun and the light. So we find ourselves in the presence of both these opposite forces.[9]

In its most basic elements, film exists as a portioned exchange between light and darkness, whose rhythm does nothing to calm the mystery of its effects. This umbral coordination remains a foundation of astronomy, which the tapestry also invokes. For the filmmaker, astronomer, magician and priest, all players of interest to Bergman, light does not simply improve what one sees, and when it does, the process from absence to presence requires an attention of a different order than what passes the time. One is compelled by the circumstances, furtive and verdant, to create a pact, swear an oath, or perform a sacrifice – all gestures that are, in their basic mold, types of duration. The distinction here is subtle as a shadow shapes, and the suffering of whatever deferral is activated might be transformed through a formal intention, or some act within the logic of ritual, to become a privileged note, or token of one's symbolic reality.

Bergman's obituary in the *Economist* begins,

> When he was filming 'Winter Light,' in 1961, Ingmar Bergman made a tour of the churches of northern Sweden. He and his cinematographer, Sven Nykvist, would sit in the hard pews from 11 in the morning till two in the afternoon, watching the light change.[10]

This ritual was not begun in service to making pretty films. This covenant that will organize Bergman's practice was begun early in youth. The obituary continues,

"From childhood, he had got up at six and noted the track of light on the wall opposite his window. After two months of darkness, a thread would reappear in January." In Bergman's autobiography, we find this situation in his own words:

> While I was making preparations for *Winter Light*, I went around looking at churches in Uppland in the early spring. I usually borrowed the key from the organist and sat for a few hours in the church, watching the light wander and thinking how I would work out the end of my film. Everything had been written down and planned, all except the actual ending … It was a misty early spring day with strong light above the snow.
>
> (2007, p. 272)

The function of light here is manifold, and yet its most familiar use, to render visible, seems to be secondary. This church scene will no doubt inform how the film is lit, but better yet, this dispensation of light alerts Bergman to how the film will end. That light wanders is a fact to which he fastens his thought, and thus his thinking moves in league with the moving light. Lastly, it signifies the day itself, though strangely in a way that makes it a whole other light, an outer radiance that hangs above the snow.

The sun accents moments in Bergman's life, and while astronomers take special notice of astral objects, appraising them and noting their positions with fervor, our fair filmmaker *is* the one here marked by light. His experimentations of it in relation to the shadings of human experience avoid the familiar trope casting the goodness of light against malevolent darkness, as mentioned in *The Magic Lantern*: "individual moments of greatness or misery are still illuminated by a mild light" (2007, p. 255). Astronomy can attest, there is in truth no such thing as total darkness. The nuance here is echoed in his early experiences in church, to which we have already borne witness. Neither secular, nor ingrained with the ecclesiastic, something precious is nonetheless transpiring. The previous scene concerning *Winter Light*, and the ones to follow are not incidental. Whether one subscribes to religious, or spiritual conceits, a refined awareness is established through the design of most churches. The structural aspect, informed by sacred geometry and allegorical mythos, is then coupled with whatever ciphers emerge through the substantiation of light.

It is true that Bergman tracked the sun on the wall of his bedroom, and from under the dining room table; he beheld it in concert with sound, but rarely in these formative years were the encounters remote from the glint of reverence. He writes, "I used to sit under the dining room table there, 'listening' to the sunshine which came in through the cathedral windows … The cathedral bells went ding-dong, and the sunlight moved about and 'sounded' in a special way" (Cowie, 1983, pp. 7–8). When one moves from a moment of acute observation to one in which the senses become mixed, there is the possibility that whatever impressions avail themselves further enmesh the psyche within the body. No doubt this experience is formative, though in being compounded it might exceed significance, and become initiatory. For as the senses mingle their function, what is typical to the point of inconspicuousness becomes stained and thus ineluctable.

Admittedly, given his father's role as a traveling minister, it was not easy to escape the atmosphere of sanctity, if not at times sanctimoniousness; he explains:

> As a child I was sometimes allowed to accompany my father when he travelled about to preach in the small country churches in the vicinity of Stockholm ... While Father preached away in the pulpit ... I devoted my interest to the church's mysterious world of low arches, thick walls, the smell of eternity, the colored sunlight quivering above the strangest vegetation of medieval paintings and carved figures on ceiling and walls. There was everything that one's imagination could desire: angels, saints, dragons, prophets, devils, humans. There were very frightening animals: serpents in paradise, Balaam's ass, Jonah's whale, the eagle of the Revelation.[11]

The church most imprinted upon Bergman's memory – and the one for which his father Erik served as parish minister (1918), then as Vicar of the parish (1934), and ultimately, as a Royal Chaplain to the court of King Gustaf V of Sweden – was Hedvig Eleonora Church. In fact, the last chapter of Bergman's autobiography reiterates the significance of a moment of sensual fusion within the confines of a church, a design that he will replicate directly, or simulate through other analogous settings. The sonic effulgence persists throughout his films, and is further memorialized as it concludes the story of his life. The vaulted roof, the sun reflected in the arches, the formation of figures, patterns, abutments, direct light, slanted sorts, the trembling and shafts, and the Bach whose intricate ratios ripple through a similar set of mathematical considerations, which can consecrate an assortment of atmospheres:

> One Sunday in December, I was listening to Bach's Christmas Oratorio in Hedvig Eleonora Church. It was afternoon. Snow had been falling, silently, with no wind. Then the sun came out.

> I was sitting on the left, high up under the vaulted roof. The gold-shimmering moving sunlight was reflected strongly in the row of windows in the parsonage opposite the church, forming figures and patterns on the inner abutment of the arch, the direct light slanting through the dome in brilliant shafts. The mosaic window by the altar flared for a few moments, then was extinguished, a soundless explosion of dull red, blue and golden brown. The chorale moved confidentially through the darkening church: Bach's piety heals the torment of our faithlessness. The trembling uneasy light patterns on the wall moved upwards, narrowed, lost their strength and were extinguished. The D-minor trumpets raised their jubilant cries to the Saviour. A gentle greyish-blue light filled the church with sudden stillness, timeless stillness.

(2007, p. 281)

Named after Hedvig Eleonara, Swedish Queen to Charles X, and sanctioned in 1737, this church, referenced above, was nonetheless designed according to a much older group of sacred geometric tenets. As an octagonal church, its design presents a number of Roman and Christian beliefs built around the number 8, often valued for the iteration of 4×2, or 2^3, the first cubic number. Principles like these, and scores of others in the field of esoteric architecture will be foundational to Tycho Brahe's unprecedented project on the Island of Ven.

Although Bergman (and Nykvist) were not as focused on mathematics, geometry, and the physics of optics as Brahe and Kepler, even if the filmmaking duo had in some ways a superior knowledge of lenses given the intervening years, they committed themselves to studying light with the utmost precision, as we shall see in Part III. Out of the many instruments that Brahe had invented and improved, there is one whose style reflects something of the church of Bergman's choice, and connects us to a youthful Brahe whose first encounters with the night sky occurred in secrecy, that essential aspect of initiation.

A constitutional scene in Brahe's history that is structured by furtiveness and, perhaps in turn, stands as a soft investiture to his future profession, concerns a small celestial globe engraved with the constellations.[12] In the Danish 16th century, astronomy was not an appropriate profession for those of an ancient noble birth, so young Tycho would sneak outside when his tutor Vedel was asleep and familiarize himself with the stellar arrangements, or consult the fist-sized globe behind his back. Brahe explains:

> In Leipzig, I began to study astronomy more and more. ... I bought astronomical books secretly, and read them in secret so that my governor should not become aware of it. By and by I got accustomed to distinguishing the constellations in the sky... For this purpose, I made use of a small celestial globe, no bigger than a fist, which I would take with me in the evening without mentioning it to anyone.[13]

This affair with the globe parallels another scene that will shape Brahe's professional life. It was a few years later, in his late teens, that he would, once again without his tutor's knowledge, witness a cosmic event that solidified his astronomical passions. Dreyer relays the following situation from August 1563:

> a conjunction of Saturn and Jupiter, which in those days was looked on as a very important one, owing to the astrological significance it was supposed to have, induced [Brahe] to begin at once to record his observations, even though they were taken with the crudest implements only. A pair of ordinary compasses was all he had to begin with; by holding the centre close to the eye, and pointing the legs to two stars or a planet and a star, he was able to find their angular distance by afterwards applying the compasses to a circle drawn on a paper and divided into degrees and half degrees ... he noted that

Saturn and Jupiter were so close together that the interval between them was scarcely visible.

(1963, pp. 18–19)

Notably, in terms of its symmetry, is the fact that Brahe's encounter here involved the exact possibility of predicting celestial movements. In 1559, he saw the eclipse of the sun, and was stunned that such a spectacle could have been foretold so long in advance. As Dreyer has it, "when Brahe saw the eclipse take place at the predicted time, it struck him 'as something divine that men could know the motions of the stars so accurately that they could long before foretell their places and relative positions'" (1963, pp. 13–14). This paradox would generate methodological features that would become indispensable for astronomy and the other positive sciences.

The import of geometry, mechanics, and machines, is not too distant from Bergman's concerns. The sole image in Bergman's theater makes as plain as a sun ray sloping along the wall of his childhood home, that the weaving of light and darkness is what endures as the "prerequisites of film," and the foundations of astronomy. The eclipse is emblematic of this weave, given its stature, and the slowness with which its hues exude. As we will see, the slicing of the solar orb into degrees of a crescent was, unlike the muted light of the moon, able to penetrate the dwellings of certain inquisitives through cracks of the wall, or cuts in the curtain. The fortune of witnessing the inverted yet perfect image of the celestial body in the face of a crooked opening in one's porch inspired the manipulation of this scene that would eventually produce the camera obscura, the magic lantern, and the film camera.

The singular moment for Brahe's course of study would occur in 1572, when he was approximately twenty-six. The point of distinction here, in relation to Bergman's initiatic moment to follow, involves the special stillness of the object at hand. It is a matter of simple presence; something is suddenly stuck in the firmament that was, the night before, absent. Dreyer recounts the situation:

On the evening of the 11th November 1572, Tycho Brahe had spent some time in the laboratory, and was returning to the house for supper, when he happened to throw his eyes up to the sky, and was startled by perceiving an exceedingly bright star in the constellation of Cassiopeia, near the zenith, and in a place which he was well aware had not before been occupied by any star. He asked his servants, assistants, who were accompanying him, and although they did not have knowledge about what stars were where, they could attest to its brightness.

(1963, p. 38)

In Brahe's own words, the situation is even more ecstatic. He writes,

Amazed, and as if I stood astonished and stupefied, I stood still, gazing … When I had satisfied myself that no star of that kind had ever shone before, I was led into such perplexity by the unbelievability of the thing that I began to doubt the faith of my own eyes.[14]

And, in another place, he mentions that the grandiosity of this incidence wrested away his alchemical work: "It was the greatest wonder that has ever shown itself in the whole of creation … the new star which flared up in 1572 made me give up my chemical labors and turn towards the study of celestial phenomena."[15]

In an interesting essay by Larry S. Fauber, "How Tycho Brahe Discovered a New Star with a Piece of String: On the Ambition of the Early Naked-Eye Astronomers" (2019), Brahe explains:

> It happened just before supper … in the middle of my walk back home, I was contemplating different bits of the sky. It seemed to me then most clear, as from a wish to guarantee continued observations after supper; when lo and behold! Just overhead, a strange kind of star from an unexpected place, blinding the eyes and shining brilliant, radiant, fulgent light. I was amazed, practically stupefied, thrown into such perplexity by the impossibility of it all that I began to doubt my own eyes.[16]

Even though Brahe was not yet a proper astronomer, he had sufficient interest and knowledge to register the brilliance of this situation for which he would spend the next years working out the math, and ultimately publishing the definitive account: *De stella nova* or *Mathematical contemplation of Tycho Brahe of Denmark on the new and never previously seen star just now first observed in the month of November in the year of Our Lord 1572.*

One might initially find Brahe's reaction to this event a touch exaggerated, as he compares it to the Bible with "Joshua's stopping of the sun in the heavens or the darkening at noon during the crucifixion,"[17] and in another place he exclaims, "It was the greatest wonder that has ever shown itself in the whole of creation," a designation that "made me give up my chemical labors and turn towards the study of celestial phenomena." The object was no doubt extraordinary, visible in daylight, and by most accounts, bright as the moon at nighttime. And while Brahe was correct to call it a star (and not a comet), the moniker *new* was ironic, as its appearance was in fact the sign of its death. When a star dies, or goes supernova, its brightness can increase sometimes with a greater intensity than is emitted from its galaxy in total. This particular supernova, which Shakespeare has been thought to reference at the start of *Hamlet*, has actually taken on Brahe's name: Tycho's Supernova.

Of course Bergman's moment of consecration differs from Brahe's in several ways. One significant point of contrast however, not uncommon to the index of those extraordinary episodes that transform one's self and life, entails an astonishing display of movement. For Bergman, the stunning aspect of his early encounter with film involved the motion of something that was previously still, if not inanimate. The supernova also appeared, or seemed to emerge from nothing, but it was then fastened to the firmament, and thus announced itself to Brahe as exceedingly static. With both figures we are faced with the plainness of light and dark, presence and absence, stillness and motion, yet there are nuanced variations of color that denote the passage of time, and mutability of objects.

There are a few accounts of Bergman's childhood induction to the mechanics of light and image, though most preserve a similar set of details. In *The Magic Lantern*, he provides the context for what he designates as the "cinematograph affair," which involved a Christmas gift given to his older brother by his aunt. Even before the present was opened, he knew what it was, and that he wanted it intensely: "At once I began to howl. I was ticked off and disappeared under the table, where I raged on and was told to be quiet immediately. I rushed off to the nursery, swearing and cursing, considered running away, then finally fell asleep exhausted by grief" (2007, p. 15). Bergman then wakes up and enters the party again, and this time the object's status is excessively existent, as it sits within a scene of lights.[18]

Later in the evening I woke up. Gertrud was singing a folk song downstairs and the nightlight was glowing. A transparency of the Nativity scene and the shepherds at prayer was glimmering faintly on the tall chest-of-drawers. Among my brother's other Christmas presents on the white gate-legged table was the cinematograph, with its crooked chimney, its beautifully shaped brass lens and its rack for the film loops.

> I made a swift decision. I woke my brother and proposed a deal. I offered him my hundred tin soldiers in exchange for the cinematograph. As Dag possessed a huge army and was always involved in war games with his friends, an agreement was made to the satisfaction of both parties.
>
> The cinematograph was mine.
>
> (2007, pp. 15–16)

It is not only the object of his desire that radiates, but, one could argue, the way it is displayed, with the various lights, the glow and glimmer, the festiveness of the holy day, the singing, all of which impress and spur him into action. Here, the glow of the nightlight, and the flare of the nativity figures orchestrate his swift decision, inspiring him to concoct a strategy.

The seriousness of this situation inclines us to note the scenic nature, and in particular, what is often repeated in his exalted moments: a catalogue of lights, the accents of a flickering lamp, or the soft blur of moonlight that spreads across the kitchen wall. Like with other ritualistic situations, what he will gain is coupled with a loss. Army soldiers may not seem too fantastic a possession, but they also negotiate his brotherly status, and at an age where such objects, and what they in turn allow, matters a great deal. As a result, his brother Dag beat him "hollow in every war afterwards." It's worth mentioning that this scene does not yet include the actual experience with the machine, what becomes a potent demonstration of brilliance. He continues:

The next morning I retreated into the spacious wardrobe in the nursery, placed the cinematograph on a sugar crate, lit the paraffin lamp and directed the beam of light on to the whitewashed wall. Then I loaded the film.

A picture of a meadow appeared on the wall. Asleep in the meadow was a young woman apparently wearing national costume. *Then I turned the handle!* It is impossible to describe this. I can't find words to express my excitement. But at any time I can recall the smell of the hot metal, the scent of mothballs and dust in the wardrobe, the feel of the crank against my hand. I can see the trembling rectangle on the wall. I turned the handle and the girl woke up, sat up, slowly got up, stretched her arms out, swung round and disappeared to the right. If I went on turning, she would again lie there, then make exactly the same movements all over again. *She was moving.*

(2007, p. 16)

The ritualistic quality at stake with Bergman, something reminiscent of the formal scenes of initiation, is not easy to describe, and for reasons that exceed the atmosphere of secrecy often pervading esoteric ceremonies. We might speculate that, beyond the repetition of sacred objects, like the sun and moon, and the metaphorical themes of darkness and light, the effects of the ceremonial allow one to perceive something patently, but with the tenor of conferment. Initiation has something in concert with revelation, for what was formerly hidden is not so much an object, but the mechanism of perception itself. One is introduced, and often at great risk, to that which grounds all appearance. An encounter with the sacred object of ritual, regardless of one's aim, though it seems intention is somewhere necessary, can change the position of the subject immediately and for a sustained amount of time, if not forever.

The sense of movement is as essential as it is distinct for Brahe and Bergman. Something changed. Something is moved. Everything moves. Something appeared where it shouldn't have. Even though Bergman has a hand in this affair, holding and turning the crank, what happens as a result is remarkable in a way that is, as he admits, impossible to describe: he feels the crank, and the girl on film, or rather, on the wall, wakes, sits up, stretches, swings around, and disappears. The fact that he can repeat the sequence does not lessen its effect. Because this is a scene, spatially drawn up, affected by smells and sounds, nothing can be replicated. The constellation of elements are, in some regard, similar; they are also not the same and can, in effect, never be the same: the smell is different, cogent, and in clumps, the lamp is stronger, or the film sticks, there is activity outside the room, memory of the last time, of the tin soldiers, of the girl asleep in the meadow who moves and in turn moves him.[19]

Part III. Glory: Cosmic Dusk

It is one thing to be compelled by the contours of the sun dancing across one's kitchen wall, or by the phases of the moon as it traverses the night sky. It is another to study such phenomena, and yet another still to design instruments that mimic the illumination or manipulate its emergence. Part of what made Bergman and Brahe exceptional was their capacity to effect what seemed to be the fundamental, and thus, unchangeable manner of appearance. Even in film the objects are often a given, in space, set to be recorded blatantly, as they are, and the devices with which to document the objects are also prescribed. Brahe and Bergman shifted the basic conditions of observation, moving what was for the most part not movable, and in this they affected not simply the things of the world, but the methods with which to keep vigil, to sanctify.[20]

Bergman, for instance, goes from being fixated on the light echoing around the churches where his father preached, to actually building a church, and thus increasing his agency over the materials of production and presentation. He is not the first to engage in set design of course, though his reasons for doing so are emblematic of his unique methodology. He states, in *Bergman on Bergman* (1973):

> Lundgren built the church in the big studio, and together Nykvist and I began working on a completely new lighting technique. We studied light and began to figure out methodologically how light functions, how it actually behaves, and how we could technically mimic its behavior. We did this as some sort of an aggression against modern photography, which has given us an artificial idea of what real light looks like. Photography using ultra-fast film makes the bright side seem much brighter and the dark side darker than in reality. All that's very interesting. When it comes to the appearance of light, we've got a new lie instead of the old one.
>
> (p. 174)

Using or adjusting light is certainly not the same as mimicking its behavior, which assumes that one must first attend to it as something that behaves, that conducts itself in accordance to the situation at hand. Figuring out how light functions, as Bergman says, requires a system of methods, and a devotion to light itself, not only as it concerns the proper set design for a specific sequence. In addition, this passage shows a working knowledge of photography, which is not unique for a director, though Bergman adds to the operational understanding, an insight on the broader cultural implications of an image's capacity to mediate the perception of reality.

His relationship with Sven Nykvist has been well documented – their closeness, and the compatibility was essential to Bergman's success. In the *Guardian*'s obituary of the cinematographer, Ronald Bergan called Nykvist "midwife to Bergman's masterpieces."[21] What is essential about their collaboration, and of note considering the theme of this essay here, is the fact that their bond was very much composed by light. Bergman describes their alliance in the film *Sven Nykvist: Light Keeps Me Company* (2000) made by the son of his partner, Carl-Gustav Nykvist:

> Sven and I saw things alike ... thought things alike ... Our feeling for light was the same ... We had the same basic moral principles about camera positions etc. – so we didn't need to talk to each other so much. I mean, I could

> say to Sven: "I think we need a ray of sunlight here." Without my having to say any more, there was the ray of sunlight.

His response is concise, but not simplistic. Seeing things, and thinking things alike is analogized, if not more directly substituted by their tactility for what is lucent. This extends into camera positions, etc., but not before these two figures are blended by light to the degree that a ray of the sun finds its place without either's declaration.

We've had cause to mention briefly at the start Brahe's groundbreaking observatories, The Castle of Urania, and the Star Castle, Stjerneborg, that were designed according to hermetic principles and sacred geometries, and which increased the accuracy in, and capacity for studying the cosmos through quite practical means. And like Bergman, Brahe's projects involved the creation of a whole atmosphere. In addition to the inclusion of instruments, Brahe's castles set the furniture, walls, windows, bushes, gardens, and ponds in such a way that their presence and place compelled one to contemplate the mysteries of natural world. We might now in this final section sharpen our focus, and contract our aperture in order that Brahe and Bergman can appear comfortably in the same picture. Our frame now lies over the development of Bergman's magic lantern and the small dark chamber in which he set it up.

As patently modern as film can seem, something of its most basic conditions has been recorded thousands of years ago. According to Laura J. Snyder's *Eye of the Beholder: Johannes Vermeer, Antoni van Leeuwenhoek, and the Reinvention of Seeing* (2015):

> As far back as the fifth century BCE, the Chinese writer Mo Ti recorded the creation of an inverted image when light passed through a pinhole in a screen. He referred to the place the inverted image occurred as a 'collecting palace' or a 'locked treasure room.' Later, sometime after the third century BCE, Greek writers observed a natural occurrence of the camera obscura effect. During a solar eclipse, they noted, if the light falls through small holes in leaves, the image of the sun's crescent is visible on the ground.

> (p.106)

Although the development of optics, for astronomy and film, were highly specialized – based on techniques within the field of mathematics, chemistry, and physics – they progressed through the investigation of simple bouts of light, not dissimilar to Bergman's childhood preoccupations, or the problems of light that shaped his cinematic style.

One of the first notated examples of this basic condition comes from Aristotle. Oscar Marshal describes the situation as follows:

> Aristotle was pacing to and fro within his study, undarkened except for the west window over which was drawn a shade to exclude the afternoon heat.

He chanced to notice a circular spot of light upon the wall opposite the shaded window. This arrested his attention and he paused to investigate its source. A small hole in the shade was found. He concluded that the sun was the light-source of the circular image on the wall, but he was amazed to find that hole was quite irregular in outline.[22]

Like with Bergman, the study of light was something done within the constraints of one's house or studio, and according to certain intentions and limitations. It was also, however, an organic wonder to access during the casual encounters about town. Marshal continues, stating that while

walk[ing] the shaded streets of the city [Aristotle] began to notice circular spots of light on the ground under the trees. These he referred to the sun as their source. Then, one day when a solar eclipse occurred the images on the ground were no longer round, but took the shape of the sun's disk as partially covered by the moon.[23]

What occurred here in a natural way was then modified, and repeated, though the problem of an inverted image persisted until Kepler added a lens to the opening.

An early log of Brahe's states, "In 1544, GEMMA observed an eclipse of the sun." From this early proponent of the pinhole camera, which he designates as the "easiest and most certain of all" methods of observation, the sun is beheld "without any visual difficulty as perfectly as if you were present in the heavens yourself" (Straker, 1981, pp. 269–270). The prominence of this feeling is reminiscent of Bergman's childhood exploits, if not his barn theater, and of course speaks to the justified esteem that he is given for making us present to the heavens and hells of earthly experience.

Though humans have been conscious of the camera obscura effect since ancient times, the device itself, apart from its analog in cement foundation cracks, and forest leaf holes, had become something of a sacred object in the intervening centuries. The Italian natural philosopher Giambattista della Porta writes in one of the two versions of his text *Magia naturalis* (1558, 1589) a glowing review that recalls Bergman's childhood visions that entered his shaded room care of the moon and sun. Like Méliès, Porta sustained his abundant empirical output on the study of magic, and what finer a device exists for exploring the interplay of nature's spectacles and the mind's processes than the camera obscura, magic lantern, and film camera?

Nothing can be more pleasant for great men and Scholars, and ingenious persons to behold; That in a dark Chamber by white sheets objected, one as clearly and perspicuously, as if they were before his eyes, Huntings, Banquets, Armies of Enemies, Plays and all things else that one desireth. Let there be over against that Chamber, where you desire to represent these things, some spacious Plain, where the sun can freely shine: upon that you shall set trees in Order, also Woods, Mountains, Rivers and Animals that are really so, or made by Art, of Wood, or some other matter . .... those that are in the Chamber shall see Trees, Animals, Hunters, Faces, and all the rest so plainly, that they cannot tell whether they be true or delusions.[24]

Because celestial objects move rather slowly, and terrestrial ones like della Porta's territory can appear fixed within one's room, it is reasonable that the camera obscura has been too often associated with a clear and clean representation of reality. However, as Jonathan Crary remarks in his excellent study, *Techniques of the Observer: On Vision and Modernity in the Nineteenth Century* (2012), the camera obscura was often praised for how it showed movement: "Observers frequently spoke with astonishment of the flickering images within the camera of pedestrians in motion or branches moving in the wind as being more lifelike than the original objects" (p. 34).[25] This seems to be a matter of attention that causes one to consider the projected branches as too real. Perhaps it is a case of the objects being made strange by virtue of the unfamiliar context, and the ethereal tone that demands the viewer to look again, and with greater intrigue than the basic act of recognition would require.

With the invention of the magic lantern in the late 17th century, rendering the tent or room sized chamber into a small box, one had access to a stable lens, and a set of slides, photographs, or painted prints to pass over the light source. The mechanics are still quite similar to what have been described above. It is worth emphasizing that although Bergman was taken by the image of the woman in the field, he was initially, and certainly throughout his career, mesmerized by the very machinations of the contraption. He writes in his *The Magic Lantern* (2007):

> As long as I live I'll never forget what it looked like, or how it was constructed. Have you ever seen one of those little machines? Well, it was just a tall tin box, black, with a simple system of lenses and a paraffin lamp and a chimney sticking out of the top. A little smoke would come out of the chimney. One of its functions was to run circular film strips – two or three metres long. Another was to project slides. These could be inserted into the lens system: coloured slides – German, done in poker-work, with Red Riding Hood and Snow White. Then there were films you could buy, the old inflammable sort. The image was as small as could be, the only source of light being a paraffin lamp.
>
> (p. 7)

> It was not a complicated machine ... the crank was attached with a cogwheel and a Maltese cross. At the back of the metal box was a simple reflecting mirror, behind the lens a slot for coloured lantern slides.
>
> (p.16)

Regardless of one's skill and commitment, no one transforms a field alone. Brahe had his Kepler, and Bergman, Nykvist, though there was also for Bergman,

Uncle Carl, a character right out of the medieval alchemical laboratory. From Bergman's description, Uncle Carl was as necessary to his pursuits as any other. And, although this education was not tainted with the monotony of schooling, it provided the young artist with that blessed trinity of prosperity: fascination, proficiency, and invention. Bergman describes Uncle Carl's role:

I admired him because he invented things for my magic lantern and my cinematograph. He rebuilt the slideholder and lens, mounted a concave mirror inside, and then worked away on three more movable pieces of glass, which he himself painted. In this way, he created mobile backgrounds for the figures. Their noses grew, they floated, ghosts appeared from moonlit graves, ships sank and a drowning mother held her child above her head until both were swallowed up by the waves. Uncle Carl bought strips of film at five or a metre, then put them in hot soda-water to remove the emulsion. When the strip had dried, he drew moving pictures directly on to the film with Indian ink. Sometimes he drew non-figurative patterns that could be transformed, exploding, swelling and shrinking ... He sat, leaning laboriously over his worktable in the overfurnished room, the film lying on a matt sheet of glass illuminated from below, his glasses pushed up on his forehead and a magnifying glass wedged into his right eye.

(2007, pp. 28–29)

Following closely Uncle Carl's inquisitiveness presented Bergman with the means to create illusions from the ground up. His devotion to light, from youthful moments in his house and the churches, to philosophical moments with Nykvist, become a foundation for a method that is very much his own.

Film perseveres for him as an investiture, and this status is now inherent to what he produces. As with the priest and magician, this venerable artist, Bergman the filmmaker, has sacrificed the complacencies in his being. His whole life has prepared him for this role, and the risk he took trading his soldiers for the magic lantern, cannot be unwagered. He is not a filmmaker by occupation, at the start, nor at the end, though there were likely some years when he would have answered to that title. However fanciful this conjecture, it is not inaccurate, nor does it seem to be something he would disavow. He states as much:

No other art-medium – neither painting nor poetry – can communicate the specific quality of the dream as well as the film can. When the lights go down in the cinema and this white shining point opens up for us, our gaze stops flitting hither and thither, settles and becomes quite steady. We just sit there letting images flow over us. Our will ceases to function. We lose our ability to sort things out and fix them in their proper places. We're drawn into a course of events – we're participants in a dream. And manufacturing dreams, that's a juicy business.

(1973, p. 44)

The great use provided by the camera obscura, beyond the whimsical feats performed for one's illustrious dinner company, involved the possibility for safely observing the sun. Its emanations are too blatant, too blustery, too burning not to damage one's eyes. This was especially true during the eclipse, an event that even today inspires superstition, dread, and an unparalleled sense of awe.

In Bergman's case, which is intensified given the sun's behavior in Sweden, the direct light was unbearable. The following quotations from him show the severity of his dealings. He declares in *Bergman on Bergman*, "For me a Swedish summer is full of deep undertones of sensual pleasure, particularly in June, the time around midsummer – May and June. But for me July and August, July especially, when the sun shines day after day, are dreadful torment" (1973, p.79). In responding to a question from Stig Björkman about his "way of experiencing the summer, the clear penetrating light," Bergman responds:

> I have a feeling that there isn't all that much difference between the summer motif and, for example, the hour-of-the-wolf motif. There's something desperate about your way of experiencing the summer, the clear, penetrating light. For me a Swedish summer is full of deep undertones of sensual pleasure, particularly June, the time around midsummer – May and June. But for me July and August, July especially, when the sun shines day after day, are a dreadful torment. Sunlight gives me claustrophobia. My nightmares are always saturated in sunshine. I hate the south, where I'm exposed to incessant sunlight. It's like a threat, something nightmarish, terrifying.
>
> (1973, p. 78)

Even in the dream sequences, Jonas Sima states, there is "strong sunshine." Bergman affirms,

> There's that same hard sunlight in *The Hour of the Wolf* and *Wild Strawberries*. When I see a cloudless sky I feel the world's coming to an end. Throughout *The Silence*, for instance, it's blazing hot and the sun scorches down.

The surface contact is one thing, and the internal emotions conjured by the hard sunlight another. And yet, as Torsten Manns asserts, "In some way the sunlight goes right through your people and their actions," to which Bergman avows, "Yes, they're eaten out."

The developments for the various cameras were often shaped in service of shielding one from the viciousness of direct sunlight, which caused blindness in some and was thought to inspire madness in others.[26] There are a host of emotional and psychic states that Bergman has dared to look into directly, and each blazes with a particular tint and heat. This essay could have been a study of how one is blinded or maddened with respect to the proximity of the many suns, and according to their internal composition, or the clarity of their respective lenses. More often than being visually impaired or spurred into psychosis, purveyors of

Bergman's work are severely dazzled. And while the fans of Brahe may be fewer in number, no doubt what his work has allowed in terms of knowledge and technology has illuminated our lives with a precious sort of gravity.

The young woman flickers into motion, swings around, then disappears. The star sticks above the moon shedding color over the course of months. Both figures maximize their receipts, take the respective contingencies into their own hands to query, curate, and create something of the splendor that befell them. However much these two shared an interest in optics, this study of disparate figures has been organized by their relationship to the sun, and therefore might provide something novel about the habits of research outside the important work of interdisciplinarity. In a sense, all disciplines "mingle their methods," and all pursuits are enmeshed in the natural world, which in turn, imbues the body, heart, and psyche – warmed into life and lit into living.[27]

Notes

1 From Georges Bataille's *The Accursed Share* (pp. 55–56), a treatise on economy that is based on the generosity and wastefulness of the sun's exertion.
2 https://bergmangardarna.se/
3 Published in *Playboy*, 11, No. 6 (1964), pp. 61–68. https://scrapsfromtheloft.com/2017/05/11/ingmar-bergman-playboy-interview-1964/
4 Cowie, P. (1983). *Ingmar Bergman: A Critical Biography*. London: Secker & Warburg, p. 8
5 Bergman, I. (2007). *The Magic Lantern: An Autobiography*. Chicago: University of Chicago Press, p. 229.
6 Although this progression is true, it is important to not take the development in too neat, or direct a line. Each of these devices has its own spread of influences based on the intention, time, and town in which they were created. Crary is clear about this in his *Techniques of the Observer: On Vision and Modernity in the Nineteenth Century*, though there is not the space in this essay to explore these lineages.
7 In his titles are ghosts, demons, hallucinations, secrets, fairies, dreams, living dolls (and other haunted objects of the home), apparitions, wagers, oracles, enchantresses, sorcery, witches, and several important pieces devoted to astronomy asserting, if only implicitly, the familial bond between these ocular systems. Of note: *The Astronomer's Dream*, or *The Man in the Moon* (1898); *The Eclipse*, or *Courtship of the Sun and the Moon* (1907); and *A Trip to the Moon* (1902); *The Impossible Voyage*, or *Whirling the Worlds* (1904).
8 Bergman, L. (2014). "The three o'clock rite: Ingmar Bergman's home cinema." *BFI: Sight and Sound Magazine*. Accessed February 26, 2022: www2.bfi.org.uk/news-opinion/sight-sound-magazine/comment/three-o-clock-rite-ingmar-bergman-s-home-cinema
9 Bergman, L. (2014). "The three o'clock rite: Ingmar Bergman's home cinema." *BFI: Sight and Sound Magazine*. Accessed February 26, 2022: www2.bfi.org.uk/news-opinion/sight-sound-magazine/comment/three-o-clock-rite-ingmar-bergman-s-home-cinema
10 "Ingmar Bergman: Obituary." (August 2, 2007). *The Economist*. doi: www.economist.com/obituary/2007/08/02/ingmar-bergman
11 www.ingmarbergman.se/en/production/seventh-seal-0 Writings, 1956 [On the Seventh Seal].
12 The Great Brass Globe, a stunning object that Brahe designed and in large part furnished, is described in his *Astronomiæ Instauratæ Mechanica*.

13 *Heavenly Intrigue: Johannes Kepler, Tycho Brahe, and the Murder Behind One of History's Greatest Scientific Discoveries*, Joshua Gilder and Anne-Lee Gilder (p. 32).

14 Gilder, J., & Gilder, A-L. (2005). *Heavenly Intrigue: Johannes Kepler, Tycho Brahe, and the Murder Behind one of History's Greatest Scientific Discoveries*. New York: Anchor Books, p. 58.

15 https://lithub.com/how-tycho-brahe-discovered-a-new-star-with-a-piece-of-string/

16 Fauber, L. S. (2019). "How Tycho Brahe Discovered a New Star with a Piece of String On the Ambition of the Early Naked-Eye Astronomers." Accessed on February 26, 2022: https://lithub.com/how-tycho-brahe-discovered-a-new-star-with-a-piece-of-string/

17 Thoren, V. E., & Christianson, J. R. (2006). *The Lord of Uraniborg: A Biography of Tycho Brahe*. Cambridge: Cambridge University Press, p. 66.

18 http://cinemathequefroncaise.com/Chapter1-1/Certain_Tendencies.html#R1.9 Reading 1.2 In Theory: Certain Tendencies in the Pre-cinema.

19 The language is reminiscent of the famous, though most likely false, anecdote concerning Galileo, when after recanting his belief in a mobile earth, utters under his breath, "… and yet it moves."

20 Relevant here is the fact that the realization of Copernicanism was not simply a statement that the Earth (and other planets) revolved around the sun, but that they moved of their own volition, through something like magnetism, or love, what became clarified as gravity. Before then it was thought that the planets were inserted into spheres that drove them around the sky.

21 Bergan, R. (September 22, 2006). "Sven Nykvist: Obituary." *The Guardian*. doi: www .theguardian.com/news/2006/sep/22/guardianobituaries.obituaries#:~

22 Astronomical Society of the Pacific * Provided by the NASA Astrophysics Data System Leaflet No. 282–October, 1952 "The Camera Obscura" by Oscar S. Marshal (pp. 253–254).

23 Astronomical Society of the Pacific * Provided by the NASA Astrophysics Data System Leaflet No. 282–October, 1952 "The Camera Obscura" by Oscar S. Marshal (pp. 253–254).

24 *Techniques of the Observer: On Vision and Modernity in the Nineteenth Century* (pp. 37–38).

25 Perhaps more impressive, though outside of my essay's scope, is Crary's analysis of the "optical regime" implied by camera obscura, and other related though distinct technologies (pp. 34–39).

26 See Jonathan Cray's remarkable *Techniques of the Observer: On Vision and Modernity in the Nineteenth Century.*

27 For the suggestion to state more directly the angle of this essay's thesis, I must thank Emma Lieber who was also kind enough to read the work and offer edits. I was not able to incorporate my own study of light, and the sun, that was, in many ways coincident with this project and a few others, though I look forward to the challenge. Often in these pandemic times, I would be pulled (like a monk to the name) and stood standing in her living room taking photos and video of the geometric flickering of the sun as it passed over the leaves of the tree outside, onto a gutter jammed with water, through the window frame, and against the wall of her living room. Or with a flashlight beaming about her crystalline kids.

Bibliography

Bataille, G. (1991). *The Accursed Share: Volume 1, Consumption*. New York: Zone Books.

Bergman, I. (1964). "Ingmar Bergman: Playboy Interview." *Playboy*, Vol. 11, No. 6, pp. 61–68.

Bergman, I. (2007). *The Magic Lantern: An Autobiography.* Chicago: University of Chicago Press.

Bergman, I., Björkman Stig, M. T., and Sima, J. (1973). *Bergman on Bergman.* New York: Simon & Schuster.

Bergman, L. (2014, February 5). "The Three O'clock Rite: Ingmar Bergman's Home Cinema." *BFI: Sight and Sound Magazine.* https://www2.bfi.org.uk/news-opinion/sight -sound-magazine/comment/three-o-clock-rite-ingmar-bergman-s-home-cinema.

Cowie, P. (1983). *Ingmar Bergman: A Critical Biography.* London: Secker & Warburg.

Crary, J. (2012). *Techniques of the Observer: On Vision and Modernity in the Nineteenth Century.* Cambridge: MIT Press.

Dreyer, J. L. E. (1963). *Tycho Brahe: A Picture of Scientific Life and Work in the Sixteenth Century: (Unabridged and Corrected Republication of the Work First Publ. in 1890).* New York: Dover.

Fauber, L. S. (2019). "How Tycho Brahe Discovered a New Star With a Piece of String on the Ambition of the Early Naked-Eye Astronomers." https://lithub.com/how-tycho -brahe-discovered-a-new-star-with-a-piece-of-string/.

Gilder, J., and Gilder, A.-L. (2005). *Heavenly Intrigue: Johannes Kepler, Tycho Brahe, and the Murder Behind One of History's Greatest Scientific Discoveries.* New York: Anchor Books.

Lindberg, D. C. (1996). *Theories of Vision From al-Kindi to Kepler.* Chicago, IL: University of Chicago Press.

Marshal, O. S. (1952, October). "The Camera Obscura." *Astronomical Society of the Pacific * Provided by the NASA Astrophysics Data System Leaflet,* Vol. 252, pp. 253–254.

Nykvist, C.-G. (2000). *Sven Nykvist: Light Keeps Me Company.* Sweden.

Sherriff, L. (2004, October 28). "Astronomers Finger Culprit in 1572 Supernova Star Spotted Fleeing the Scene." *The Register.* https://www.theregister.com/2004/10/28/ runaway_star/.

Snyder, L. J. (2015). *Eye of the Beholder: Johannes Vermeer, Antoni van Leeuwenhoek, and the Reinvention of Seeing.* New York: W.W. Norton & Company.

Straker, S. (1981). "Kepler, Tycho, and the "Optical Part of Astronomy": The Genesis of Kepler's Theory of Pinhole Images." *Archive for History of Exact Sciences,* Vol. 24, pp. 267–293.

Thoren, V. E., and Christianson, J. R. (2006). *The Lord of Uraniburg. A Biography of Tycho Brahe.* Cambridge: Cambridge University Press.

Ullmann, L. "The Bergman Estate on Fårö." https://bergmangardarna.se/.

Chapter 5

The Truth about *The Silence*

Ingmar Bergman's Masterpiece about the World

Peter Jansson

In relation to a traditional film analysis, where the film and the filmmaking are interpreted, analyzed, and reconstructed based on an *already* formulated theoretical framework – within which the narratives, the images, and the words are incorporated – my intention in the following is the reverse: to illustrate how "*one theory*" *operates* and takes shape *in* the cinematic world of Ingmar Bergman.[1] In the words of Ola Sigurdson, it is a matter of "speaking about film as a conceptual investigation in its own right," which in virtue of a contemporary comment "can be a tool for 'looking awry' at the existing reality."[2] In viewing *The Silence* (1963) from that perspective: what can Bergman's cinematographic work *teach* us about the world and life? What picture of society and culture emerges from *The Silence*, in a psychoanalytic sense? What ideas and fantasies dwell inside the narrative and the representations of human beings, the world they inhabit, their bodies, spirituality, desires, doubts, loneliness, silence ...? This amounts to posing the following questions: how can we judge and evaluate Bergman's testament? What significance and meaning does *The Silence* contribute to his legacy? It is my fundamental conviction that the film speaks to elements that constitute Bergman's originality, allowing us to better understand why he has left such a durable and powerful imprint on cinematic culture. In a sense, he himself brought forth his dreams, his reality, and his own style, which combined to make his artistry as a filmmaker recognizable at first glance.

Here I intend – in accordance with the theories of Jacques Lacan, who, in conjunction with the existentialist philosophers and the pessimists, will serve as a guiding light in this present account – to shed light on that which falls away and conceals itself, evading language and image, in *The Silence*; all this in order to evoke the intangible and the void by conferring human traits on the abyss. In this sense, my project is situated in the field that Lacan has come to call *the real* – what has not been expressed in words or language, evades all symbolization, and has not acquired an imaginary form – the space beyond the silence, the hole in heart of the symbolic order, the void concealed by the visible, whose eye, beyond all human meaning, in the unbearable disorder of being, our eyes cannot endure.[3] If film is a window to the world, *The Silence* opens the door a little to the *impossible* crack. It is not about treating the misery of lack or suffering as an object for

DOI: 10.4324/9781003200246-6

fiction. It is, rather, about discreetly and in an authentic sense, seeing the human beings, hearing their voices, seizing their secrets ... all of this in order to reveal the truth of cinematography in the tortured, desiring, and excluded bodies. My intention is to show how *The Silence* depicts a world that is falling apart, where God is dead, and how people – in darkness, emptiness, and despair – try to give meaning to this world.

But why *The Silence*? In an article, "Whatever Happened to Ingmar Bergman," Harlan Kennedy says:

> In many ways *The Silence* is cinema's answer to Camus's *L'étranger* ... A new generation of directors would inherit the rich and difficult freedom this thought embraces. For Bergman's trilogy wasn't just a masterpiece of self-destruct art of and for itself ... It was a shudder in the culture that would go on to engender a whole cinema of visionary anti-narrative, from Tarkovsky's *The Sacrifice* ... to Mike Leigh's *Naked*, from Eustache's *The Mother and the Whore* to the bleakest tragicomic yarns of Kieslowski and von Trier.

The Silence, he concludes, "is the great watershed movie of Ingmar Bergman's career, perhaps of Sixties art cinema."[4] Those are big words, but they say something about the greatness of *The Silence,* and about the fact that it has a crucial place among Bergman's works, and also among the films that were produced during the 1960s. Maaret Koskinen, who has written a brilliant and deeply insightful book about *The Silence*, points out that

> *The Silence* remains a classic and, as such, is one of the important European modernist art films of the 1960s, rich enough for scrutiny from a variety of perspectives, methodologies, and interpretative matrixes ... *The Silence* offers an excellent entry into the cinematic, cultural, and sociopolitical issues of its time.[5]

I have brought along Krzysztof Kieślowski, the Polish film director and scriptwriter, who has written an in-depth article about *The Silence*.[6] He perceives Bergman's film as a riddle and the Swedish film genius himself as being at a loss for answers to all the questions that the film raises.[7] But *why* and *how* does a silence appear *before* and *in The Silence*?[8] *What* does *silentium* and this stillness refer to in this case, according to Kieślowski? "The silence in Bergman is as painful as Death in Fellini, as Absence in Buñuel and Tarkovsky, as the beautiful but no longer moving films of Kurosawa or the failures of Wajda."[9] Mikael Timm, who had access to Bergman's workbooks when working on the biography *The Lust and the Daemons: A Book about Bergman*, points out that the director aimed for a "non-literary" lyrical film, exceedingly visual, but without interruptions: "The new film was born between two opposite poles that he [Bergman] called the stillness and the violent movement."[10] This quiet silence in *The Silence* is nevertheless infinitely painful and sorrowful – it is, according to Kieślowski, a fundamentally tangible and discernible *atmosphere* that made the narrative different from all others at the time and explained why so many people in so many countries all over the world wanted to see this film about two sisters, Anna (Gunnel Lindblom) and Ester (Ingrid Tulin), and the former's eleven-year-old son Johan (Jörgen Lindström), who are on a night train on their way home to Sweden from a holiday.[11]

It is a painful but at the same time incomprehensible and menacing silence that in a concrete sense corresponds to the fact that neither of the sisters, nor the boy, understands the language spoken in the foreign country. Ester has suddenly fallen ill and they are forced to stay at a hotel in a small city where they cannot converse with others or make themselves understood; they feel abandoned and homesick. Even the name of the city, *Timoka*, is incomprehensible and unfamiliar.[12] The spoken language in the foreign city resembles no recognizable language, and the first phrase with which the viewer is presented is written on a piece of paper in the train compartment: "*Nitsel stantnjon palik.*" At the hotel, it is the elderly and friendly room service waiter, who Johan runs into during his explorations of the corridors and rooms of the turn-of-the-century building, who speaks this unknown language and manages to teach Ester a few new words (she is after all a professional translator) while aiding her with food and care.[13] Through Ester we learn that "*kasi*" means "hand," "*naigo*" "face," and "*hadjek*" "fate." The words are very different from the corresponding Swedish words, with one exception, "musik," which, apart perhaps from the pronunciation, is the same word in the foreign language, "*muzik.*"

Although the silence in *The Silence* – through its irrefutable and dark glow of pressing unease and pain – denotes the fact that the characters find themselves in a place with an unknown language, this uncompromising chamber play about two sisters who are biologically and physically close, at the same time symbolizes a merciless muteness between two women who, in a sense, are strangers. Anna and Ester are each other's opposites and, despite the fact that they live in close prox- imity to one another in the hotel room, an existential abyss has opened up between them. The words do not bring them closer to each other, and when they do speak, what takes place is not a conversation but rather statements and vocalizations that are mechanically, soullessly, reproachingly and/or spitefully uttered in a violent way. Concrete in their brutality, covering an abyss of painful feelings and experi- ences of humiliation and loneliness, their deadly lines are like a coral reef spread- ing out in the dark waters beneath the surface of language. This extreme lack of contact gives body and shape to a wordless narrative, as shown already in the initial scene, when we see a boy between two silent women in a train compartment while the train slowly rolls into a foreign city. In his *Workbook 1955–1974*, Bergman writes as he is working on the script for *The Silence*: "Words are something damn boring and irritating and the constraint is hard. Words are nearly always double and prostitute and inflationary ... Every word feels harsh and meaningless."[14] In the film we recognize this fact in a deep-seeded fear of language *and* silence, where words are drained of love and meaning, while at the same time filled with violence and emptiness. In Koskinen's words:

The human voice, and language itself, seems fragmentary and unarticulated, and is often marginalized or threatened by nonhuman sounds: running water, typewriting, sentimental music from a crackling transistor radio, the wispy sigh of clothing against skin. This fragmentation is emphasized by the use of sound in the scenes set in the streets of the city, which seems pervaded by persistent noise: cars, horns, drills, sirens, the constant hoarse shouts of newspaper vendors – all becoming part of the city's nonhuman roar.[15]

A frightening and painful silence has spread in this dirty, gray city, and it is easy to perceive the aggressive muteness between the sisters as a result of the vulnerable predicament in which they have landed through having been involuntarily forced to stop in this unfamiliar and menacing place. Here, a war is being waged or ended, a war that, according to Kieślowski,

> is conveyed to the viewers just through a few signals. The close-up of a water decanter and a glass next to it. The decanter and the glass vibrate. On the surface, the first, soft ripples appear, you hear the unpleasant, loud engine noise. After a while, Anna (maybe Ester) sees through the window how tank columns roll on a street.[16]

The city that Anna, Ester, and Johan arrive in truly has something of the Eastern European state about it, and the fact that we do not know where the drama takes place what country the hotel and the square that Anna visits are situated in – creates an anxiety-laden feeling of insecurity in the sisters and the boy but also in the viewer. We are in the City that embodies and shapes the disorientation, blindness, rootlessness, and estrangement of the contemporary human being and that, in Kieślowski's words, creates a black hole of silence by asking questions without giving any answers:

> We never learn why and where the sisters have travelled We don't learn why they stop in a city that is unknown to us, where neither German, English, French nor Swedish is spoken and where the passers-by don't exchange a word with each other. We are not told what country it is and why there is a war. We won't get to know if Ester is going to die in this city, or what Ester's letter to Johan says. I don't think Bergman knows either.

The dream which gave rise to *The Silence*, of "sinking into an enormous city, absorbing it, experiencing it, becoming anonymous within it" originates from a short story by Sigfrid Siwertz.[17]

When we listen to Bergman's own reflections about *The Silence* – the dreams and ideas hidden behind it that infuse it with life and then enter the film – we realize how his own experiences and impressions have impacted the narrative, the images, and the voices. It is as if we are witnessing a dissolving world – everything is collapsing and the ground gives way under our feet. But the houses, the abysses, and the streets that crumble, yawn, and crack open are not real; it is the thin film over a vertiginous and unbridgeable chasm in the culture that has burst. The images, the symbols, and the mirrors have been dissolved and an impalpable abyss is revealed.[18] The veil that was supposed to envelop the void of death has been torn asunder. Civilization has crumbled and become a brutal, savage, and crude world, and in this remote, barbarian place Anna, Ester, and Johan can no longer recognize themselves – they are transformed into shadows that waste away along with the other lost souls in space. An unbearable gulf closes around their victims, where we can trace the root of social madness, and the struggles for life and death can be acted out in violence, as the regulated boundary that has prevented us from blindly responding to the rushes of our blood has been eroded and we witness a war between two women.[19] This film, which is perhaps the most photographically outstanding film made by Bergman and Sven Nykvist, portrays the confrontation between two sisters in an incestuous relationship in a nameless country. The meaningful words and the trusting conversation seem to have lost their value, and in terms of Lacan's theoretical framework, Anna and Ester have – in their quest for merely imaginary forms of recognition and confirmation, of similarity rather than difference – come to mirror themselves in each other.[20] The words and the signs that confirm who I am have lost their power, their significance as a barrier between me and the other having collapsed and withered. The Hegelian struggle for life and death can no longer be reduced to an *inner* struggle but is immediately acted out in concrete dueling situations. In their longing for companionship and love and in the absence of confirmation, Anna and Ester, full of fury and hatred, find themselves in a situation of rivalry and strife.

What is so ingeniously disturbing about *The Silence* is after all that nothing violent actually happens, which means that the intrusive silence does not happen outside but *within* Anna, Ester and Johan, Bergman, and the viewer. Although the bodies of these human beings, their concrete actions and events can be specified with regard to time and space, there is a catastrophe we can sense occurring behind the doors of our *inner* world. There, it is quiet and still, loud and violent. The sisters and the boy are on a train and then immediately afterwards at a hotel, but, as Kieślowski emphasizes,

> We don't see them get off the train, go through the city or look for a taxi. When Anna walks through the streets – not in order to go somewhere else – it is because we are supposed to become aware of her growing desire.[21]

Johan roams the long, labyrinthine hotel corridors, which, in contrast to the claustrophobic hotel room, seem like an imaginary landscape, and Bergman had already written in the *Workbook*: "The corridor as a switch and a secretive transformer. The hotel rooms as islands of reality in this stream of sensory impressions."[22] A sense of unreality comes creeping in the city that does not exist. Besides the three protagonists, the hotel seems to house merely a troupe of dwarves, and when Anna goes out and arrives at the square where things are lively, we do not hear any voices and the humans resemble sleepwalkers with empty and tense faces. In *The Silence* it may be that we witness the inner process of only *one* human being.

The absence of an actual plot in a concrete sense sheds light over the fact that in the film *time* seems to have halted and frozen to ice. We do not see Anna, Ester, and Johan leave the train and make their way through the menacing city, where silence and stillness reign – the world that Bergman has half opened a window to seems like a hallucinatory dream landscape that has, in the Lacanian sense, lost all its meaning, where the whole of being has curled around an engulfing hole and all temporal reference points have vanished. Tied to what is perceived as an objective reality, the surface of ordinary time has dissolved, and in contrast to an existing and continuous time horizon, the hallucinatory *Silence* spreads out in a strange, imaginary time without duration, subject, and symbolic point of orientation.[23] Note the absence of film music, which has been replaced by sleepy ticking clocks that establish a kind of dreamlike timeless silence.

> The film, as Bergman explained it to Nykvist, was certainly meant to be dreamlike, but there were to be no hackneyed dream effects such as soft focus images or fades. The challenge lay in the fact that the film itself must have the character of a dream.[24]

Bergman's *Images* recounts a recurrent dream that had served as a source of inspiration for the film:

> I am in an enormous, foreign city. I am on my way towards the forbidden part of town. It is not even some dubious area of ill repute … but something much, much worse. There the laws of reality and the rules of society cease to exist. Anything can happen and everything does.[25]

Another dream from this time seems to have been embodied in the film as well, if briefly:

> When putting the final touches to *Winter Light*, Bergman wrote down a dream he had about an old man being pushed around some hospital grounds by four women. In her exertions, one of them falls down and lies flat on the ground, whereupon the others laugh uncontrollably.[26]

In my eyes, Bergman depicts a hallucinatory dream world.[27] But *whose* dream or dreams does he portray? In *See Bergman*, Leif Zern writes that

> Johan drifts about in the empty hotel corridors and encounters his fantasies as in a dream landscape … No other film by Bergman balances as skillfully

between the real and the fantasized. The incidents at the hotel are symbolic and are reminiscent of the reversed perspectives of dreams. Johan appears alternately small (when he stands beneath a man perched on a ladder) and big (in relation to the dwarves).[28]

When we witness, through the window of the train, the columns of tanks rolling along on a street, even they appear to exist in a dreamlike landscape, and in the square it is silent among the sleepwalkers.

Anna enters a variety theater where the circus dwarves perform. Confronted with this spectacle, a surrealist unreality seizes us, and when we analyze *The Silence* as a whole, the film is transformed into a frightening and sharp depiction of the onset of madness when the sense of reality is disrupted – the film narrative comes across as if a patch has been attached where there was originally a tear in connection to reality. Fully oriented in time and space, it is still as if an eerie madness has been hovering around our souls – not that *The Silence* is merely an ominous case study about the mechanisms of madness and its often tragic out-comes; if we thought so, we would overlook the deeper meaning of the drama – what is eerie about it is that, in an existential sense, this delusion casts a doubt on the credibility and solidity of the real world. Is there no truth in what we think we have heard or seen? As a result of the doubt and fear that haunt us, suspicion is also cast on our belonging to, and our faith in, what we perceive as an objective reality. Beyond our blinkers, *The Silence* exposes the truth of reality, where, in Bergman's words, the laws of the socio-cultural order are cancelled. The ghosts of the apocalypse pursue the viewer, too, and a gap opens up in our reality, where the eyes of death itself observe us and we are haunted by an inexorable truth about our own blind and miserable condition. When we hear the strange noise on the street, when the decanter clinks and the whole house shakes – is it not our own image of the world that trembles and cracks? Bergman is well aware of the abysmal depth of truth in madness when he, in the *Workbook* on February 20, 1962, points out that the women and the boy are one and the same person "as they are three faces on the same body."[29]

Nearly a month later, he writes:

> Penetrating to the hot core. Visions and overall pictures are not enough, they can be like the confusing reflections on glazed paper. Then, underneath, there is the emptiness or the fabrications or the lies ... One has to penetrate to the hot core where all moral and aesthetic speculations are burnt away and are no longer obstructing the truth.[30]

And a further two days later:

> I believe I have an extra ear sunk into my body, a nose entangled in my bow-els, an eye staring into my brain and hopelessly bloodshot for lack of light. This film is more and more getting to be a case of first-rate suffering. My

congratulations. At the same time, I think it is shaping up somewhere inside my head.[31]

And when we hear and see Ester deliriously talking in her illness, it is as if she lends contours to this psychotic confusion that pervades the film and also affects the viewer, and that Bergman verbalizes in his *Workbook*: "The confusion of complete madness …"[32]

If *The Silence* gives body and shape to Lacan's theory of psychosis, it is because the holding ground that offers an anchoring in a cultural and linguistic order has been *rejected*, and in the film we encounter this enormously frightening and serious condition in the feeling of a world catastrophe that has *already* taken place, where the symbolically structured reality of the human being collapses.[33] The linguistically conveyed order of culture is in a state of dissolution and has collapsed into an obscure abyss, where the bizarre and incomprehensible language spoken in Timoka comes across as an illustration of the linguistic impairments of the schizophrenic testifying to a kind of speech beyond speech. In *The Silence* we experience an imprint of how words lack access to the metaphorical significance of language; insufficient and meaningless, insubstantial and flat, they have ossified and been transformed into *objects* – as in the language of the schizophrenic – the concrete speech being synonymous with violence, and Anna and Ester use words like blows to their bodies. In a Lacanian sense, the sisters are faced with a situation or an *appeal* and have been placed in opposition to *the Name of the Father* that was rejected earlier in their history and to which they now have no possibilities to relate and respond.[34] Their gestures and violent expressions cannot be identified with neurotic symptoms and acting out – where earlier wishes and desires have been repressed and return in the shape of guilt and underlying conflicts of love and hate in relation to an Oedipal father – it is rather about deeper and more damaging experiences of abandonment and loss and the absence of a (symbolic) recognition from a father whose name has been excluded and thus opened up an abysmal hole in their world.[35]

Unlike the traditional Oedipal drama, with symbolically charged conflicts in relation to a father who in an imaginary sense can be seen as prohibitive, here we find a failed outcome of this triangular relational structure and a related absence of identification with a father, resulting in a full manifesto, undisguised and *non-repressed* pleasurable hatred in connection to a radically rejected *Name of the Father*. It is in the figure of Ester that we recognize this madness that surfaces in the scene in the hotel room when, lying down, she talks to the room service waiter – who, as we know, does not understand her words – about her father and his death:

Ester: I must say that now I feel really well. Do you know what my state is called, old man? Euphoria. Father was the same. He laughed and told funny stories. Then he looked at me: 'Now it's the eternity, Ester,' he said. He was so kind, although he was terribly big and heavy, weighing almost two hundred kilos. One would have wanted to see the faces of the men carrying the coffin.

About the above scene, Vilgot Sjöman writes:

> In *The Silence*, the dying Ester thinks … about the death of her old father. He weighed two hundred kilos when he died. She would have liked to see the expression of the pall-bearers who had to lug him; and on his way home from a trial run in a cinema in Rättvik … Ingmar laughs at this farewell of the symbol of the old safety-father-figure god: *all that remains* of it is a dead old man who weighs two hundred kilos.[36]

In a kind of euphoric mania, *the Name of the Father* has been reduced to a piece of charred body; Ester cannot talk and sublimate in the *name* of the father, and the fact that she is a translator can be perceived as an expression of how she quite *concretely* has to "translate" the words, as the rejection has meant that she no longer has inner access to a linguistic (symbolizing) network. Anna reminds her that *she did not want to live* when their father died – the possibility to replace what has been lost by a reconciling grief process in terms of a *metaphor of the father* fails to materialize and the loss itself is reduced to a form of bodily amputation. Unlike Anna's physical, passionate, and suffering figure, Ester is perceived as stiff, cold, and hard, and are we not able to here sense an expression of her having, in Lacan's parlance, established merely a strictly formal and "external" relation to the symbolic? She has identified with the flinty imperative of the superego without connection to – as it is not integrated into our symbolic universe – an emotional psychological depth, something which results in a kind of "malevolent neutrality," a basic indifference to our empathies and fears, to Anna's love and hatred. Ester has compensated for the absence of a recognition of the *Name of the Father* by, in a narcissistic imitation, using the closeness to her sister as a fragile imaginary prosthesis, and now that Anna, in her rebellion, refuses to uphold this function, it is questioned and lost, and the path to the psychotic breakthrough is open, when her symbolic universe, whose warrant is this fatherly name, collapses. Perhaps this unfortunate circumstance interacts with the fact that the sisters have now arrived in a foreign country and language, and that Ester – since where the *Name of the Father* should have been, there is simply a gaping void – does not have access to the symbolic tools with which she would have been able to handle the vulnerability and abandonment that now hit her with a violent force and let her fall into the abyss.

But there is maybe another figure concealed in the shadow of the father whose hopeless puppets the sisters have become. We listen to Kieślowski:

> Some time, somewhere, a mistake has been made. By whom? By the father? One of the sisters? The mother, who is not once mentioned in the film? Today – with *Fanny and Alexander* in focus (where the mother soon finds her feet

after the death of their father and remarries a strict bishop) – the answer must be that it was *the mother.*

In this sense, it is the desire of the mother that lurks in the background and plays out in the sister's (Ester's) rivalry and hatred.[37] The foundation for envy and rivalry is laid and the simultaneous presence of two children in relation to an engulfing and omnipotent mother can only be resolved through the obliteration of the other. Regardless of whether it is the mother or the father who bears the ultimate guilt, the result of an imaginary duel situation is that when speech and sentences lose their symbolic meaning, a ghostlike disembodied voice emerges, a voice that is not connected to any person inside the reality of the narrative – and that is not simply the voice of an external commentator either – but a voice belonging to a dead person who hovers about in a mythical in-between space and acquires a terrifying dimension of ubiquity and omnipotence, the voice of an invisible master. Bergman himself claims in the *Workbook* that "loud sounds are supposed to be heard as faint and the faint sounds are supposed to be perceived with extreme acuity ... sometimes people speak and no lines are heard, the mouth is moving but no lines."[38] Already now we can say that it is the dead father's (or mother's) voice that cuts a hole in the visual reality, hollowing out the being of the women, speaking of its own accord through the sisters, and sounding, or stuck, in their throats like a silent cry. We hear their grief over what they have lost – it is the void that resounds when they are silent – but when they attack each other it is as if the screen, the last veil, the fabric falls apart and collapses in Ester's psychotic confusion, becoming a pure, inarticulate scream. In this respect, *The Silence* confirms Lacan's words about how it is the "[r]upture, split, the stroke of the opening [that] makes absence emerge – just as the cry does not stand out against a background of silence but on the contrary makes silence emerge as silence."[39] Through Anna and Ester, the voice of their dead father tears apart the shackles of law and order. In *The Silence,* "we hear the scream with our eyes" or see the silence that indicates the end of life.

*

Through the breakdown of language and culture in *The Silence* we can recognize Lacan's algorithm for the process and structure of psychosis: "What is refused in the symbolic order re-emerges in the real."[40] When *the Name of the Father* does not gain recognition and no longer has any symbolic effect, it returns beyond the order of language into a hallucinatory world where the words are transformed into objects, in a massive and ghastly silence that envelops *The Silence* in a mysteriousness which makes Bergman and all of us speechless, in Kieślowski's sense. From the horizon of the symbolic, we meet *the real* in the form of absence or lack: a veiled, enigmatic, and mythically lost object that evades linguistic sense and imaginary form. With images and words, Bergman nevertheless manages to evoke an imprint of the space of the real beyond the visible and the symbolic. This is to sketch the silhouette of a gaping void, a frightening silence at the heart of the reality of language and meaning, to conjure up the dimension of lack and loss, and decipher an inaccessible truth that is incompatible with the illusion that makes living possible, not by shyly examining it at the edge of the abyss, but by seeking it at the very bottom of the crack of madness.[41]

Yet it is not the presence of the real in terms of absence or something repressed or denied that returns in *The Silence*, but here we are haunted by the real in a brutal and total *presence* in the shape of body, meat, uninhibited pleasure, death drive … We have, with Lacan, entered a zone that human life may only enter for a short while, where "a being remains in a state of suffering."[42] It is to be placed face to face with a pure death drive in virtue of the endpoint of the real, where our symbolic reality falls apart.[43] In *The Silence* there is a short interlude – without actual meaning and taking place early in the film when Anna, Ester, and Johan have just arrived at the hotel – that gives body and image to this unconditional drive in which the object is transformed into a part object of an "undead" striving beyond life and death.[44] Ester is resting on her bed, Anna arranges things in the room and Johan, bored, sits down on the floor and (through the camera) gazes at her feet:

Anna: What are you looking at?
Johan: I'm looking at your feet.
Anna: Why is that?
Johan: They walk around with you all the time, all by themselves.

In *The Silence*, we no longer experience reality at a safe distance but are forced to confront the absolute closeness of the real – where we leave an established rendering of a harmonious reality behind, "over there," and are hurled against the unpleasant presence of the real in the shape of the revolting substance of pleasure: groveling, sticky, indestructible life.[45]

It is, however, above all the pure incarnation of pleasure – in the form of a stale and dissolute sexuality, pervaded by the rot of death – that is present in *The Silence*. Several long scenes show how Anna, in contrast to Ester's sterile, cold, and formal figure, acts out this crude carnal voluptuousness. Left alone, Ester experiences a severe attack of suffocation, due to her illness, and seeks solace in cigarettes and alcohol. Anna goes out to explore the hot, sunny, crowded, noisy city. Outside the hotel there is a lively square, where the only thing that seems to engage the interest of the visitors is sexual pleasure. While picking up some coins from the floor by her table, a waiter at the bar that Anna visits discreetly touches her knees. She then enters a variety theater – an adjacent cabaret hall where the troupe of dwarves perform – and sees at the back of the theater a couple beginning to making love, which soon turns into heavy copulating. Affected by the atmosphere, and heavy with lust, she returns to the bar and seeks out the waiter.

Anna returns to the hotel and, in Kieślowski's words, goes

> into the hotel room, observed by Ester. She removes her underpants and puts them in the sink in order to wash them. It almost happens *off* – outside the image. It is not due to any prudishness on the part of Bergman – we see exactly as much as is needed for us to imagine that she removes her underpants because she is revolted by what may have remained after her intercourse with the bartender.[46]

Ester jealously wants to know where she has been. She suspects what has happened and exclaims:

> Erectile tissue! It's a question of engorgement and mucus. A confession before the last anointing: I think semen smells bad. I happen to have a sensitive nose, you see. I found that I stank like a rotten fish when I had been impregnated. It's optional, after all.

Angered, Anna tells her that she has made love with a man in a church, but then claims that it is a lie. The relationship between the sisters is tense. Anna walks away and meets the nameless waiter again in an adjacent hotel, where they make love. She tells him: "How good it is with you. How good it is that we don't understand each other." Later, after having run around in the long corridors of the hotel and when he is in bed for the night, Johan tells Ester that he has seen his mother enter a room with a strange man. Upset, she seeks out her sister, and a bitter scene ensues, while Anna's lover watches and listens, and their conversation ends in words of abuse and tears, and no reconciliation takes place. After Ester leaves and breaks down, Anna flies into a rage, and the waiter, as if in an attempt to console her, penetrates her from behind.

It is obvious that Anna, with respect to her personality and her actions, has come to incarnate the figure of crude, forbidden, sexual pleasure, in contrast to Ester's cold, formal, and asexual figure. The fact that she – in a scene considered by many to be highly unpleasant – lays drunk in her bed masturbating, indicates how she is not part of a sexual *relation* but has to act out her desire in loneliness and with her own body, in what psychoanalysis defines as the figure of autoeroticism. As a result of their narcissistic and aggressive mirror relationship, it is as if Anna acts out the pleasure that Ester has come to reject but which returns in the jealousy of madness.

> *Ester*: Can't you refrain from meeting him? Just tonight. It torments me.
> *Anna*: Why?
> *Ester*: Because I feel humiliated. You mustn't think that I'm jealous.
> *Anna*: I have to go now.

Already the famous initial *mise-en-scène* of the film, where Johan sits between the two sisters in the train compartment, gives an anticipatory hint of their mutual relation. Cool and contained, Ester sits in what looks like an office outfit, while

Anna, sweaty, appears in a low-cut, thin dress. The drops of perspiration come across as a bodily expression of the sticky and unpleasant substance of pleasure that leaves its mark on the explicit sex scenes (such as the masturbation scene), and the fact that we can sense the rot of death behind them and the frightful presence of the real in the shape of the death drive, may explain the violent reactions to *The Silence*.[47] Kieślowski sees:

> the ambiguous portrayal of the feeling we all have when we are constantly shaken and torn between love and hate, between fear of death and longing for peace, between jealousy and generosity, painful humiliation and voluptuous vindictiveness. *The Silence* is played out in that fuming atmosphere during a hot day and a hot night, where there is room for eroticism and for desire, but not for love, and where the lack of mercy and empathy has become a completely natural state.

The presence of the death drive in *The Silence* can be felt and described in virtue of the difference between "two deaths," which, according to Lacan, is the exact, theoretical concept for the representation of the possibility of a "second death" originating from the Marquis de Sade's idea of a radical, absolute rupture that liberates the creative powers of nature: the distinction between a natural death and an absolute death that annihilates, cancels nature's eternal cycle – described by Lacan as something that takes place when death is completed and as "the point at which the very cycles of the transformations of nature are annihilated."[48] He sketches a topology in terms of the transition between life and death, "a death lived by anticipation, a death that crosses over into the sphere of life, a life that moves into the realm of death."[49] It is in this border zone between life and death that we meet the living dead, the phantoms, and in *The Silence* we behold, in this nightmarish reality, sleepwalkers with empty and tense faces, the sisters having been reduced to shadows in an apocalyptic ghost world.

> *Ester*: I don't want to accept my pitiful role. But now it's really lonely. One tries out attitudes and finds them all meaningless. The forces are too strong. I mean the forces, the ghastly ones. One has to move carefully among ghosts and memories, I should say. I talk. But there's no need to discuss loneliness. It's really unnecessary.

Sweaty and drunk with lust and sexual desire, Anna has entered the place of this second death and she confirms, in the Lacanian sense, de Sade's fantasy about the female victim, who in a certain sense is immortal and (by her sister) exposed to "eternal suffering," she is endlessly tortured, yet survives. It is as if she has, besides her natural body and death, been given access to another body: an indestructible bodily substance, free from the natural cycle of life – of life and death, regrowth, and decay – a sublime beauty, but one which also frightens us in its monstrous shape of unqualified crude sexual pleasure, and which for Lacan "suggests in its very form the presence of what one might call petrified pain," opening "onto that limit where a living being has no possibility to escape."[50] Anna has entered this domain between two deaths, she has been exposed to Ester's hatred, and she asks her to leave and be quiet, but her sister smilingly pats her on the head, saying, "Poor Anna."

With *The Silence*, Bergman puts into words and images the truth of the death drive, which does not correspond to a psychopathological symptom but is a fundamental human condition to do with the fact that the human being is "sick until death," an animal plagued by an insatiable parasite, and which, thus, defines *la condition humaine*. Kieślowski writes:

> In many of his films, Bergman deals with Death. His deceased characters have even been able to visit the living (*Fanny and Alexander*). In *The Silence* too, death is constantly present. "If father had still been alive …," "Before father died …," Ester says, very ill herself and in the penultimate scenes close to death. Death is the theme of the film, just as it is that of life.

After all, the very name of the city denotes a place belonging to the executioner. *The Silence* is shrouded in the veil of death. When Johan wanders around in the corridors and rooms of the hotel, he discovers death in the face of the room service waiter. In the *Workbook* Bergman writes: "Then the boy sees Death walking about in the corridors and greets him, bowing and saying something. The old man stares at him with an inquiring look, stuttering. But Johannes [sic!] is scared and runs from Death."[51] At the first encounter he is scared, but quite soon he calms down. The waiter tries to scare him by sticking sausages into his mouth, like incisors, a trick that does not frighten Johan. So the elderly man finally pulls a photograph from his wallet, a photograph showing a dead person in a coffin surrounded by people. Johan hides it under the carpet in the hotel corridor. When death manifests itself in its frightening reality, he sweeps it under the carpet.[52]

This is to represent death and transience as fundamental existential conditions. Johan's wanderings, Anna's journey out into the city, and Ester's fatal illness remind us of the fact that contemporary human beings   in our extreme quest for happiness and preoccupation with immortality in a tyrannical and narcissistic culture of compulsive joy – do not want to acknowledge the end of life. We deny the inevitability of annihilation and decay, and death has been medicalized, institutionalized, and dehumanized as an objectively physiological phenomenon. Bergman, however, depicts the human being's own *subjective* death – as an unremittingly frightening existential potentiality. We are not confronted with our mortality for the first time when we die, it is part of life from the beginning. But the loss of life is not essentially a bad thing; death inhabits life, giving it light and meaning. Otherwise, *The Silence* would be meaningless.

When Anna and Johan leave the city on their own at the end of the film it is because their (and our) lives are played out against the finite horizon of death, and when we see Ester writhing in the mortal disease of madness, I hear the echo of the most well-known line in Samuel Beckett's absurd drama *Waiting for Godot* (1953): women "give birth astride of a grave, the light gleams an instant, then it's night once more."[53] As Charles Baudelaire writes:

It's Death comforts us, alas! and makes us live.
It is the goal of life, it brings us hope,
And, like a rich elixir, seems to give
Courage to march along the darkening slope.[54]

The tragic and inexorable truth of death makes visible and embodies our existential conditions and fate. As Kieślowski says, Bergman has "almost like no one else, and perhaps he is the only one in the the world, had as much to say about human nature as Dostoyevsky or Camus."[55] The human being is a suffering creature, the dimension of lack and loss being forever inscribed in our tragical existence. In writing about *The Silence,* I am reminded of the leitmotif of August Strindberg's play and pilgrim drama *A Dream Play* (which the author himself called "my most beloved drama, the child of my greatest pain") that Indra's daughter, Agnes, repeats again and again: "Humankind is to be pitied." Following the fates of the protagonists in *The Silence*, I also listen to the philosopher and religious writer Blaise Pascal when he scans the silence of space:

When I see the blindness and the wretchedness of man, when I regard the whole silent universe, and man without light, left to himself, and, as it were, lost in this corner of the universe, without knowing who has put him there, what he has come to do, what will become of him at death, and incapable of all knowledge, I become terrified, like a man who should be carried in his sleep to a dreadful desert island, and should awake without knowing where he is, and without means of escape.[56]

The abandoned human being, enveloped in silence, darkness, and emptiness, as described by Pascal, has left a powerful imprint among the existential philosophers – Søren Kierkegaard, Friedrich Nietzsche, Martin Heidegger, and Albert Camus among others – who have all pointed to the human being's lack of anchoring and belonging, and to our alienation, lethargy, and existence in loneliness and absurdity. When we, in *The Silence,* follow the fate of the sisters and Johan – marooned in a foreign city whose language they do not understand, without any myth about who they are and how they came into existence – it is as if they have, in an existential sense, landed in exile among spiders and are perceived as intruders, whose arrival constitutes a hemorrhage in the inhabitants' world of illusory freedom. Their actual abandonment and homesickness provide a contour for how they once were, through an original act of violence, thrown out into the world as rootless, wounded and helpless creatures. Behind the brutal, erotic scenes shrouded in the decay of death and pleasure and the violent duel between the sisters, lurks the strange and frightening presence of our peer, the unremitting possibility of death, where we – in the desperate figures of Anna and Ester – can discern the fundamental existential challenge and dilemma of reaching the other and attempting to bridge the abyss between human beings. Bergman himself wanted to show that:

Sexual perversion – that is hell. When sex is isolated from other aspects of life and from other feelings, it creates an enormous loneliness. That is what *The Silence* is about. The devaluation of sex that opens the way for brutality and cruelty.[57]

*

Ultimately, the existential conditions and challenges of *The Silence* converge in questions to do with religious faith and the existence of God.[58] The film is part of a trilogy and was preceded by *Through a Glass Darkly* (1961) and *Winter Light* (1963), and when Sjöman wonders about how this film could conclude the trilogy, Bergman exclaims:

> But that's obvious, isn't it? In *Through a Glass Darkly*, it's God and love that reign. Then comes *Winter Light* which criticizes this and ends in a stripped-down nadir with a prayer addressed to an unnamed god. A god beyond formulas, the living religion represented by Frövik. And then *The Silence* – everything is even more stripped down, a world completely without god. Where only the hand – the fellowship – remains. And music.[59]

Or as Bergman expressed it on the flyleaf of the published film scripts, *A Film Trilogy* (1963): "These three films are about reduction. *Through a Glass Darkly* – conquered certainty. *Winter Light* – penetrated certainty. *The Silence* – the silence of God – the negative imprint. That's why they constitute a trilogy."[60] The silence that prevails in *The Silence* is ultimately the silence of God, but how can we understand it? In a sense it denotes "the absence of God" or "the death of God," and we remember that Nietzsche already at the end of the 19th century exclaimed: "*We have killed him* – you and I! We are all his murderers!" In their rejection of *the Name of the Father*, God has never existed for Anna and Ester. In Vilgot Sjöman's book, Bergman explains: "Squarely expressed: Anna is the body, Ester is the soul. He laughs at how flat it all becomes when it is supposed to be explained and reluctantly mumbles something about the battlefield of *The Silence*: the tumult that arises between the body and the soul when God is gone."[61] When God is dead, a struggle between body and soul ensues, shown in the ever-present confrontations and conflicts between the sisters – when a divine legal system (the ten commandments) is no longer valid, it is as if the film *from within* a monotheistic perspective wants to illustrate how we are exiled to a barbarian backwater in the world, where the legally regulated boundary between humans has been chewed to pieces and violence and oppression have been given free rein. On seeing Anna's half naked figure in a hotel room with a stranger, and her son in an adjacent room, it is as if the door has been opened to bodily pleasures and as if the protection of morals, civilization, and spiritual rationality has been eroded *from without* a biblical order. When Johan points out that Anna's feet walk around of their own accord, he accentuates the corporality and mobility of his mother, in contrast to Ester's bedridden soul.[62] In the struggle between the sisters, the body wins, while the soul is left to die in a hotel room in a foreign city.

Bergman laughs when Ester herself expresses the death of God by, in a farewell to the symbol of "Father God," reducing their dead carnal father to a two-hundred-kilo corpse. In the confrontation between the sisters, he is also referred to in terms of the rejected *Name of the Father* – a basically religious reference – which in this respect can be perceived as a patricide, seen by Lacan as a "myth of a time for which God is dead."[63] Furthermore, when Johan, early in *The Silence*, ventures out into the corridors of the hotel and runs into a porter who is busy changing a light bulb, we get a hint about the boy's and Bergman's negative view of God. Johan stands under the old man's ladder, sticks out his tongue and then shoots him with a cap pistol. We witness the scene from an *above* perspective – which is reminiscent of God's all-seeing eye – and an uncomplicated interpretation is that it is Bergman as a child that kills God in a patricide. God's death (in the death of the father) may be seen as a reference to a vision of God that Bergman had carried for many years and believed in since he was a child and that he here pronounces dead:

> At that time I lived with a number of withered remains of a childish piety, a completely naive idea of what you could call an *otherworldly* salvation. My present conviction had also manifested itself during this time. The human being carries his or her own Holiness which lies within the realm of the earth, it has no otherworldly explanations.[64]

It is the silence that ensues on God's death that arises in *The Silence*. In my eyes, traces of God's silence return when Ester, agonizing, is left behind on her own – exposed to the terrible fate of death, she embodies Pascal's ghastly image of the predicament of the human being who has been abandoned by God in a decayed and empty world. God, severe and hard, does not care about her cries for help, in his absence. He does not reach out to her, and she is thrown into the darkness of despair.

Bergman's reduction-whittling down of an authoritarian and severe transcendent God in the shape of "the death of God," leads, in Lacan's parlance, to the loss and breakdown of the symbolically founded reality in *The Silence*, and we sink down into an abyss of anxiety, threatened by *spiritual death* and dissolution. Following Hegel, it is possible to perceive in God's death what the mystics called "the night of the world," when they experienced the dissolution of the (symbolically structured) coherent "earthly" reality itself.[65] Here we recognize the fear of darkness, hell and damnation that has emerged in the spirituality of the Christian church and in the saints' dread of being separated from God. It is this secular darkness that we experience in *The Silence* and that Hegel in a much-cited passage spoke of as *the Night of the World*:

> Man is this Night, this empty Nothing, which holds everything in its simplicity – a kingdom of endless representations, images, none of which appears

immediately to him – or which are not immediately present. This is the Night, Nature's inner, which here exists – pure self – phantasmagorical representations are surrounded by Night, here shoots out a bloody head – there another white figure suddenly comes forward, and disappears just as suddenly – One catches a glimpse of this Night when one looks others in the eyes – into a Night which would be frightful – here hangs over against one the Night of the world.[66]

In the terrible night that already darkens *The Silence* in a quite concrete sense in the night train compartment, I also see a rotten and cancerous world with the bloodied heads and frightening phantoms of human beings, where we, in a hallucinatory dream world, *inwardly* experience the suffering that humankind has been exposed to at all times and in all places. It is consequently not to be wondered at that we, in the violent and, for many, sexually revolting scenes, can witness an expression of drives and wishes – as opposed to ascetic coldness (in Ester) – that, due to demands and obedience and in a state of subjection and self-denial, have been denied in compliance with "the only good will" according to the belief in the otherworldly salvation in the Holy Spirit of the Christian *community*. In this sense, *The Silence* confirms Lacan's perception that

the myth *God is dead* – I am much less certain about this myth than most contemporary intellectuals, which is not a declaration of theism or of faith in resurrection – this myth is maybe only a shelter against the threat of castration ... the true formula of atheism is not that *God is dead* ... the true formula of atheism is that *God is unconscious*.[67]

The death of God is not an atheistic explanation, because God is unconscious, and this circumstance testifies to the fact that Dostoyevsky's assumption – through Ivan in *The Brothers Karamozov* – that *if God does not exist, everything is permitted*, is not true. Lacan writes:

As you know, his son leads [Karamazov] into those audacious avenues taken by the thought of the cultivated man, and in particular he says, *if God doesn't exist ...* – *If God doesn't exist*, the father says, *then everything is permitted*. Quite evidently, a naive idea, for we analysts know full well that if God doesn't exist, then nothing at all is permitted any longer. Neurotics prove that to us every day.[68]

Even if *The Silence* is enveloped in God's silence, there exists in Anna and Ester an *ambivalence* in relation to God. They are not believers who harbor secret doubts and devote themselves to forbidden fantasies; instead the film openly exhibits desires and pleasures: it is the *prohibitions* themselves that are denied and rejected. "If God does not exist, then everything is permitted" lives in Ester's soul in the shape of empty prohibitions and restrictions that want to prevent and destroy her sister's possibilities to experience pleasure and joy. In reality, Ester embodies the predicament of the religious fundamentalist in that she perceives herself as God's tool, and because her actions are blessed in virtue of a higher will, she can do as she likes and oppress her sister. In Bergman's workbook Anna exclaims: "She torments me, she torments me."[69] It is Ester's soul and not Anna's body that is soaked in perverted pleasure when the former, like a saint, radically rejects the position of sexual object for another human being – a rejection that concerns merely her material (corporeal) body – whereby she with even greater passion can offer her spiritual (pious) body to God. Ester takes up the position of the pure object, conjures up nothing but simply endures with her immobile presence (she is constantly in bed) – turning herself into a fetish for the absolute Other. Through her devotion and her sacrifices she wants, like a sublime object (Lacan's *objet petit a*), to heal Him, be what He lacks, at the same time as filling her own void and acting out an "uncastrated," parasitical and destructive pleasure in relation to her sister. Behold the scene where Anna rapidly puts out her cigarette, rises and puts on her jewels, Ester turns off the music of the radio set, her sister still fiddling nervously with her jewels while she speaks in a rushed voice:

> *Anna*:   I'm going outside for a while. It's so hot in here. You know I can't stand … I'll be back soon. [*to Johan*:] Why don't you read aloud to Ester in the meantime?
> *Ester*:   Go now, before your bad conscience makes you scream.

In *The Silence*, God's absence throws us out into the darkness of despair and doubt, in an experience of the death of God in *the Night of the World*, where we have withdrawn into the darkness of the pure ego – where reality ruptures – and experience a radical loneliness, as we in this moment leave the Christian symbolic community's faith in God. When I, seemingly abandoned by God in Pascal's world, driven to despair, am thrown out into a completely solitary world, I *can* identify with Jesus Christ on the cross, as he cried: "My God, my God, why hast thou forsaken me?" ("*Eloi, Eloi, lema sabachtani?*"). In contrast to the salvation of faith in relation to God as a transcendent beyond in the community of the church, faith is here transformed into a purely *existential* experience. It is no longer the object of knowledge (as in the Christian doctrine) but encompasses a lived inner-worldly experience beyond Reason – the logics of the rational symbolic order – that, in Lacan's words, situates itself in the field of the real: "God is encountered in the real."[70] *Beyond himself in himself*, the knight of faith experiences God in the heart of holiness. In Bergman's words: "[P]eeling off theology, the Holy remains."[71] Immersed in God's otherworldly absence, in *The Silence* we leave the silence of reason and the darkness of lovelessness in order to reveal the inner-worldly, radiant, and wordless name of love. Although the relation between the two sisters, framed by brutality and lovelessness, is surrounded by the silence of God, Kieślowski senses the presence of sparks of love and humaneness:

> In this bleak, fiercely sad film, a ray of hope nevertheless penetrates, beyond the dialogue and the plot, seemingly without reason. I know where this light

streak, despite the bleakness of the film, comes from: from Bergman's strong belief in humanity even in situations where the actors are forced to cruelty and ruthlessness. The hardly noticeable and yet constantly present hopefulness in the film lies in Ester's tender, almost fleeting gesture on seeing Anna naked and asleep, little Johan cuddling up to her. Ester makes a gesture as if to caress Anna, but changes her mind and withdraws her hand. Why? Does she not want to allow herself to make a gesture that could reveal a feeling? Apparently. Does she fear all signs of love?

In an interview with *Playboy* magazine, Bergman summarizes the message of love at the end of *Through a Glass Darkly, Winter Light*, and *The Silence*:

Bergman: It's not God that is our salvation, it's *love*. That's all we can place our hopes in.
Playboy: How is this shown in the other two films?
Bergman: Each film, you see, contains moments of contact making: the line "Father spoke to me," at the end of *Through a Glass Darkly*; the pastor conducting the service in the empty church for Märta's sake, at the end of *Winter Light*; the little boy reading Ester's letter on the train, at the end of *The Silence*. A short episode in each film, with the decisive moment. What means more than anything in life is the ability to *approach another human being*. Otherwise you are dead, just like all other people nowadays that are dead. But if one can make that first step towards *contact*, towards understanding, towards love, then it doesn't matter how difficult the future looks – and one shouldn't have any illusions; even if one has all the love in the world, life can be damn difficult – one is liberated. That's all that means anything, isn't it?[72]

Alone, completely abandoned and waiting for death in a foreign city, Ester still manages, in an act of love, to hand over a gift to Johan – a letter with new words that the boy spells out in the foreign language.[73]

Anna: What's that?
Johan: Ester wrote me a letter.
Anna: A letter? May I see? "For Johan. Words in the foreign language." That's kind of her.

In Bergman's words, the plot testifies to the need for human contact, an attempt to *come close to another human being*, and in this sense it represents an inner-worldly divine gesture. The agonizing sister on her death bed is filled with God's inscrutable mercy that has at this moment given her the Word and when Johan reads the new words and enters a foreign world, we witness the blessing and liberation of the miracle of God leaving traces in the real. God's mercifulness and loving goodness are manifested beyond the individuality of human beings in their fateful fellowship across cultural and geographical borders, because one of the holy words that the mystic Johan reads is "*kasi*," which means "hand" and in Bergman's sense denotes companionship. Through the sheet of paper in the boy's hands, Ester, Johan, and Anna (in her role as his mother and her sister) are swept into the forgiving and selfless love of Christianity through *Agape*. This plea, a gift and an act of affection, symbolizes the moment when a transcendent God is humanized in word and speech and transformed into an inner-worldly *Name of the Father*, which, after having been rejected in the shape of the silence of an appeal that has failed to materialize, now gains Ester's recognition. In a redemption from doubt, in "penetrated certainty," and after having been in a position where she could have died abandoned, without meaning, she has re-entered the symbolic, her father's name being transferred from one generation to another; in a *sublimating* action, the suffering (the lack, the loss, and the desire) acquires a *sublime* expression, she is liberated from the weight of herself, and, in Lacan's words, she elevates "an object ... to the dignity of the *Thing*."[74] From the wordlessness of silence, from the void of language, the universe of the word, *Logos*, is born, and from *the Night of the World* and the darkness of lovelessness, the light of love springs forth. From the silence of the symbolic and the darkness of the imaginary, the door to the emptiness of the real is ajar ... From the meaninglessness of the silence and the unreflected mirror image of obscurity, the miracle emerges in a kind of *impossible* metaphor, when, according to Lacan, "a glimmer of signification springs forth at the surface of the real, and then causes the real to become illuminated with a flash projected from below its underpinning of nothingness."[75] The clearing (*Lichtung*) of Being – in terms of Heidegger's philosophy of existence – opens the world, and what has till now been forgotten and hidden in a movement of *aletheia* is once again covered in a (divine) light in the clearing of the sublime.[76]

If *The Silence* is about the silence of the symbolic and the darkness of the imaginary, we travel from the domain of *hearing* and the ear to the world of *looking* and vision. The film shows a reality *beyond* the visible.[77] Bergman teaches us to see this *real* nothingness, and *The Silence* gives form and body to how an object is elevated to the dignity of the *Thing*. It is through the eyes of Johan – in one respect the most important character in the film – that the images and the symbols have been dissolved and an abyss is revealed. Throughout the film, he is like a "sleepwalker," interjected from nowhere, that suddenly rises and sees the truth of reality. Symbolically, Carol Brightman articulates this fact, when she describes Johan's look as unfocused: "When he looks out at us, it is as if he sees as far as the flat screen which delimits him, no further. His eyes never really focus."[78] This gap in reality is, in Koskinen's words, "emphasized in Anna's apathetic stare straight into nothingness, Ester's forced blinking, and Johan's persistent rubbing of his eyes."[79] An unbearable gulf closes around us when Johan, with his "awakening" eyes, goes wandering through the labyrinthine hotel corridors, where he constantly gets lost, and as expressed by Koskinen: "Johan seems to be looking out into a world that looks like a flat painting, while he himself is circumscribed by frames, as if caught in a painting."[80]

Thus this boy is a "pilgrim," a "guide" into the world, a kind of interpreter of our existence – the extended eye of the viewer and, I believe, of Bergman as well, and through *The Silence* the image appears as a decoy, a snare, and a mirage for our eyes.[81] But behind this embellishing veil lies the horror of life. *The Silence* simultaneously shows how death looks at us *from another direction* ... The ghosts of the apocalypse pursue us, a gap opens up in our reality, where the eyes of death itself observe us and we are haunted by an inexorable truth about our own blindness. This reversal occurs at the moment when we realize that Johan is also someone who is *observed*.[82] In this sense, *The Silence* reveals Lacan's basic view that it is not the human beings who see the world, but the *world that looks* at them.[83] Johan sees only his mother's feet, not the rest of her – he sees a world in fragments.[84] We do not endure the mortal and basically unbearable look from the world, and all our images, symbols and mirrors are ways to hide this elusive and deadly void.

Johan becomes the bridge; he encompasses hope and through him we are in a process of meaning and a desire for "unity."[85] With the night comes the promise of a new day and his soul has been given access to a light beyond the sun of reason. So has Anna. Her decision to depart with Johan and leave Ester at the mercy of loneliness and death, can be seen as a brutal and inhumane escape, but it is not. At the core, it is a truly separating and deeply humane act – an expression of an authentic insight that she no longer *wishes to* maintain this narcissistic and imaginary duel relation and be *the object* of her sister's pleasure in order to fill her lack. Exposed to a destructive death drive in the rift between two deaths, Anna leaves this no man's land where no human life may set foot, and follows her desire to the point where the emptiness behind its object emerges and is reconciled with the truth of lack, loss, and grief. It is Anna's act that opens up the possibility for Ester to hand over a letter to her son, and when she, together with Johan, leaves her sister in the hands of the city, it is due to a will to start anew and to – in a sublimating desire – create something out of *nothing, ex nihilo*. This is the true gift of love – rather than benevolence, Anna lets Ester meet loneliness – and both of them corroborate Lacan's maxim: "Love is giving what you don't have ..."[86]

*

When Bergman seeks to sketch the outline of this gaping void in the real, this vast and incomprehensible silence, beyond all conversations and meanings, he meets the silence of God in ... *the music.* After finishing *Winter Light*, Bergman had planned to devote a year to investigating and immersing himself in the music of Bach. This intention was not realized, however; instead, he created *The Silence*, where the musical works of the German composer have a crucial function and meaning, and in this respect the film testifies to his love of Bach.[87] The idea for *The Silence* did *de facto* spring from the music:

> Just as in *Winter Light*, *The Silence* started with a piece of music, namely, Bartók's concerto for orchestra. The original idea was to make a film that followed musical laws rather than dramaturgical ones. A film that worked

associatively – rhythmically with a main motif and subsidiary themes. During the construction of the film I thought in musical terms much more than I had done before. The only thing that remains of Bartók is really the very beginning. It follows Bartók's music quite closely, with that deep, sustained tone and then the sudden explosion.[88]

We hear the music – at a low volume, almost inaudible – when Ester at the beginning of *The Silence* watches the narrow streets of the city at night through the hotel window. She walks away from the window, stops at the desk with a radio and a pile of books, and lights a cigarette. In the foreground, there is the back of a chair and, at the far end of the room, a plant. Ester takes the radio with her, places it on a table and sits down. In the background, in the adjoining room, Anna sits in front of a mirror with Johan at her side, both of them turning their backs to Ester. The volume of the music is raised. Johan asks: "When are we going home?" Anna answers: "Tonight perhaps." Ester has turned her eyes to them. Johan wonders if Ester will accompany them, but Anna replies evasively that she does not know. Ester's face is shown in profile, she raises the volume of the radio, whereafter we behold Anna and Johan in a close-up when she applies cream to his hands, they embrace and she kisses him all over his face. Ester holds the radio with both hands. There is a knock on the door, Ester looks up. The room service waiter enters the room with a tray and puts it on her table. Johan lies in Anna's lap. Ester asks the waiter:

Ester:	What is it called? Music?
	The Waiter: 'Muzik'… [clarification:] 'muzik.'
Ester:	Sebastian Bach?
The Waiter:	Johann Sebastian Bach.

The waiter and Ester are still for a few seconds before he leaves the room. Ester stands up and walks towards the headboard of the bed, Johan leaves his mother and moves towards the door, Anna turns to Ester and explains that Johan is going to ask her for cigarettes, whereupon he fetches them on the desk and then sits down on the threshold. Ester says that she thinks they should leave, Anna objects mechanically and half-heartedly, then says:

Anna:	What music is that?
Ester:	Bach. Sebastian Bach.
Anna:	It's beautiful.

Anna rapidly puts out her cigarette, rises and puts on her jewels. Ester turns off the music on the radio.[89] The viewer has listened to Bach and booming church bells, the inscrutable murmur of human beings, car horns, and the clatter of hooves from a horse that is wasting away. But from within Ester's room, it is – with the exception of the almost inaudible musical piece – totally quiet.[90] We hear the music streaming out of the radio, see Ester handling it, turning up the volume and turning it off, and yet it seems disconnected from the reality in which it exists.[91] Irrespective of what happens, the notes ripple across the scene and acquire an otherworldly dimension. Evasive and lyrical, the piece of chamber music seems to expand the room in which the sisters and the boy are located: the images are linked together and the space shrinks. The spatial boundlessness of the music also has a symbolic meaning. If the words distance the sisters from each other and their conversation is cold, reproachful, and violent, there occurs in this scene, while they are listening to Bach, a *shift* – an approach – between them and an attempt at benevolence and love; it is the music that unites them. At a distance from each other, they sit each in their own room (Ester is in focus, while Anna and Johan are not), often turning their backs on each other – yet the music bridges the spatial gap. Untrammeled by the laws of space, it travels intact and freely between the siblings, and it is as if Bach's notes – which existed on board both of the Voyager spaceships that traveled out into actual interstellar space – are no longer sounds that exist *in* the room but sounds keeping the room as such *open*. If the sound was obliterated, the empty space itself, with all its "inner-worldly" phenomena, would vanish. The music of Bach in *The Silence* is therefore in a sense *the sound of silence*, which creates the ontological horizon, the texture that keeps the symbolic reality together, and what happens when Ester turns off the music? Then the war between the sisters starts all over again. The sublimely beautiful musical veil collapses and the voice of the dead father comes alive.[92]

The words in *The Silence* are meaningless, both between the sisters and in relation to the waiter; they do not understand each other's language, but they are both familiar with Bach, and after a brief verbal exchange they look at each other in recognition. Though they are total strangers to each other – in the linguistic, cultural, and historical sense – the music unites them. Beyond the symbolic, beyond the hopeless struggle and all the differences and hate in the darkness of the imaginary, Anna reveals through a small but miraculous gesture, surrounded by the silence of light, the universal link of music, in a speech to an all-encompassing, deeply human inner world. Let us listen to Bergman:

> Johann Sebastian Bach. People can't cope with all the words that belong to the rituals of religion. Partly because they have lost their reality, their complete conviction, and partly because today it is more difficult than ever to accept the vision of God presented by Christianity. People who must reject dogmas and rituals, who are indifferent and averse to the acts of religious services and their meaning, now experience a feeling of emptiness or hunger. It is the disorientation of the religious feeling that follows on the debacle of the struggle for faith. In the music of Sebastian Bach, our homeless longing for God finds a security that isn't disturbed by the ambiguity of words or the pollution of speculations. We allow our wounded thought to calm down, don't have to mount a resistance before a faith that in its boundlessness encompasses all our ambivalent anxiety. Bach's music lifts us beyond the crude tangibility of rituals and dogmas, taking us to a communion with defenseless holiness.

If I have started in the train compartment and end in the compartment. The boy has got hold of the will left behind by Ester. And initiates investigations with great stubbornness.[93]

His name is Johann Sebastian Bach, but Ester cannot say his full name, in front of either the waiter or Anna, she leaves out Johann – it is as if she wants to emphasize the difference between the boy on earth and the dead person in the sky, but by doing so she reveals that the words she *would* offer Johan are in the name of God and Bach. Bergman himself has all the time been in the train compartment, looking out at the world through the eyes of Johan in order to film God in the space of the real, through Bach, about whom Cioran has said:

> Without Bach, theology would be devoid of an object, Creation would be fictive, and Nothingness peremptory. If anyone owes everything to Bach, it's God.[94]

And Bergman.

Notes

1 I would like to thank Katarina Graah-Hagelbäck for her help with the English translation.
2 Ola Sigurdson, *Žižek, Augustinus och zombier. En essä om subjektivitet och hopp* (*Žižek, Augustine and zombies. An essay on subjectivity and hope*) (Malmö: Eskaton, 2016), p. 10.
3 See Jacques Lacan, *Psykoanalysens fyra grundbegrepp. Bok XI* (*The Four Fundamental Concepts of Psycho-Analysis. Book XI*), trans. Carin Franzén & Mats Svensson (Hägersten: Tankekraft förlag, 2015), pp. 85–136; see also Peter Jansson, "Vad finns bakom draperiet?" ("What is behind the curtain?"), in Georg Klein (ed.), *Nya tankar om kreativitet och flow* (*New thoughts on creativity and flow*) (Stockholm: Brombergs, 2012), pp. 160–176; Sven-Olov Wallenstein, "Ögat och blicken. Om Jacques Lacans bildteori" ("The eye and the gaze. On Jacques Lacan's picture theory") *Divan. Tidskrift för psykoanalys och kultur* (*Divan. Journal of Psychoanalysis and Culture*), no. 2, 1996, pp. 20–29.
4 See Maaret Koskinen, *Ingmar Bergman's The Silence. Pictures in the Typewriter, Writings on the Screen* (Seattle: University of Washington Press, 2009), p. 6.
5 Koskinen, *Ingmar Bergman's The Silence*, p.137 f. Koskinen's valuable information and reflections on the film have left traces in the present study.
6 Krzysztof Kieślowski, "Bergmans *Tystnaden*" ("Bergman's *The Silence*"), trans. Carl Göran Åhlund, *Chaplin*, 4–5/1994, p. 28; if nothing else is indicated, all quotations and references to Kieślowski derive from this article.
7 From January 1962, Bergman works on the script for *The Silence*, among other places at Siljansgården Hotel outside Rättvik. The film is shot during the summer; see Ingmar Bergman, *Arbetsboken 1955–1974* (*The Workbook 1955–1974)* (Stockholm: Ingmar Bergman and Norstedts, 2018), p. 127.
8 Koskinen writes: "*The Silence* is a film *about* just that – sounds and various auditory phenomena (and lack of them): silences"; Koskinen, *Ingmar Bergman's The Silence*, p. 16.
9 Kieślowski writes: "Those of us who are one or two generations younger, have to be frank about the fact that we have not been able to replace them. When I think about the films of today, more often than not I visualize a churchyard. Tombs and a few old

people who support each other with cautious movements, and close by, a motorway, full of fast, technically perfect but confusingly similar cars"; author's translation. If nothing else is indicated, all translations of the quotations are the author's.

10 Mikael Timm, *Lusten och dämonerna: Boken om Bergman* (*The Lust and the Daemons: A Book about Bergman)* (Stockholm: Norstedts Förlag, 2008), p. 347.

11 The leading roles were played by Ingrid Thulin (1926–2004) and Gunnel Lindblom (1931–), the latter in her greatest ever performance for Bergman. She had been a key player in his band of actors since *Don Juan* at the Malmö City Theatre in 1955, and had played minor parts in *The Seventh Seal*, *The Virgin Spring*, and *Winter Light*.

12 The director himself talks about its origin in *Bergman about Bergman*: "Timoka, the name of the city, I saw in a book belonging to my wife at that time. She's Esthonian. It was a book of poetry. The word 'timoka' stood there on a line by itself, and without knowing what it meant I baptized the city Timoka. Then I asked her what it meant, and she said – there are a lot of cases in Estonian – it means 'appertaining to the execu-tioner.' Otherwise it was just a language I made up"; see www.ingmarbergman.se/en/production/silence.

13 The old room service waiter was played by the veteran Håkan Jahnberg (1903–1970), formerly the leading actor at the Gothenburg City Theatre. He had a problem remem-bering his lines in Bergman's made-up language, and struck a deal with the director that he could revive his childhood ability to speak backwards. Attentive Swedish-speaking listeners might notice that some of Jahnberg's lines are well-known Swedish nursery rhymes recited backwards!; see www.ingmarbergman.se/en/production/silence.

14 Bergman, *Arbetsboken 1955–1974 (The Workbook 1955–1974)*, p. 131.

15 Koskinen, *Ingmar Bergman's The Silence*, p. 113.

16 In his *Workbook*, Bergman writes: "Tanks, armored cars and jeeps pass through the city. The feeling of constant threat and insecurity [...] Out in the street there is a strange noise. The decanter starts to clink, the whole house trembles." Have we beheld such a scene in any other film? Kieślowski is struck by a feeling of *déjà vu* when he "see[s] *The Unbearable Lightness of Being* directed by Philip Kaufman, more specifically the scene where the vibrating glasses in the cupboard announce the arrival in Prague of the Soviet armoured forces in 1968"; cf. the last scene in Andrei Tarkovsky's allegorical science fiction film *Stalker* from 1979. Kieślowski recog-nizes the shadows that sweep over Johan's face from the passing tanks, from one of the world's first films, *Arrival of a train at a station* (*L'arrivée d'un train en Gare de la Ciotat*) by the Lumière brothers.

17 See www.ingmarbergman.se/en/production/silence. In *The Circle* (1907) there is a story set in Berlin and entitled "The Dark Goddess of Victory" which, Bergman writes, "must have hit me like a bullet straight into my young consciousness"; see www.ing-marbergman.se/en/production/silence. This is easy to understand. Siwertz's short story exhibits some similarities with the authorship of the young Bergman.

18 See Pierre Legendre, "Den västerländska människans tillblivelse" ("The Fabrication of Western man"), trans. U. Jakobsson, P. M. Johansson, U. K. O. Nilsson, and A. Holme, *Psykoanalytisk Tid/Skrift*, no. 1, 2002, p. 11.

19 See Pierre Legendre, "Bilden och uppdelningen mellan heligt och profant" ("The Image and the Division between the Holy and the Profane"), trans. M. Leffler, *Psykoanalytisk Tid/Skrift*, no. 22–23, 2008, p. 6, 9.

20 See Jacques Lacan, "Några reflektioner över jaget" ("Some Reflections on the Ego"), trans. Jurgen Reeder, in *Divan. Tidskrift för psykoanalys och kultur* (*Divan. Journal of Psychoanalysis and Culture*), 3/95.

21 Shortly before, Kieślowski writes: "He has constructed *The Silence* simply. Everything superfluous has been removed. There is no *establishing shot*, no shots that aim to situate the action."

22 Ingmar Bergman, *Arbetsboken 1955–1974* (*The Workbook 1955–1974*), p. 142.

23 See Jacques Lacan, *The Psychoses. The Seminar of Jacques Lacan. Book III 1955–1956,* trans. Russell Grigg (London: Routledge, 1993), p. 13; Jacques Lacan, "Response to Jean Hyppolite's Commentary on Freud's 'Verneinung,'" in *Écrits,* trans. Bruce Fink (New York: W. W. Norton & Company, 2006), p. 325 f.

24 See www.ingmarbergman.se/en/production/silence. The director and cinematographer decided to use Eastman Double-X negative, developed to a higher gamma than usual. Coming after the ascetic imagery of *Through a Glass Darkly* and *Winter Light,* they decided to be far less restrained.

25 See www.ingmarbergman.se/en/production/silence.

26 See www.ingmarbergman.se/en/production/silence.

27 And that is why, in Koskinen's words, "while *The Silence* is perfectly plausible on a purely narrative level … it is at the same time so sparse and enigmatic that it seems to call out for (further) interpretation"; Koskinen, *Ingmar Bergman's The Silence,* p. 10.

28 Leif Zern, *Se Bergman (See Bergman)* (Stockholm: Norstedts förlag AB, 1993), p. 138 f.

29 Bergman, *Arbetsboken 1955–1974 (The Workbook 1955–1974),* p. 129 f.

30 Bergman, *Arbetsboken 1955–1974 (The Workbook 1955–1974),* p. 133.

31 Bergman, *Arbetsboken 1955–1974 (The Workbook 1955–1974),* p. 133.

32 Bergman, *Arbetsboken 1955–1974 (The Workbook 1955–1974),* p. 144.

33 See Lacan, *The Psychoses. The Seminar of Jacques Lacan. Book III 1955–1956*; Jacques Lacan, "On a Question Prior to Any Possible Treatment of Psychosis," in *Écrits,* trans. Bruce Fink (New York: W. W. Norton & Company, 2006), pp. 445–485.

34 See Mathias Alvidius' perceptive and condensed article, "En not om det psykotiska genombrottet" ("A note on the psychotic breakthrough"), *Psykoanalytisk Tid/Skrift,* 2–3, 2002, pp. 75–78. It is important to underline that it is primarily Ester who testifies to the rejection of the *Name of the Father,* which becomes evident further on in my presentation.

35 Kieślowski writes: "Ester makes a gesture as if to caress Anna, but changes her mind and withdraws her hand. Why? Does she not want to allow herself to make a gesture that would reveal a feeling? Apparently. Does she fear all signs of love? Yes, the answer is to be found in Anna's violent reaction after having humiliated Ester by, in the embrace, appearing to be a temporary lover and now, with cruel satisfaction, laughing at the pain inflicted and suddenly passing from shrill laughter to tears. Tears whose despair equals the hatred with which her earlier laughter was brimming. Why does Anna laugh? Because she hates her sister. Why is the laughter followed by tears? Because she loves her. How big must Ester's and Anna's love not have been when they were children, before discovering that the father's love for one of them was greater than his love for the other one? When did this happen? When did they understand? Was it simply through a gesture or word from the father? Maybe just a look that sparked the jealousy, a jealousy that later switched to pleasurable hatred."

36 Vilgot Sjöman, *L 136: Dagbok med Ingmar Bergman (Diary with Ingmar Bergman)* (Stockholm: P. A. Norstedt & Söners Förlag, 1963), p. 38 (footnote).

37 My thoughts go to the church father Augustine, who in the face of the small child who had been torn apart by the tortures of jealousy, witnessed original evil: "I myself have experience of a jealous little toddler. He could not speak yet, but he glared, pale and with hateful eyes, at his suckling brother"; Augustinus, *Bekännelser (Confessions),* trans. Bengt Ellenberger (Skellefteå: Artos Bokförlag, 1990), p. 43.

38 Bergman, *Arbetsboken 1955–1974 (The Workbook 1955–1974),* p. 133.

39 Jacques Lacan, *The Four Fundamental Concepts of Psycho-Analysis,* trans. Alan Sheridan (London: The Hogarth Press and the Institute of Psycho-Analysis, 1977), p. 26.

40 See Lacan, *The Psychoses. The Seminar of Jacques Lacan. Book III 1955–1956,* p. 13; see also Lacan, "Response to Jean Hyppolite's Commentary on Freud's 'Verneinung,'" p. 324.

41 See Piera Aulagnier, "Anmärkningar om den psykotiska strukturen" ("Remarks upon the psychotic structure"), trans. Mats Leffler and Håkan Liljeland, *Psykoanalytisk Tid/ Skrift*, 2–3, 2002, pp. 61–70.

42 Jacques Lacan, *The Ethics of Psychoanalysis 1969–1960. The Seminar of Jacques Lacan. Book VII*, trans. Dennis Porter (London: Routledge, 1992), p. 262.

43 See Slavoj Žižek, *Om Lacan* (*Žižek on Lacan*), trans. Oskar Söderlind (Hägersten: TankeKraft förlag, 2016), pp. 75–79.

44 See Žižek, *Om Lacan* (*Žižek on Lacan*), p. 77; Sigurdson, *Žižek, Augustinus och zombier. En essä om subjektivitet och hopp* (*Žižek, Augustine and zombies. An essay on subjectivity and hope*), pp. 21–24.

45 See Slavoj Žižek, *Njutandets förvandlingar. Sex essäer om kvinnan, kulturen och makten* (*The Metastases of Enjoyment. Six essays on woman and causality*), trans. Margareta Eklöf (Stockholm: Natur och Kultur, 1996), pp. 166–169.

46 Kieślowski continues: "In order to depict the scene in the street, Bergman has used four takes. The scene with the underpants is done in five takes. In his book *Images*, Bergman says that he had too little money to realize the scene at the café and at the variety theatre, and he points out that lack of money is not always a drawback for the filmmaking. Both scenes are, in their unpretentiousness, expressive as well as dramatic. The film montage is dense and effective, with clear switches between the cuts. Bergman repeatedly used parallel montage in order to maintain the suspense. Twice he tries, if I remember correctly, to stage a montage inside the image. And the grey-toned faces of Ingrid Thulin and Gunnel Lindblom are captured with perfect timing by means of the exact focus of Nykvist's camera."

47 A passage in *Bergman on Bergman* is telling: "After *The Silence* I received an anonymous letter containing filthy toilet paper; so one could say that the treatment accorded to this film, which by today's standards was pretty innocuous, was rather fierce. There were even people who called up and threatened to kill both me and my wife at that time. Besides being subjected to telephone terror, I suppose I must have got about a hundred letters. So the sexual trauma in Sweden must have been acute. Things have changed radically in these last few years"; from Koskinen, *Ingmar Bergman's The Silence*, p. 48 (see also pp. 43–54).

48 Lacan, *The Ethics of Psychoanalysis 1959–1960. The Seminar of Jacques Lacan. Book VII*, p. 248.

49 Lacan, *The Ethics of Psychoanalysis 1969–1960. The Seminar of Jacques Lacan, Book VII*, p.248.

50 Lacan, *The Ethics of Psychoanalysis 1969–1960. The Seminar of Jacques Lacan, Book VII*, p.60.

51 Bergman, *Arbetsboken 1955–1974* (*The Workbook 1955–1974*), p. 140. In *Bergman on Bergman*, the room service waiter symbolizes death; see Bergman, 1970, p. 71.

52 If we look at the room service waiter from this perspective, *The Silence* appears to be a remnant of the struggle with the fear of death that had characterized Bergman's earlier films, not least *The Seventh Seal*, where death – unlike its symbolic presence in the previous film – has more of a concrete character.

53 Samuel Beckett, *I väntan på Godot* (*Waiting for Godot*) (Stockholm: Albert Bonniers Förlag, 2002), p.109.

54 Roy Campbell, *Poems of Baudelaire* (New York: Pantheon Books, 1952).

55 Koskinen writes: 'The Silence, then, deals with highly worldly issues, both Corporeal and carnal'; Koskinen, *Ingmar Bergman's The Silence*, p. 42.

56 Blaise Pascal, *Pacal's Pensées*, trans. W. F. Trotter (New York: Dutton, 1958), p.198.

57 From Hans Nystedt, *Ingmar Bergman och kristen tro* (*Ingmar Bergman and Christian Faith*) (Stockholm: Verbum Förlag AB, 1989), p. 97.

58 Throughout Bergman's filmmaking, there are recurring themes that more often than not relate to the big existential questions – death, the meaning of life, the significance of

art for the lived life and the conditions and existence of love as well as the problematic of religion, faith and God. This is a thread that runs from *The Seventh Seal* (1957) to *Cries and Whispers* (1973) and that is crowned in the 1960s by *Through a Glass Darkly* (1961), *Winter Light* (1963), *The Silence*, and *Persona* (1966).

59 Sjöman, *L 136: Dagbok med Ingmar Bergman* (*Diary with Ingmar Bergman*), p. 220; Bergman was, however, critical of the idea of a trilogy. Koskinen writes: "But whereas this film and the first one, *Through a Glass Darkly*, explicitly mention the notion of 'God's silence' in the dialogue – the theme supposedly linking the films, according to the epigraph of the published screenplay – the religious theme (or, the word 'God' itself) is not referred to at all in *The Silence*. Instead, this third film is in its frank sexuality so different from the previous two that had Ingmar Bergman, and numerous scholars in his wake, not insisted on this link, one would never have discerned any connection"; Koskinen, *Ingmar Bergman's The Silence*, p. 41.

60 The idea was first formulated in Bergman, *Film Stories 1. Through a Glass Darkly. Winter Light. The Silence.* (Stockholm: Pan/Norstedts, 1973), p. 4.

61 Sjöman, *L 136: Dagbok med Ingmar Bergman* (*Diary with Ingmar Bergman*), p. 220.

62 See Ludvig Lindelöf, *'Guden tiger och människorna pratar'* – *en studie av gudsbilden i Ingmar Bergmans filmer* (*'God remains silent and the people speak'* – *a study of the images of God in the films of Ingmar Bergman*), p. 50 f.

63 Lacan, *The Ethics of Psychoanalysis 1959–1960. The Seminar of Jacques Lacan, Book VII*, p. 177.

64 Ingmar Bergman, *Bilder* (*Images*), p. 237 f. From the very beginning, Bergman wanted to "clean up his act" regarding his faith in God, the "heavy religious superstructure"; Stig Björkman, Torsten Manns and Jonas Sima, *Bergman om Bergman* (*Bergman on Bergman*) (Stockholm: Norstedts, 1970), p. 237.

65 See Žižek, *Njutandets förvandlingar. Sex essäer om kvinnan, kulturen och makten* (*The Metastases of Enjoyment. Six essays on woman and causality*), p. 78 f.

66 Quoted in Žižek, *Njutandets förvandlingar. Sex essäer om kvinnan, kulturen och makten* (*The Metastases of Enjoyment. Six essays on woman, culture and power*), p. 206.

67 Jacques Lacan, *The Four Fundamental Concepts of Psycho-Analysis*, 2015, p. 27, 59.

68 Quoted from Žižek, *Om Lacan* (*Žižek on Lacan*), p. 114; Lacan also says: "God is dead, nothing is permitted anymore. The decline of the Oedipus complex is the mourning of the father, but it leaves us with a durable consequence: the identification known as the superego"; Lacan, *The Triumph of Religion, preceded by Discourse to Catholics*, trans. Bruce Fink (Cambridge: Polity Press, 2013), p. 25.

69 Bergman, *Arbetsboken 1955–1974* (*The Workbook 1955–1974*), p. 143.

70 Jacques Lacan, "Introduktion till Fadersnamnen" ("Introduction to the Names-of-the-Father"), trans. Carin Franzén and René Rasmussen, in *Divan*, 3–4, 2006, p. 27.

71 Bergman, *Bilder* (*Images*), p. 246.

72 Paul Duncan and Bengt Wanselius (eds.), *Regi: Bergman* (*Direction: Bergman*) (Stockholm: Max Ström, 2008), p. 320.

73 In the workbook it says: "The dying man has gradually learnt a few words of the foreign language. With some kind of passion he has tried to penetrate this closed secret. He has written a few words on a sheet of paper. Those words are a poem or a message to his wife crystallised through fear of death, jealousy and immense physical suffering. A formula that she is unable to decipher but that she perceives as something to help her go on living"; Bergman, *Arbetsboken 1955–1974* (*The Workbook 1955–1974*), p. 128 f.

74 Lacan, *The Ethics of Psychoanalysis 1959–1960. The Seminar of Jacques Lacan, Book VII*, p. 112.

75 Lacan, "On a Question Prior to Any Possible Treatment of Psychosis," in *Écrits*, trans. Bruce Fink (New York: W. W. Norton & Company, 2006), p. 468.

76 See Martin Heidegger, *Konstverkets ursprung* (*The Origin of the Work of Art*), 2001, (especially) pp. 30, 50 f, 53 f, 63. See also Wallenstein, "Lacan, Heidegger och det

psykoanalytiska sanningsbegreppet" ("Lacan, Heidegger and the psychoanalytic concept of truth"), *Divan. Tidskrift för psykoanalys och kultur* (*Divan. Journal of Psychoanalysis and Culture*), no. 4, April 1992, pp. 44–51; Daniel Birnbaum and Sven-Olov Wallenstein, *Heideggers väg* (*Heidegger's Way*) (Stockholm: Thales, 1999), pp. 100–103.

77 Koskinen writes: "If *The Silence* is a film about *hearing* and the domain of the ear, and thus about language, talking, and listening (and the lack thereof), it is also very much a film about *looking*, and the sensorium of vision. As noted, Bergman scholars have pointed out that there is in this film a shift toward a more visual style, as opposed to the more verbal style of his earlier films. But one could go further and claim that there is in *The Silence* a theme as well as an aesthetic of vision: this is arguably the first Bergman film in which the act of seeing constitutes the core of the narrative as well as of the narration"; Koskinen, *Ingmar Bergman's The Silence*, p. 114.

78 Quoted from Koskinen, *Ingmar Bergman's The Silence*, p. 115.

79 Koskinen, *Ingmar Bergman's The Silence*, p. 116.

80 Koskinen, *Ingmar Bergman's The Silence*, p. 118.

81 See Koskinen, *Ingmar Bergman's The Silence*, p. 118 ff, 124.

82 See Koskinen, *Ingmar Bergman's The Silence*, p. 118.

83 Lacan, *The Four Fundamental Concepts of Psycho-Analysis*.

84 See Koskinen, *Ingmar Bergman's The Silence*, p. 124.

85 This structure extends to all the protagonists in the film. Koskinen says: "At the most extreme, Ester's and Johan's relationship to Anna could be said to be analogous to the viewer's relationship to the film itself. The viewers are continually placed in situations in which they find themselves observing Anna – and are reminded of this fact by all the numerous mirrors, windows, and frames in the film. Like Johan, the viewers are driven by a desire for 'wholeness,' seeking to meld together a totality from those fragments supplied by the narrative. Perhaps, then, Anna can be said to metaphorically signify this fullness, the fictive world that the viewers try to piece together: she is the body of fiction"; Koskinen, *Ingmar Bergman's The Silence*, p. 132.

86 Jacques Lacan, *Transference. The Seminar of Jacques Lacan, Book VIII*, trans. Bruce Fink (Cambridge: Polity Press, 2015), p. 34.

87 Timm, *Lusten och dämonerna* (*The Lust and the Daemons*), p. 342.

88 Stig Björkman, Torsten Manns and Jonas Sima, *Bergman om Bergman* (*Bergman on Bergman*), p. 195.

89 This piece of classical musical is performed diegetically via the radio set during three minutes, that is, it is perceived as part of the fictive reality, and it is heard on site in the filmed situation.

90 The viewer does not see the source of the music and thus automatically assumes that it is *non-diegetic*; when Ester then walks up to the writing desk, the viewer sees the source (the radio) and realizes – possibly at once – that the music is *diegetic*.

91 The interaction between the music and the room and the depth of the room is an important dimension in *The Silence*. The spatial depth of the room is created by Anna and Johan being placed far away in another room (the side of the door is clearly visible).

92 See Slavoj Žižek, "Rösten och blicken som kärleksobjekt" ("Gaze and Voice as Love Objects"), in Slavoj Žižek & Renata Salecl, *En liten bok om kärlek* (*Gaze and Voice as Love Objects*), trans. Maria Fitger and John Swedenmark (Stockholm/Stehag: Brutus Östlings Bokförlag Symposion in collaboration with Nordisk Sommeruniversitet (NSU), 1997), p. 47, 56; Žižek, *Njutandets förvandlingar. Sex essäer om kvinnan, kulturen och makten* (*The Metastases of Enjoyment. Six essays on woman and causality*), p. 168.

93 Bergman, *Arbetsboken 1955–1974* (*The Workbook 1955–1974*), p. 131.

94 Cioran, *Bitterhetens syllogismer* (*Syllogisms of Bitterness*), trans. John Milos (Stockholm: Symposion, 1989), p. 172.

Chapter 6

Three Sisters

Sibling Knots in Bergman's *Cries and Whispers*

Andrea Sabbadini

A father proudly shows a newly born baby brother to his little two-year-old girl, expecting her to rejoice. Instead, she asks: *"When will he die again?"* Reporting this story, Anna Freud comments that children's jealousy should be taken seriously and attributes its origin to the relationship of the child to the mother:

> This wish for his brothers and sisters to be dead is thoroughly natural on the part of the child ... An emotional conflict arises within him only when he realizes that his mother ... demands that he give up these evil wishes, and even love [his siblings]. Here is the starting point of all the difficulties in the emotional relations among children within a family.
>
> (1930, pp. 84–85)

With the exception of cursory references to "sibling rivalry," psychoanalytic writings about brothers and sisters have been scanty, the main emphasis having been on the child's Oedipal relationship with parental figures. However, a number of recent publications (Bank and Kahn, 1997; Coles, 2003, 2006; Mitchell, 2000, 2003; Volkan and Ast, 1997) have given relationships among siblings a new prominence in our understanding of development. For instance, stressing the *lateral* relationships of siblings (and, later, of peers and affines) rather than the more conventional *vertical*, generational ones between children and parents, Mitchell challenges the psychogenesis of the Oedipal complex. "In Freud's account," she states,

> love and hate derive from the parental relationship and are subsequently transferred to siblings. I read these events the other way around: faced with a sibling, the child regresses to its wish for infantile unity with the mother; it is then that it finds the father in the way ... Feelings for siblings and peers cast their shadow over relations with parents.
>
> (2000, p. 23)

While not necessarily sharing these rather extreme views, other authors also suggest that "sibling relationships form a vital and lively part of the internal world

DOI: 10.4324/9781003200246-7

and provide a blueprint in which an individual thinks about, creates and sustains relationships" (Silverstone, 2006, p. 244).

With these psychoanalytic considerations in mind, let us now look at the "treatment" of the relationship among sisters by Ingmar Bergman, a filmmaker especially sensitive to the minutest details of his characters' complex psychologies; here, in the devastatingly painful soul-searching description of their conflicting longings, frustrations, hopes, and guilt, we discover the power of great cinema.[1]

Three sisters, like on Anton Chekhov's stage and Woody Allen's set, dominate the screen of *Viskningar och rop* (*Cries and Whispers*, 1972), one of Bergman's masterpieces. This film is a powerful exploration of one of those deep-rooted family knots where love is inextricably (con)fused with cruelty, and neediness with anguish. The Swedish director's women – Agnes, Karin, and Maria, and the wonderful actors playing them: Harriet Andersson, Ingrid Thulin, and Liv Ullmann, respectively – are entrapped inside an even bleaker universe of suffering, emotional no less than physical, than those of either the Russian playwright or the New York comedian.

The sisters' agonizing pains – their cries and their whispers,[2] no less than their secrets and their lies – are inside them. Agnes's body is devastated by the cancer from which she is dying. Maria's mind is troubled by her neurotic compulsion to manipulate and exploit those nearest to her for her own selfish gratification. Karin's disordered personality is affected by such a paralyzing coldness of heart that it deprives her of any capacity for humane gestures or words of comfort, a "kind of rigid inflexibility and aversion to intimacy that can only come from being irreparably emotionally wounded" (Berardinelli, 2002). Their dramas unfold within their family home, the luxurious version of a Vermeer interior, with its closely observed everyday-life little objects, such as the *memento mori* of a gilded clock on which the camera enjoys resting its eye. As the narrative unfolds this mansion, no longer large enough to contain the sisters' suffering, fills itself with the sort of memories that make it almost claustrophobically suffocating. What allows us, the film spectators, to survive the experience of watching these women's agony being dissected in front of our eyes is the messianic function of the mother-earthly housekeeper Anna (Kari Sylwan). This fourth woman, by reminding us of humankind's potential for compassion, comes to rescue us with her faith when our despair has almost reached the edge of the precipice.

In contrast to Anna, the sisters are sick, though each in different compartments of their selves. If their personalities are too complex to fit into easy pathological categories, our analytical understanding of psychological problems still entitles us to suspect that they, while remaining responsible for their present circumstances, are also likely to have been the victims during childhood of considerable emotional, if not also physical, abuse. Bergman only hints at a few details about their upbringing; but the fact, for instance, that nothing at all is revealed about their father suggests that he was as absent from the girls' early life as he is from the film, and this fact alone must be of great importance. Bruce Sklarew (1987) convincingly argues that, in this film, "Bergman reveals how difficult it is for each sister to establish intimacy, a cohesive self, and mature feminine identity *because of preoedipal struggles* to survive an inconsistent, narcissistic mother" (p. 169, *my emphasis*). I would add that unresolved oedipal issues must also have played a significant role, as indicated by their problems in establishing and sustaining satisfactory relationships with their husbands and with each other, free from severely neurotic, perverse, reparatory, or conflictual connotations.

We watch them interact with one another at the dramatic juncture in their lives – that of Agnes's last days on earth – on which Bergman focuses his slowly moving camera, transformed into a magnifying lens for the observation of the human soul. This cinematic scrutiny is not, as it may at first appear, a morbidly voyeuristic or even sadistic operation, but the documentaristic (if also dream-like and lyrical) equivalent of our own psychoanalytic work of uncovering the uncomfortable truths buried inside our patients' unconscious – not to cause them unnecessary suffering, embarrassment, or guilt, but to help them come to terms with themselves. Some filmmakers, Bergman *in primis*, may be keen to distance themselves from psychoanalysis; yet, the sincerity and depth of their explorations of unreachable corners of the human minds have much in common with our own analytic endeavors.

Occasionally, even Karin and Maria can show genuine affection, for instance when they wash Agnes, change her nightshirt, comb her hair, read to her from a novel. But to truly emerge from their emotionally deprived selves, sisters Karin and Maria would have to develop a capacity to accept themselves and others, and to experience empathy for their predicaments, as Anna does. It is indeed in their final insensitivity to the maid who for twelve years had cared for Agnes, better than they could have ever done themselves, that Karin and Maria, together with their husbands, show the worst side of their character, dismissing her with hardly a word of thanks. An important ingredient in what makes us all human, the capacity to feel gratitude, is missing in them, and one wonders if anybody – a friend, a therapist, or a pastor (such as Bergman's own father, a Lutheran minister) – could ever break through their indifference and reach their hearts. For them, life, as Karin exclaims several times, "*is nothing but a tissue of lies.*" Nor is there much hope that the death of their sister Agnes would represent one of those epiphanic events that could transform their existences. Their bitterness and cynicism, as they become evident in the second half of the film, are far too deeply embedded in their souls to allow them to experience true grief for their loss. The only tangible manifestation that Maria and Karin are undergoing at all a process of mourning can perhaps be found in their attempt, aborted but nevertheless significant, to relate differently to one another and to overcome what must be their long-standing and extreme form of sibling rivalry.

Because of the narrative center-stage position of Agnes's overwhelming distress and her eventual passing away, two other losses in the film risk going almost unnoticed; yet their psychological function is important to our understanding of some of the existential, personal, and interpersonal dynamics of all the main *dramatis personae*. The first one is the death of a child, Anna's daughter. We learn about it early in the film when we are shown the housekeeper praying the Lord to have angels guard her little girl in heaven, as the camera focuses on a photograph of the two of them together. Later we meet this child herself, in a flashback sequence, when we are introduced to the doctor who is visiting the sisters' home to care for the sick young girl. We could suggest that such a traumatic loss as that of a child may have contributed to Anna's sensitivity to Agnes's suffering, as if by helping and comforting her charge she could also, through the unconscious mechanism of displacement, still be of help and comfort to her own deceased girl. The other crucial loss in *Cries and Whispers* is that of the sisters' mother, described as a beautiful, narcissistic woman, dead for twenty years but still in Agnes's thoughts "*almost every day*" even if "*she could be cold and playfully cruel.*" We meet her in a flashback scene when Agnes, as a child, usually feeling left out and jealous of her mother's favorite, Maria (a point emphasized by the fact that both are played by the same actress, Liv Ullmann), remembers a rare occasion when she was, for once, accepted rather than scolded. "*I almost burst into tears,*" Agnes recalls, "*I put my hand to her cheek. We were very close at that moment.*" I may add that, in that memory, it is Agnes who ends up comforting her mother once she notices her sorrowful look. Here, their functions are reversed, with Agnes mothering her own mother: a situation we frequently come across in our work with analysands who were neglected as children.

I will now offer a few words about the intense sensual connotations of *Cries and Whispers*, not surprisingly perhaps in an *auteur* so influenced by Ibsen's and Strindberg's dramas, and most specifically by their austerely nordic version of the Romantic association of death with sexuality. The screen, far from being silver, is dotted here with moving black or white images in a crimson interior environment. Red, the color of passion and sin and blood, but also a color which, as Bergman stated, "represents for me the interior of the soul," seems to flood everything, sparing only a few brief, more peaceful scenes in the garden.

On this crimson background, erotically charged scenes abound, such as Maria's artful seduction of the doctor, weak as all the other men in the film: the first time (in flashback) when he comes to treat Anna's dying child, and again a few years later when his patient is Agnes, dying in the bedroom next door. Infused with sensuality is also the sequence when Anna, responding to Agnes's panicked request for physical closeness to assuage her suffering, offers her the only form of human contact which could still give the dying woman some relief. We watch Anna unbutton her nightdress, caress and kiss Agnes, talk reassuringly to her, and gently guide Agnes's face, no longer twisted now with pain and fear, on her generous naked breasts. As she holds her there for a long quiet moment, Anna almost looks like a *mater dolorosa* in a Renaissance statue of the *Pietá*. In contrast, following the long ceremony of Karin's undressing for the night and getting into bedclothes with Anna's help, we are presented with the shockingly erotic violence of Karin's deliberate self-harming gesture of inserting a shard of wine-glass between her legs. Her initial masochistically ecstatic reaction to pain is complemented by her grotesquely spiteful grin of sadistic satisfaction as she smears blood from her genitals over her mouth in front of her bewildered husband.[3]

Perhaps more intensely sensual than all, if less manifestly so, are those instances in the days following Agnes's death, inhibited but not for that reason less intimate, when Maria tries to find access to her sister Karin's heart through physical contact with her body. In those touching (in both meanings of the word) moments when they attempt to discover a sense of closeness between them – responding to a longing which must exist somewhere in the depth of their beings, yet remains seemingly inaccessible – we watch them struggle with their feelings, from hatred to tenderness, from greed to suicidal rage, and hurt themselves in the process no less than they torture each other. Here are some extracts from those excruciating scenes, with Ullmann and Thulin shot in merciless close-ups, mostly on a red background.

Maria: "*Karin, why won't you be my friend? ... We could embrace each other ... Karin, couldn't we use these days in getting to know one another? Karin! I can't stand distance and silence ...*" Karin gets up and walks away from her. Maria follows her towards the door, tries to reach her, pleads with her: "*Have I said something to hurt you?*" As Karin doesn't answer her and goes next door to read from Agnes's diary, Maria approaches her again and tries to caress her sister's face. Karin turns away and screams at her (with as much anguish as anger in her voice): "*Don't touch me! Don't come near me. I hate any sort of contact!*" Then she seems to allow Maria to get closer, to hug, stroke, and nearly kiss her ... though at the same time Karin also begs her not to be kind to her. Then, suddenly, she burst into tears and turns her face to the wall; as she turns around again towards Maria, overwhelmed by her own inner conflicts, she cries (or are they whispers?): "*I can't! I can't! It's constant misery and torment, it's like in hell. I can't breathe anymore because of the guilt ... Leave me alone! Don't touch me!*"

Later, Karin, having hurt her sister again with hateful, unforgiving words in a scene around the dinner table, apologizes: "*Maria, forgive me. Perhaps you mean well. Perhaps you just want to get to know me ...*" and we see them for the first time touch and embrace and caress each other with what appears to be true reciprocal warmth. They even smile at each other for a moment, and talk – their words now inaudible to us as they are covered by the somber notes of Bach's Saraband for cello.

Later yet, as they part after Agnes's funeral and abandon their house, Karin, the older sister who was throughout the film the harsher of the two, tells Maria: "*You touched me. Remember?*" hoping perhaps for a final reconciliation. But Maria retorts, cold as ice: "*I can't remember every silly thing, or be made to answer for them.*"

Notes

1 Of the countless films centered around sibling relationships, and also relevant to a psychoanalytic discourse, I shall limit myself to mention Hitchcock's *The Shadow of a Doubt* (1943), Siodmak's *Dark Mirror* (1946), Visconti's *Rocco and His Brothers*

(1960), Truffaut's *Anne and Muriel* (1971), Allen's *Hannah and Her Sisters* (1986), and Levinson's *Rain Man* (1988).

2 "The 'cries' for help express the yearning for closeness and attachment, for intimacy. The 'whispers' are the torment of the frustrated longings, the hovering unattainable fulfillment" (Sklarew, 1987, p. 175).

3 A similar scene can be found in Michael Haneke's *La pianiste [The Piano Teacher]* (2001), where sexually repressed musician Erika (Isabelle Huppert) inserts a razor blade inside her vagina.

Bibliography

Bank, S. P., and Kahn, M. D. (1997). *The Sibling Bond*. New York: Basic Books.

Berardinelli, J. (2002). "Review: Cries and Whispers." http://movie-reviews.colossus.net.

Bergman, I. (Dir.) (1972). *Viskningar och rop [Cries and Whispers]*. Sweden.

Coles, P. (2003). *The Importance of Sibling Relationships in Psychoanalysis*. London and New York: Karnac.

Coles, P. (Ed.) (2006). *Sibling Relationships*. London and New York: Karnac.

Freud, A. (1930). "Four Lectures on Psycho-Analysis for Teachers and Parents." In *Introduction to Psychoanalysis, 1922–1935*. London: Hogarth Press, pp. 71–134.

Mitchell, J. (2000). *Mad Men and Medusas. Reclaiming Hysteria and the Effects of Sibling Relations on the Human Condition*. Harmondsworth: Penguin Books.

Mitchell, J. (2003). *Siblings: Sex and Violence*. Oxford: Polity.

Silverstone, J. (2006). "Siblings." In *Sibling Relationships*, edited by Prophecy Coles. London and New York: Karnac, pp.225–246.

Sklarew, B. H. (1987). "Ingmar Bergman's *Cries and Whispers*: The Consequences of Preoedipal Developmental Disturbances." In *Images in Our Souls: Cavell, Psychoanalysis, and Cinema*, edited by Joseph H. Smith and William Kerrigan. Baltimore: Johns Hopkins University, pp. 169–182.

Volkan, V. A., and Ast, G. (1997). *Siblings in the Unconscious and Psychopathology*. New York: International Universities Press.

Chapter 7

The Seventh Seal

Bergman and the Frenchmen

S. Alfonso Williams

The work of Ingmar Bergman will be the subject of discussion over the next few pages. Specifically, his film *The Seventh Seal* (1957) will be explored. Bergman composed a great number of films, many of which are worthy of equal study due to the careful attention he puts into the lives of the characters. *The Seventh Seal* is one film that represents a special cross-section of qualities ripe for philosophical and psychoanalytic analysis. Bergman possessed these insights, even if completely unexposed to first-hand experience of the domains and ideas into which we will be delving.

Our discussion will loosely revolve around the ideas of three principal thinkers: Jean Baudrillard, Gilles Deleuze, and Jacques Lacan. The "French Triad" we have here is a significant one, all dealing with poststructuralist discourse in some way or another. Each will deal with a specific theme, respectively: Chance, Time, and Death.

Through Baudrillard, the theme of Time will be dealt with tangentially through his concept of Seduction. The idea revolves around the play of games and signs as a façade and dance. We will probe this concept to see what happens when two subjects engage by Chance in such a dance and drive each other to a point where one cannot be without the other.

Deleuze perhaps offers the most tricky and idiosyncratic concept of the three. His notion of Time is a-synonymous with conventional notions of time and is structured upon his idea of Difference that pervades every aspect of his thought. His dissertation, *Difference and Repetition* (1994), is a whole 350-page treatment on the subject of time and differential relations. Naturally, we will not recount that here. We will muse on the idea of what happens when one's notion of Time requires a forfeiting of exactly what one desires.

Lacan, ironically, of the three, takes the more straightforward approach. Death is pursued through the perspectives of the hysterical and obsessive subjects, which approach the object of desire differently. Our case presents both entities within the same subject, our knight, and offers a lucrative set of questions regarding the context.

The Seventh Seal offers great opportunities to pique our interests, if only for a brief moment. Chance, or Contingency, Time, and Death, are all major structural themes in both philosophy and psychoanalysis and lenses through which

DOI: 10.4324/9781003200246-8

significant catalytic ideas pass. Our three thinkers deal with the notions in their own syncretic ways. Put into dialectical and interpretive dialogue with film, their usefulness brings out further indebted links to visionary filmmakers like Ingmar Bergman, who, given optimal conditions, are able to produce the kinds of films they desire with the proper integrity and care good films deserve. It's not even that Bergman intended his films to be analyzed in this way, as he assuredly did not. He was not that kind of fellow. Nevertheless, films of such merit offer up the occasion to pop open the hood and see what we can see, given our skill set.

Bergman: Chance

It is difficult to imagine a more ironic place to negotiate the circumstances surrounding one's demise. The notorious "deal with the devil" invites more speculation than first appearances reveal. The knight had already arrived from a culture of death that probably felt like a planned obsolescence, religiously speaking. His own moment could only have been an advanced antecedent to his own future, the limit that would bar him from knowing exactly the when, where, and how. To be seduced by Death is a miraculous feeling.

Death is pure difference, and does not make chance encounters. Not even for the knight whose random, rhizomatic encounters seem accidental. But given the chance – at the level of the subject – if contingency is held at bay by fate, and Death and the knight are forced into a situation neither may exit, what implications would arise from this complex? Sisyphus is the model example, as even though his fate is gruesome, for a brief moment, he achieves the unachievable: he stops the unstoppable force. Our knight is not so lucky. Fortunately for us, we get to learn from his example.

Knight: Pardon me, I was detained for a few moments. Because I revealed my tactics to you, I'm in retreat. It's your move.

Death: Why do you look so satisfied?

Knight: That's my secret.

Death: Of course. Now I take your knight.

Knight: You did the right thing.

Death: Have you tricked me?

Who tricked who? If accidents are contingent, was this a truly contingent outcome on the knight's behalf? Surely the knight is putting Death on, because, rationally speaking, there is no practical way for the knight to "put on," or out-trick, Death, if we are taking this story as an exploration of the *real* and not simply an allegory. Or is Death putting the knight on? This seems the more logical outcome, given the scope of Death's epistemology. The audience watching the events play out knows both what the knight does not (or knows unconsciously) and what Death does know.

Marshall McLuhan said that a funny man is a man with a grievance. The grievance our knight had must have been fairly strong for him to conjure up such a clever, or not so clever, scheme. Though the same must be said if Death, knowing what the knight was up to, decided to play along anyway. It is at this point where we reach a sort of strange symbiosis of character, a deliberate willingness by both parties to engage in a tango of mutual deception (or delusion).

Here we have a strange relationship that should be taken rather seriously. The knight and Death have entered into a dialogue that one cannot put forth without the other. Without Death, there is no knight, and no knight without Death. The knight's questions possess no urgency or deadline without a perilous end waiting to take all knowledge he has accumulated. Death, with nothing and no one to consume to formulate the time it does not have, is left unemployed as an agent of nothingness, trapped in its own void. We can in a way call this a dance of contingent necessity. Each party is forced into a paradigm exceeding them, reducing the agency of each to a mutual state of inertness that makes it difficult to say who exactly is in control of the situation. That is to say, we have a *deadlock*. With no way to go back, they can only move forward, exacerbate the circumstances, and drive the other to the point of transgression. Though we used the word agency to describe their actions, role is perhaps a better fit, given that the ontological script is predetermined. It is maddening in a way to think that the answers to one's questions are achievable only by transgressing an impasse of no return. All the more for Death, as the only way for Death to be itself, to achieve movement, is through constant transgression. Death almost becomes a parody of itself, trying to live up to its own image ....

Bergman: Time

The knight stands in unsolicited but immanent anxiety because he desires the one thing he cannot have: knowledge. It is the belief in knowledge that drives him halfway across the world in the untold story that is cut off from the film narrative. We do not need this particular backstory. It is enough to be compressed within the history that opens the doors of perception into the unknown future, formulated by the extant present, choosing, deciding where to go and what to do. But it is neither the past nor the future which ultimately concerns him. He is stuck, or rather unconsciously desires to remain stuck, in the present, toward a goal which is impossible to attain: true knowledge of God.

Yet, the knight must know that what he desires is impossible to achieve. Even more startling is that Death himself is the recipient of these dis-confirmations of belief. Still even more curiously are the responses of Death throughout the interaction:

> "And yet you don't want to die" ... "You want guarantees?" ... "But He remains silent" ... "Perhaps no one is there" ... "Most people never reflect about either death or the futility of life" ... "How will you outwit Death in your game?"

> (Bragg, pp.12–13)

Death's responses provoke one to wonder if he is really putting on the knight, as it is nearly impossible to invoke the name of God apart from Death itself, for Death opens the door to be received by God. So how could Death not know of the intimacies of God's operations being an integral co-conspirator?

This is not Death's first time around the block, however. It must be taken into consideration that the questions the knight offers are neither novel nor pertinent to Death at all, having been in the business of being the most prestigious gatekeeper since the beginning of time.

Then what is the knight to Death in the present time? The knight searches for answers to which Death is indifferent. Whereas the knight searches for a sense of novelty to break the conditions of redundancy of habit, Death is condemned to redundancy. It shouldn't be assumed that Death is bored, however, as Death achieves novelty through creativity in choosing the points at which people enter his passageway. Death performs this with the knight by indulging him in a game of chess. The bargain seems absurd at first, for Death outlasts a session of any length. Even if the knight were to cause delays until the end of his life, Death still awaits. The knight wishes to operate on borrowed time while Death, numb to time, uses novelty to re-create time within itself.

Our poor knight is in a much more difficult position, unfortunately, to achieve the novelty he seeks. There is a synthesis of past events at work in his present, generating the pressing questions he conveys. However, this present reaches an impasse through the figure of Death, who orients and restricts the contingencies of the knight's perspective toward one dimension – Death. And yet as Death contains the undivulged answer sought, blocking the knight's access to novelty, the knight, in a twisted way, becomes the answer he seeks by being absorbed into Death's formation of novelty that is the future. What the future is as a terminal impasse for the knight, the knight turns around and uses, as Death itself is the only access point to this knowledge as future novelty. In turn, Death uses the knight as the creative expression of time itself in the present. Death only feels time by being absorbed up into the syntheses of time experienced by the knight, as a medium from which the knight is the content. An embedded synthesis within the spectrum of time is the expression of the bargain between the knight and Death. Each uses the other to further their syntheses of time and novelty formation. Ironically, the knight will achieve his answer without experience, while Death, indifferent to knowledge, chases experience for experience's sake.

Bergman: Death

Our hero seems to have hit a snag. One wouldn't necessarily notice it at first, but he does state it at various times. The second instance of meeting Death in the church provides an interesting moment in getting to know the condition of the knight's mind. He and his squire have come back from overseas and are physically, and no less spiritually, exhausted. War has the tendency to do this.

They have not escaped Death, however. Despite their best efforts to flee the main site of the trauma, Death has followed them home in various forms: drunkenness, theft, rape, murder, murals, and Death-as-figure itself. The knight meets Death in the place considered to be ideal for relaxation – the beach. The knight is even praying before the encounter. But what happens when they meet? Death is propositioned with a game of chess.

Under most circumstances, propositioning Death with an extended game of chess would be considered absurd. Though to accept the absurdities that come with life, it is no less absurd than taking the quests of Odysseus in *The Odyssey* seriously. The only difference between the knight and Odysseus is that the knight's encounter with Death is intended to be *real*.

The specific usage of chess as opposed to any other game is less important than what the nature of the game signifies between two players. Chess is a game of time that carries the potential to go on forever. To *delay* this inevitability, the timer was introduced to track both the movements of the players and the overall progression of the game. The purpose of the timer is to speed up the inevitability of the game – in other words, to counter the desire of the obsessive. Stuart Schneidermann makes an interesting remark about the obsessive:

> Note that if it should happen that the desire of death is not for the obsessional's life, then he certainly has a problem. Better, the fact that death's desire is not for life is what creates the problem. Like any other desire, death's desire is to be recognized and taken into account.
>
> (1984, p. 146)

Taken literally, the chess game as point of delay on the knight's behalf serves a double purpose: it allows the knight to seek the answers to his unanswered questions, and allows Death the time to be properly recognized by that which allows it to feel time pass. Lacan says the following about the difference between desire in the hysteric and obsessive:

> Whereas the relation to desire in hysteria has an instantaneous structure, the obsessive always puts off until tomorrow committing his true desire.
>
> (2021, p. 428)

The knight shows hysterical and obsessive tendencies: hysterical in the source of his questioning, and obsessive in the execution of answering those questions. Despite sharing characteristics, the chess game stands as the point of signification of the delay of Death, in a literal sense. Death delays himself by directly engaging in the game to the benefit of the knight.

We are left to question, however, whether the knight is aware of his appeal to delay death on an unconscious level. Do not mind the contradictory statement, that of being aware of the unconscious. That was a provocation to suggest that perhaps the knight overestimated his ability to truly believe he would find the answers to his questions. He surely knows he is "living on borrowed time." This borrowed time is effectively the barrier set between the endpoint of Death as the delay that puts off the object of desire: knowledge.

Living on borrowed time in pursuit of a vain search is not the recommended way to go about a life encounter with Death, with an "IOU" strapped across one's back. Others have taken worse routes. But the debt to Death is not one that is ever repaid in the act of acknowledgment. The moment it occurs, the game is over, and one never gets to experience *the discovery made too late*. This is the awkwardness that the obsessive wants to avoid. Building the anticipation over a long arc of suspension is of prime delight. To push forward, however, into the moment of contact – only for that contact to be denied in the final instant – is an act of unforgivable devastating cruelty. Finality. Death may not be the end, but in the pursuit of the end, Death is THE end of the end.

We remind ourselves that it was not our intent this go 'round to delve into the depths of critical analysis. This was only the light entertainment before the main event which takes place sometime in the distant future, a "purview to preview." Yet, here we find ourselves, like the obsessive, delaying that which we desire, until future notice. The structural spell of Death invites us into its master plan. It cannot complete those plans without us, for without, there is no plan.

We are delaying knowledge. Why? What is it that this knowledge will give us? All the more, what do we gain in its abeyance? Is there something in the role, in the play of appearances that allows us to achieve a sense of *jouissance*, a bout of negative excess pleasure?

Even if we achieve this pleasure, what novel aspect is produced from it? Our current activities are already setting the stage for the future in a non-linear fashion. It is not that we are waiting to experience this *jouissance*, but that its beginnings were already in preparation through the potentialities of the present and the habits set forth to bring that possibility into fruition.

As obsessives, however, our true aim is not achievement, because that is Death itself. The cessation of desiring, the acquisition of the Truth we lust for, is the ultimate price we cannot afford to pay. Crossing that threshold means the end, and everything was for nothing.

The warning makes itself clear in presenting itself to us. Knowledge is not what we want. It is not our object of desire. Death is. We play with appearances and create novel opportunities only to end up right back where we started – in pursuit. We chase the signifier for the repetitive delay. To hope that this time around, this is not the end. Like the knight, even if we did achieve our end, it would not satisfy us. Another query would eventually replace the satisfied ones.

Do not forget, *jouissance*, our temptation to pursue Knowledge to the end, is what gives Knowledge its power. Without desire stretched over contingent possibilities of time, it means nothing. The knowledge would have meant nothing to the knight were he not in his present state of hysterical urgency. Urgency as compressed time makes all the difference in the world between the hysteric and the obsessive. Combined into one, it is a strange play of roles, appearances, and games with the self. The subject is divided into multiple positions depending on which state of events is dominant.

Are we aware of the switching of these roles as events? For that answer, we must engage the unconscious to find out – obviously, a contradiction in terms.

Bibliography

Baudrillard, J. (1991). *Seduction*. London and New York: Palgrave Macmillan.

Bergman, I. (Dir.) (1957). *The Seventh Seal*. Performances by Max von Sydow, Gunnar Bjornstrand, Bengt Ekerot, Nils Poppe, and Bibi Andersson, AB Svensk Filmindustri.

Bragg, M. (1993). *The Seventh Seal = Det sjunde inseglet*. London: BFI Publishing.

Deleuze, G. (1994). *Difference & Repetition*. Translated by Paul Patton. New York: Columbia University Press.

Homer. (2018). *The Odyssey*. Translated by Peter Green. Oakland: The University of California Press.

Lacan, J. (2021). *Desire and Its Interpretation: The Seminar of Jacques Lacan, Book VI*. Edited by Jacques-Alain Miller and Translated by Bruce Fink. Cambridge: Polity Books.

Schneidermann, S. (1984). *Jacques Lacan: The Death of an Intellectual Hero*. Cambridge: Harvard University Press.

Chapter 8

Serpentine Conceptual Autophagia

Lesbian Contrapuntal Dialectics in *Persona* and *The Silence*

Alireza Taheri

The theme of self-reflexiveness is central to *Persona* (1966) and *The Silence* (1963). We note countless allusions to the films where images of reels and cameras point to the cinematic process. Moreover, *Persona* is a film about a theater actress and, one must remember, Bergman was then very involved with theater. In fact, his decision to create *Persona* was bound to a needed break from theater, something echoed in Elisabet's refusal to act and her lapse into silence. Like Bergman, she returned to theater after a life-saving hiatus. The train, with which *The Silence* begins and ends, is an allegory of the film akin to a reel that reveals *pictures in motion*. Also, insofar as both films relate stories of unrequited lesbian love one can see, basing oneself on the controversial claim linking *homo*sexuality to narcissism (the prefix "homo" points to *sameness*), that the theme of *self*-reflexiveness is reintroduced through that subterfuge. Like the homosexual object–choice which hinges on a narcissistic self-reference, *Persona* and *The Silence* refer to themselves and, more crucially, to each other. Indeed, my decision to consider the two films together is tied to the theme of lesbian love. The two films constitute a pair much like Anna and Ester in *The Silence* and Alma and Elisabet in *Persona*. They are lesbian lovers in the grips of a powerful intertwinement. The title of the earlier film (*The Silence*) constitutes an essential feature of the second film, Elisabet's refusal to speak. Historically, too, the films are inextricably connected. As aforesaid, Bergman completed *The Silence*, then moved on to theater projects before returning to cinema with *Persona*. Moreover, the two films share a preoccupation with the central themes of the love–hate relation between two women and that of the feminine rejection of maternity.

According to Sontag (2016), the "element of self-reflexiveness … states on a formal level the theme of doubling or duplication – that is present on a psychological level in the transactions between Alma and Elizabeth." Translated into Lacanian diction, the theme of doublings constitutes an "imaginarization" of self-reflexiveness. In Hegelian parlance, the doublings constitute an expression of *inner contradiction* in the derivative mode of *external opposition*. In "The Snakeskin,"[1] Bergman states that "literature, painting, music, film, and theatre give birth to and feed upon themselves" (1990). For Bergman, an *autophagic* tendency is intrinsic to art; the two films devour themselves. In *Persona*, fire burns

DOI: 10.4324/9781003200246-9

the film reel while in *The Silence* the train evokes the idea of a snake, namely the motif that Bergman associates with *Persona*. Train and snake evoke the idea of a creature biting its own tail. The theme of autophagia thus returns as a further imaginarization of the theme of self-reflexiveness. Here, imaginarization functions according to the logic by which a symbolic operation (the gaze turned upon the self – inner contradiction) is expressed in the modality of carnal incorporation, namely autophagia. The two forms of imaginarization here outlined (1. the projective process by which inner contradiction is viewed as external opposition and 2. the unconscious coloring of the psychic mechanism with the fantasy of incorporation) combine such that the originary mechanism of self-reflection comes to the fore in the derivative mode of *being eaten* (the second imaginarization) *by an Other* (the first imaginarization). The theme of self-reflexiveness is thus disparaged, by virtue of these two processes, to the theme of vampiricism, a common horror film motif. In fact, many commentators have held the mistaken view, aptly critiqued by Sontag (2016), that *Persona* is about Elisabet's vampiric consumption of Alma. Such simplistic reduction of the predator–victim model – a hallmark of *beautiful soul*[2] mentality – diminishes the richness of the film and depreciates its veritably philosophic import.

The autophagia of Bergman's "The Snakeskin" should be read as a dialectical–philosophical autophagia where the concept devours itself until it veers uncontrollably to its opposite. For Freud, the psychoanalytic symptom is a compromise formation between the law and a wish that inexorably deviates towards the fulfillment of the latter to the detriment of the former. The very effort to resist one's wish (*jouissance*) becomes the very locus of the satisfaction of that self-same wish. Resistance is co-opted by the wish for the sake of its gratification. Nietzsche (1998), with the signature prescience of the genius of his nostrils, sniffed out a similar mechanism in the manner that the ascetic ideal becomes co-opted as a means to lascivious *jouissance*. Likewise, the two films put on stage for us the space of vicious dialectical reversals where in every opposition the so-called "lower" term triumphs over the "higher" element whose truth it represents. What I call the "lower" term represents the "truth" of the "higher" term. For instance, in the opposition of truth and lies, everything slowly veers towards the dominance of lies, which, despite being the "lower" or "corrupt" element of the opposition provides the truth of the "higher" term. Cast aphoristically, the lie provides the truth of truth or, as Lacan renders it, "there is no truth that, in passing through awareness, does not lie" (Lacan, 1977). I consider the following oppositions in this paper: adult and child, masculine and feminine, power and impotence, semblance and the real, truth and lie, beauty and ugliness, innocence and guilt, identity and fragmentation, Eden and the fall, light and darkness, reality and fiction, good and evil, love and hate, faith and atheism, sense and non-sense.[3]

In *Le Sacrifice*, Rosolato isolates three principal differences that organize mental and social life, namely sexual, generational, and power difference. Firstly, we have the opposition of man and woman. Secondly, we have parents distinguished from children and finally, we have, to put it in Kojève's words, "the principle of the essential difference between those who exert it [authority] and those who are subject to it" (2014). I consider the way these boundaries are subverted in the two films thereby rendering a social space hinging on madness. In *The Silence* the incestuous tension between the mother and son is emphatically highlighted when the boy scrubs his mother's back and then enjoys having cream spread all over his body. Earlier he is fixated on her feet and remarks that it is as if they walk alone separated from her body. We not only get a glimpse of the incestuous wish but also a lucid expression of the partial nature of human sexuality, namely its perverse fixation on aspects of the body not centralized by the genital. The film also ends with Anna seized by rapture in the train as she gazes incestuously at her son. Incest is that which disturbs generational difference most traumatically. The father's role is that of separating mother and child such that the mother is *deprived* of the child and the child is *castrated* from his/her position of centrality in the mother's desire (Lacan, 1994). Interestingly, the two films mark a radical absence of paternal figures. The male progenitors are alluded to very vaguely in the films (e.g. Johan speaks briefly to Ester about his father). In *Persona*, we hear the tale of Alma's orgy/foursome on the beach and her eventual pregnancy and abortion. She evidently lied to her partner, leaving him to believe that he was the father of the aborted child. Paternal figures waver from absent men buried in toil to the duped fools of feminine guile.

A central theme of both films, *Persona* in particular, is the rejection of maternity. In her monologue to Elisabet, Alma accuses her of rejecting maternal duties. Earlier in the film, Alma makes a similar reproach to herself as she tells Elisabet of her abortion. What began as melancholic self-reproach transforms into a moralistic attack on her alter ego. The rejection of maternity at once unites the women who are both guilty in this respect and functions as a desperate means to maintain a modicum of separation as Alma desperately insists on her difference from Elisabet. However, the moment of Alma's firmest insistence on difference (she screams, "I am not like you") coincides with the facial fusion of the two as if to suggest that Alma's accusations are tantamount to a displacement of her own guilty conscience. Alma's monologue thus replicates the drama of the *beautiful soul* projecting her own disorder on the world and attempting to cure this very same world – perhaps an unconscious motivation for her decision to pursue a clinician's vocation. The moment of the fusion of the faces and Alma's desperate exclamation of innocence – a veritable avowal in the disparaged form of negation – is the moment of dialectical reversal where truth emerges in the modality of misrecognition. Interestingly, *Persona* begins with Elisabet playing the role of Electra, namely the woman after whom Jung re-named the female Oedipal complex. Elisabet is thus depicted as someone held in the grips of an infantile wish and whose identity is thereby bound up entirely in her relation to her parents. Her refusal to speak renders her literally *infant* (one who cannot speak) and marks her regression and concomitant unwillingness to assume adulthood. It is therefore no surprise that *the symbolic permutation of roles*[4] required to achieve maternity is drastically rejected. At the heart of Elisabet's hate of her son is the fear of the loss of her own infantile position. Following Lacan's idea that "behind every mother there is a Medea," we may quip that behind every parent is a child. Indeed, Elisabet's husband expresses his wish to be a child both in his letter and when he visits her by the sea. Also, according to Alma's testimony, Elisabet had her child in order to abide to a social norm; her decision to bear a child was rooted in the infantile attitude of succumbing to peer pressure. The confusion around generational difference is highlighted in *The Silence* through the motif of the dwarves who occupy an uncanny liminal position between adult and child. Likewise, the old man in *The Silence*, depicted as Johan's principal playmate and counterpart, is another failed adult. Aunt Ester, too, remains stuck in infantile passion to her father. Her maturity is reduced to the sole quality of literacy and intellectual prowess. Johan not only reads to her, thereby inverting the expected adult–child roles but also entertains her with his marionettes. The subversions of adult–infant and parent–child roles render for us the unexpected truth that the child is the truth of the adult. To quip Brecht as Žižek often does, we may ask: what is the infant's failure to reach adulthood in comparison to the infantilism of adulthood itself?[5] This paradoxical inversion is something well known to Lacan who once quipped that "there are no other children in the family but the parents" (Lacan, 2006, p. 482). Bergman renders for us the truth regarding the *semblance* of adulthood; it is a fake behind which rests the *infantile real*. Indeed, an adult is a fiction that only a child is naïve enough to believe in.

Persona and *The Silence* also subvert our usual conceptions of sexual difference, thereby creating spaces of androgyny and ambiguity. *Persona* starts with a scene with a very old man and woman as well as a young boy, scarcely pubescent, lying on hospital beds thereby representing the two ends of the spectrum of life. These are the ages where secondary sexual traits hold little sway. In *The Silence*, the dwarves dress the little boy as a girl. He is taken as their object, thereby repeating his mother's will to fashion him as the object of her desire. The head dwarf puts an end to the masquerade in a rare moment of the emergence of the paternal function. Immediately after, the child urinates in the hall as if to demonstrate his acquisition of phallic power as he is helped to emancipate from maternal caprice symbolized here by the dwarves. That this paternal function is carried out by a dwarf, in the absence of the boy's actual father, highlights the essential theme of phallic demise. The men in *The Silence* are stripped of phallic power; the little boy is still in latency and the old man is a pitiable character lacking the insignia of power. The two coincide as the circle of life joins together the opposite poles of age. The laborer with the ladder is ridiculed by the little boy who shoots him while making fart sounds to further heighten his triumph. The waiter, the only man in the film with sexual prowess, is debased by his profession. The lack of a common language with Anna reveals his import as a mere appendage to her enjoyment. In *Persona*, Elisabet's husband's blindness clearly evokes his castration while the person with the greatest authority is a woman (the psychiatrist). Some of the dwarves dress as women, thus further sealing their emasculation. Johan's gun, generally placed in his crotch, reveals the farcical nature of masculinity reduced to a mere semblance, a child's toy. Quipping Brecht again, we ask: what is the feminine objection to the masculine in comparison to the femininity that is the masculine?[6] Indeed, man is a fiction that only a woman could believe in.[7]

Where men are deprived of masculinity and women veer from phallic maternity to femininity proper. The theme of the rejection of maternity is a further aspect of the general movement towards feminization. For Freud (1924), the maternal position is paradoxically masculine insofar as a baby is a penis substitute. A mother occupies a masculine position with respect to her child which she reduces to an object of her desire. The mother enjoys the fact of *having* while the woman surrenders herself to enjoying *not having*. Earlier, we considered the theme of the rejection of maternity in light of the rejection of the parental position; the refusal to be a mother is contiguous with a stubborn wish to remain a child. In the context of sexual difference, the rejection of maternity consists of a refusal of masculinity and an embracing of femininity, namely the contrary to what Freud (1937) called the "rock of castration" which hinged on a repudiation of femininity. We thus veer away from maternity towards femininity. Men are effeminized and women are deprived of maternal desire, surrendering themselves to the enjoyment of *womanly insufficiency*. We thus enter a realm of pure femininity.[8] The films render the idea that femininity is the truth of masculinity. Indeed the theme of lesbian love, central to both films, provides a concrete rendition of the ubiquity of the feminine. This general feminization extends to the so-called "male" gaze of the spectators of the film. When Alma and Elisabet repeatedly pose for us in front of the camera thereby awakening our gaze, are they merely passive or are they, as Lacan (1977) would have it, *making themselves seen*, thereby reducing us to the passive position? Are the women not precisely toying with us? Has Bergman not here achieved, by contrast to what Mulvey (1975) says of traditional narrative cinema, a *castration* and *feminization* of our gaze? Is the masculine not precisely ridiculed and exposed in its effeminacy? In *The Silence*, Ester tells Johan, "We both love your mother." In fact we, the spectators, love her too. The film is in part about Ester's *jalouissance*[9] but it is also about our *jalouissance*. If the male gaze is what Alma and Elisabet target, one must not forget that the women actively *provoke* this gaze thereby making it their object. The male gaze is castrated into a lesbian gaze; we are in the place of Ester and Alma, two women trapped in the suffering longing of unrequited lesbian love. Just as Johan and Ester cannot possess Anna for lack of an adequate phallus, the viewers are also robbed of that possibility while tantalized into desiring it. If we are the possessors of the proverbial "male" gaze, it must be conceded that this gaze is veritably lesbian and deprived of phallic power; it is a gaze of feminine longing.

Received notions regarding power dynamics and relations of authority are also subverted in the films. One cannot tell without ambiguity who, Alma or Elisabet, occupies the position of authority. We witness an inversion of the usual transference relation. Elisabet takes Alma as her patient. Alma cries in Elisabet's arms; she is, as Elisabet puts it in her letter to the psychiatrist, "a little in love" (perhaps one may specify *transference love*). Alma "free associates" while Elisabet maintains (analytic) silence. Interestingly, the psychiatrist too falls into a kind of transference love.[10] She is convinced of Elisabet's sanity and takes her refusal to speak as testament of moral courage. It is likewise with respect to the relation between the viewer and the film. Alma and Elisabet pose for our gaze but, in so doing, they also rob our gaze of its power.[11] Interestingly, in the very next scene the viewer becomes the object of the actress' gaze when Elisabet directs her camera straight towards us and coquettishly snaps a quick photo. The juxtaposition of these two scenes suggests that the second scene renders the truth of the first. Though the women pose for the camera, we are the object of the gaze. We have a rapid dialectical shift from spectator to object, from voyeurism to unsolicited exhibitionism or from active to passive. The spectator is placed in the position of the lower term, namely the position deprived of power and knowledge. Elisabet's grin after taking a photo of us reveals the smug satisfaction of one in control, thereby undoing the general commonplaces regarding the spectator–performer relation. Indeed, *Persona* begins with a kind of "let there be light" moment with the camera lamps burning bright. We are urged out of the Platonic cave into *the blinding daylight*, literally the place where we cannot see for excess of truth. Our gaze, much like that of the blind husband, is that of the king who cannot see. Lacan (2006) argues that the position of the king, though endowed with the highest symbolic power, is intrinsically that of the blinded gaze. The position of the king immanently includes its own dialectical reversal. The spectator, the clinician, and the man (Elisabet's husband) are reduced from their position of sovereign power thereby rendering for us the idea that the truth of power is impotence. What is the impotence of the loss of power in comparison to the impotence that is power? Power is indeed bliss only when viewed from the position of powerlessness; the master is a fiction that only a slave may believe in. This is the drama of Alma's slow awakening. She begins imagining that Elisabet enjoys highest bliss and power; slowly she realizes that her soul is more "rotten" than common folk.

The subversion of these principal differences leads to a space where boundaries are faulty. Many scenes in *Persona* make explicit reference to borders and frontiers such as a brick wall, a fence, doors, and doorframes. Bergman reminds us that a boundary is a merely symbolic object, something that finds its meaning by its position within a larger network rather than by an intrinsic property. Anyone who takes the door to be a real object, Lacan (1988) jests, may take one to the desert hoping to cool him/herself by "opening" it. Since a door is symbolic, the locus of its placement is the outcome of a contingent will. Every boundary conceals the conceit of the will that placed it there. If the subversion of the aforementioned symbolic differences involves the transgression of crucial boundaries, one must also critically note that a boundary is itself the height of transgression: what is the transgression of a boundary in comparison to the transgression that is a boundary? The subversions of the differences required for social coexistence renders a space akin to Bakhtin's (1984) *carnivalesque*, a zone where the symbolic law is suspended and boundaries eliminated. The carnival marks the reign of the "lower" term; its relation to the comic and the grotesque stems precisely from the subversion by which what is lower takes the dominant position and reveals itself as the truth of the higher term.

The theme of autophagia arises again in the opposition between social *semblance* and the "underlying" *real* where Alma and Elisabet represent, respectively, the two poles of the antagonism. Most notably, there is a scene where Alma talks to herself about her plans of marriage and children while putting on make-up, the quintessential insignia of (pseudo)-feminine semblance. Alma plays the role of the cliché wife. Rather than explore the singularity of her femininity, she casts herself into the mold dictated by the social Other. Her choice of professional vocation too was dictated by the model provided by her mother. It is rather questionable whether she has any authentic interest in the work at all; her utter lack of professionalism, her infatuation with Elisabet and art as well as her wild youthful adventures suggest a desire that points elsewhere. Interestingly, in the scene immediately following Alma's soliloquy of alienated maternal/familial desire, we see Elisabet captivated by the news. A cursory reading points to the staging of the fall of semblance and entry into the domain of the terrifying real. The opposition between semblance and the real can be theorized in two contrasting ways. Firstly, we have the idea that once semblance is abolished we *fall* into the real. The other view posits a less stringent antagonism insofar as semblances themselves are considered as inherent to the real. Following Žižek, I reject the first view, in favor of the second interpretation insofar as it allows for the crucial fact, observed both clinically and existentially, that semblance has the propensity *to eat away at itself* as semblance. Semblance, precisely by virtue of its intimacy with the real, provides a very weak protection from the real. Like the autophagic film reel, the self-consuming semblance eats into itself, thereby revealing itself as akin to the real from which it strives to provide respite. The Alma–Elisabet opposition–fusion represents the intermingling of semblance and *jouissance*, the paradoxical manner in which semblance sheds its own skin in the very effort to dress itself up. Semblance, like art, – the most sublime and cunning semblance of all   feeds upon itself and enjoys this self-consumption.[12] If *Persona* begins with the illusion of the false divide between semblance (Alma) and the real (Elisabet), it slowly stages and develops their eventual fusion as the aspiring mother and trophy wife confesses to her seaside adulterous orgy and, by the end of the film, the would-be caring nurse morphs into an abusive tyrant. The real that is semblance is certainly more ominous than the "real itself"; the pretense to idyllic serenity is more threateningly portentous than the explicitly menacing.[13] The real thus provides the truth of semblance. What is the real behind semblance in comparison to the real that is semblance?[14]

Bergman explains that "Mrs. Vogler desires the truth" and, furthermore, that the "truth had dissolved and disappeared or had, in the worst case, turned into a lie" (1990). Regarding Elisabet, Bergman continues: "The only thing is, she refuses to speak. In fact, she doesn't want to lie" (ibid.). The refusal to speak is here equivalent to the refusal to lie and yet, precisely thereby, it sharpens into a ubiquitous *constitutive* lie. The truth thus becomes the apotheosis of the lie rather than its alleged antidote. If, as Lacan claims, "language is the instrument of lying" then one would expect that *not to speak* would entail the abolition of lies. However, what *Persona* shows us is that silence (the refusal to lie – for all one can do with speech is lie, truth being relegated, as Lacan held, to the mercurial realm of the *half-said*) is the biggest lie of all. While Alma delivers her monologue to Elisabet, the latter finally breaks her vow of not lying: she shakes her head in denial when accused of hating her child. Ironically this may be the cure, the exit from *the constitutive lie of not lying at all*. Here an isolated lie functions as a greater holder of truth (it opens the space of Elisabet's eventual recovery) than the falsity of her previous heroic denial of speech marked by the *beautiful soul*'s bad faith in projecting her own inauthenticity onto language itself. Thus the lie, held beneath the truth in the hierarchy of moral worth, here reveals itself as less imbued in falsity than the truth itself. Repeating our Brechtian refrain, we ask what is a lie against the truth in comparison to the lie that is the truth?[15]

In *The Ethics of Psychoanalysis*, Lacan christens beauty as the last defense against the real. In *Persona* and *The Silence*, beauty slowly degenerates into the real that it protects us from. As Rilke (2017) puts it, with the rapture of poetic fervor, "beauty is nothing but the beginning of terror which we are barely able to endure". When the masks of social semblance are threatened, the terror of the real surfaces in the midst of semblance. With respect to the tension between beauty and ugliness, *Persona* is an immensely contradictory film. We have two gorgeous actresses starring in a film that is largely about ugliness. *Persona* begins with close-ups of facial profiles of an old man and woman. The camera is so closely zoomed in that what one perceives resembles more a rugged landscape than a face. Bergman stages for us the *face without the mask*, raw flesh devoid of the semblances that make intersubjectivity bearable. Likewise, Levinas' ethics of the *face* involves the face without the mask. That is the true ethical test: can one take responsibility for the *naked* face devoid of ornamentation? This is perhaps where Levinas' notion of the *face* (rendered here as *mask-less face*) meets Lacan's *Das Ding*, the zone of pure *jouissance* where the garnishing of semblance is removed. When Elisabet is asleep we get again the face minus the mask. Alma gazes at her closely and describes the horror of the face. She discovers Elisabet's ugliness thereby undoing the initial idealization. We have similar encounters with the *facial Ding* in *The Silence*. The film begins with Ester vomiting, thereby grossly undermining the physical beauty of her face with hysteric convulsions. Later we witness her vile snoring and her awkward smile terrifying little Johan.[15] Johan's drawing truly testifies to the simplest form of the face; it is plain, ugly, without mask or semblance. It is, to quip Lacan (interviewed by Miller in Benoit Jacquot, 1974), quite literally a mere "grimace of the real." The setting of the start of *Persona* is totally barren and white. We have from the start the depiction of an aseptic world devoid of façade and bereft of color – Bergman's consistent choice of making black and white films is inseparable from his drive to reveal the *Thing* ordinarily obfuscated by the vain accessories of quotidian life. Black and white, though further from the colors of "reality," is more attuned to the real. The modern aesthetics of *Persona*, by contrast to the old European landscape of *The Silence*, points to the fall of semblance with modernity.[16] The moment of the merging of the faces in *Persona* marks the final triumph of ugliness over beauty. In his memoirs, Bergman explains that the two halves of a human face are not identical. Every face has a side more beautiful than the other and, in the famous fusion of Alma and Elisabet, Bergman precisely chose to bring the uglier sides together. Interestingly, the ugly side of the face is the side one is less inclined to recognize as one's own. In Lacanese, we may say that the hideous side is *negativized* from one's self-image. Bergman attempts to undo this negativization and bring to the fore the abject within the beautiful. He thus masterfully renders for us the ugly within the splendor of the two women and shows that ugliness provides the truth of beauty. Nietzsche had already come to this most terrifying truth, locating the womb of sacred beauty in monstrosity: "What would be 'beautiful,' if the contrary to it had not first come to awareness of itself, if ugliness had not first said to itself: 'I am ugly?'" (1998). What is the ugly in opposition to beauty in comparison to the ugliness that is beauty? Beauty is a myth that only the naked and the ugly could believe in.[17]

Alma's twice-repeated monologue is a kind of mirror stage; Bergman (1990) calls it a "mirror scene." What is remarkable in this cinematic mirror stage, however, is precisely how it *differs* from the traditional Lacanian version. According to Lacan, a certain object (christened as *object little a*) is effaced from the image in the mirror. The object *a* is the part that is repressed so that the image can retain dignity and integrity. The object *a*, much like the unconscious itself (the object *a* is a quasi-material correlate to the unconscious) disrupts our conscious self-image. More accurately, the object *a* at once disrupts and paradoxically, through that very hindrance, gives the image its consistency. The achievement of the mirror scene in *Persona* is that it manages to give body to the object *a*, namely the object that puts into doubt how we see ourselves. Unlike the traditional Lacanian mirror stage there is no jubilation here; one does not have a subject glancing amorously at him/herself in proud triumphant elation. The object *a*, insofar as it disrupts and paradoxically holds together the self-image, also holds (by disrupting it) the dual relation. This scene can thus shed much light on what binds the two women together precisely by also setting them in conflict. What then is the object *a* here? What holds together, at once, the dual relation and each woman's identity? The answer is guilt which Lacan (2004) lists as one of the incarnations of the object *a*. The identity of both women and therefore what brings them together in a conflictual *battle of pure prestige* is the denial of the guilt of the rejection of maternity. Alma projects all her guilt onto Elisabet as if she were herself entirely innocent. Alma's desperate plea of difference ("No, I am not like you") fails in the face of the truth of their shared guilt thereby culminating in the fusion of their faces. Throughout the film the Alma–Elisabet opposition superficially coincides with the dualism of guilt and innocence, thereby straying interpreters, as aforesaid, into the erroneous notion of vampiricism. What is missed is that Elisabet provides the truth of Alma insofar as the famous mirror scene functions as a confession in the disparaged mode of accusation – as many confessions sadly do. Here the so-called "innocent" young nurse, "prey" to the predatorial actress, reveals herself as the beautiful soul seeking to remedy in the Other the faults of her own soul. Innocence is thus reduced to *the conceit of innocence*: what is the guilt of lost innocence in comparison to the guilt of the conceit of innocence?

The very beginning of the film shows images akin to the Lacanian *fragmented body*, disparate body parts (hands, penis) rapidly succeeding one another. In Freudian terms, the film begins with the *primary process* as images roll one after the other without obvious thematic links connecting them together. Eventually, Sontag notes, the images slow down to the viewer's pace. The primary process gives way to the *secondary process*, namely the everyday mode of cognitive functioning where repression, censorship, and revision slow the onslaught of sensory and mental stimulus. *The Silence* also begins with the fast moving train revealing the external landscape rushing rapidly by. The two films are situated on the interstice of repression and its undoing. Interestingly, the first "slow" scene of *Persona* culminates with the boy at the screen, namely another "mirror scene."[18] We thus get an allegory of the Lacanian mirror stage staging the movement from the fragmented body to the formation of an ego through the encounter with the screen of the mirror. This shows the gradual rise of the "I" out of the chaos of infantile incapacity. As noted above, this is a very paradoxical mirror stage without jubilation. This, I think, is the central achievement of Bergman's films; by eliminating the factor of *jubilation* in self-formation, Bergman shows the impasses inherent to identity. *Persona* is a tale concerning the crisis of identity or, more precisely, *the crisis that is identity*. The film begins with a stringent opposition between the mute Elisabet who has lost all the bearings of self-hood – prior to her breakdown she was an actress, namely the vocation *par excellence* for those without fixed identity – and the loquacious Alma who, by contrast, secured her identity in strict compliance with social and familial norms – she choose the vocation of being a nurse, a woman's profession (and her mother's) if there ever was one. This facile opposition is gradually undone as Alma's comfortable refuge in prefabricated identities (mother, wife, nurse) slowly unravels internally. Elisabet has little to do with this deconstruction; to blame her for it would be to succumb to the error of confusing *inner contradiction* for *external opposition*. The drama of *Persona* arguably mirrors the psychoanalytic process by which *the passion of ignorance* inherent to external opposition is slowly mitigated by Alma's gradual realization that her struggles are rooted in the impasses of her own identity. Identification without dis-identification is as fragile as the proverbial unbending tree. Fragmentation thus provides the truth, rather than the contrary, of identity. What is the fragmentation of identity by contrast to the fragmentation that is identity?

Persona is a religious film about the fall; it provides a dialectical–paradoxical theory of the fall by inverting the Biblical story. Rather than begin with Eden and then fall from grace, here the fall occurs first as Elisabet, refusing to speak, is hospitalized. After the fall, Elisabet is urged to move to the seaside – a kind of symbolic Eden – in the hope of finding her health again. Interestingly, the move away from city life is the only action of the film that is narrated. Nowhere else in the film does a narrator's voice appear. Perhaps Bergman wanted to intensify the theistic motif by introducing the voice of the Other precisely at the moment where a return to Eden is taking place. Bergman's decision to invert the Biblical story points to the radically dialectical aspect of the notion of the fall. The fall is a dialectical notion insofar as *the fall is nothing but our refusal to accept the fall.* The lesson of the film may simply be that once we accept the fall we paradoxically surmount it and achieve grace. Elisabet's refusal to speak is tantamount to a refusal to fall and thus, paradoxically, it is equivalent to the fall itself. To speak is to fall and to fall is the only grace available to the human being. What unites Alma and Elisabet is a common refusal to truly speak; both subjects revolt against the imperative of full speech. Alma and Elisabet represent, respectively, meaningless chatter and silence. Neither subject *truly* speaks. Where Elisabet *does not speak*, Alma, by contrast, *speaks nothingness*. At the end of the film Alma urges Elisabet to say the word "ingenting" (nothing); now it is Elisabet who literally speaks nothing, thereby completing the mirroring function she held for Alma. The inversion of the Biblical story is, I believe, a critique of the idea that a *return to nature* can cure. This ideological error, which I christen the *pre-lapsarian fallacy*, is the veritably non-dialectical idea that falsely opposes fall and grace. What Bergman shows, by contrast to this ideological obfuscation, is that the return to Eden (the refusal to fall) is the biggest fall of all. What is the fall from Eden in comparison to the fall that is Eden?

If we follow Kleist's lead, the theme of marionettes could be said to reference the motif of the fall in *Persona*. In his seminal paper, Kleist's interlocutor argues that a boy dancer falls from grace precisely at the moment of the advent of consciousness. The dancer's grace, by contrast to the marionette's awkwardness, is an index of non-consciousness rather than the opposite. The fall from grace, a central idea of both films, occurs when the light of consciousness robs the human from the innocence of ignorance. *Persona* thus begins with a "let there be light" moment as the film lamps touch reminiscent of creation when God's hand meets Adam's. Where Plato's allegory highlights principally freedom from the clutches of lies and illusions, the Biblical story highlights the *dark side of the light*. *Persona* is in this sense more Biblical than Platonic insofar as the drama that unfolds after the dawning of light is the catastrophe of consciousness corroding sanity. Oh Lord, Bergman seems to ask, what is the darkness before the light in comparison to the darkness that is the light? The motif of the fall is evoked repeatedly throughout the films in various guises: Elisabet's fall into silence, Ester's fall into depression, the Lermontov novel which is, moreover, referenced in Camus' *La Chute* (literally *The Fall*) written before both films, thereby leaving open the possibility that Bergman read it. Most importantly, however, the motif of the fall from grace is carried by the theme of self-reflexiveness, namely the very expression of lost grace as it involves the rise of consciousness.[19] It is, moreover, an ambiguously cinematic operation which forces us to question the relation between film and theater. As Elisabet falls from grace into the silence of melancholy she abandons theater and enters the cinematic realm. Is cinema then not theater that has fallen from grace? The relation is not so simple as theater is quintessentially the domain of self-reflexive oddity where actors' gestures are veritable gesticulations signaling self-consciousness' autophagic self-encroachment restraining the performer to the idiosyncrasy of over-acting. By contrast, film is colored by the grace of reality where the awkward machinations of theatricality give way to the "natural" poise of everydayness. Cinema's verisimilitude is gained paradoxically through a technological *artifice*; this renders for us the truth – invisible to the premodern eye – that reality is itself a dream requiring the artfulness and cunning of a motley of filmic devices. It is precisely the spontaneity of theater that alienates it from reality – reality, this great imposture of naturalness, this hypocrite dressed in the guise of artless sincere mere being-there. What, may we ask, is the falsity of fiction/fantasy against reality in comparison to the falsity that is reality?

Self-reflexiveness is perhaps film's way of returning to theater, of reintroducing theater's fallen-ness within the idyllic kitsch of cinema. If cinematic realism is an assault on the real, self-reflexiveness restores that real. The dialecticity of the fall implies that cinema's denial of the fall is tantamount to a more devastating fall. Cinema that is not self-reflexive is a pre-lapsarian form; it is a denial of the fall which, paradoxically, entangles us more deeply into the vicissitudes of fallen life. The theme of self-reflexiveness brings to the fore cinema's central contradiction; it is the art form that has fallen by virtue of its denial of the fall. Bergman's strict use of black and white evokes the fall through the expulsion of color. The vain search for false paradises – kitsch art may be the name of such hollow pursuits – is more fiery hell than the flames it flees. What is the fall from grace in comparison to the fall that is grace? Freud's *common unhappiness*, namely the wisdom to refuse the promise of deceptive utopias, is the last modicum of grace available for fallen humanity. Cinema is more fallen than theater insofar as it avoids the fall. However, self-reflexive cinema regains a measure of grace by paradoxically biting *again* the apple of knowledge. Kleist's interlocutor–companion admirably renders this paradox:

We see that in the organic world, as thought grows dimmer and weaker, grace emerges more brilliantly and decisively. But just as a section drawn through two lines suddenly reappears on the other side after passing through infinity, or as the image in a concave mirror turns up again right in front of us after dwindling into the distance, so grace itself returns when knowledge has as it were gone through an infinity. Grace appears most purely in that human form which either has no consciousness or an infinite consciousness. That is, in the puppet or in the god.

To this, Kleist remarks: "Does that mean … that we must eat again of the tree of knowledge in order to return to the state of innocence?" His friend answers thus: "Of course … but that's the final chapter in the history of the world." The self-reflexive cinema of Bergman marks that paradoxical point at infinity where grace is finally regained, not through the false ideology of a forced *return*, but through a second biting of the apple. If the self-reflexive cinema of *Persona* provided Bergman with respite from the dread of *the theatrical real* after completing *The Silence*, it is not through an escape from that real but, rather, through deeper immersion in it. The cinematic gaze turned upon itself marks the second *autophagic fall*; cinema bites itself rather than the proverbial apple. Here Bergman's metaphor of the snakeskin takes on the meaning of rebirth, the shedding of old skin. If, as Schelling (quoted in Žižek, 2009) holds, "man is nature's way of looking at itself," then *Persona* and *The Silence* are cinema's way of turning its gaze upon itself. These films undo repression and subject us once again to the pain of self-awareness. The human being arguably invented repression to eschew the task of being nature's self-observer. If Lacan and Freud held that the artist prefigures the psychoanalyst, it is precisely because he/she is the one who undoes repression. Self-reflexiveness in film is a profanation against the aesthetics of repression; it aligns humankind, once again, with the task of self-reflection.

The opposition of the sacred and the profane provides another pivotal thematic axis of the films: Anna tells Ester of her sexual exploits and Alma recounts the foursome on the beach. What is essential is the fact of narrating the story to another woman. It would be an error symptomatic of the liberal hedonistic superego to assume that the locus of enjoyment lies in the sexual acts. The correct psychoanalytic insight is that *speech* provides the sweet *jouissance*. More precisely, it is the *jouissance* of profanatory speech that drives Alma and Anna's rapture. It is *the ecstasy of separation through profanation*. Alma separates from her self-imposed incarceration in the ideology of family life by confessing her sins to Elisabet. Alma's alleged guilt testifies to her bad faith; it is a false mask intended to hide her desire for profanation–separation. Guilt comforts Alma's conservatism; it is an index of her moral cowardice; it is the consequence of *"giving ground relative to [her] desire"* (Lacan, 1992, p. 319). Anna separates from the grips of Ester's jealous possessiveness by narrating scenes of sexual exploits (no less than in a Church). *Persona* testifies to the eventual degeneration of the good/sacred into evil/profanation as it recounts the saga of a simple-minded nurse complacently playing the role of the good daughter, wife, and eventual mother who ineluctably morphs into an abusive and slandering caretaker. If, as Lacan (1986) claims, the good is the penultimate defense against the real (beauty, we saw, is the last barrier), here the sacred/good fails in this function and degenerates into the real. Alma veers toward evil after reading the letter; she becomes the embodiment of cruelty and profanation. The moment of reading the letter is the dialectical turning point of the film where semblance veers towards the real, good degenerates to evil, and, more generally, the pseudo-grace of Eden reveals its true face of horror. As Alma's "love" descends into the *Thing* of amorous hate, we realize that love and hate as good and evil are false opposites. The "lower" term stands for the truth of the "higher" term. We enter here the Nietzschean paradigm of a radical *revaluation of all values* leading us to ask: what is an act of evil against the good in comparison to the evil that is the good? What, furthermore, is the violence of hate against love in comparison to the violence that is love?[20]

Let us now take a foray into the dialectics and erotics[21] of power. Psychoanalysis has taught us that power and eroticism belong together such that sexual tension can only be maintained through an *ambiguity* within power relations between subjects. Power, much like the mercurial phallus, is a *symbolic* "object" that flutters equivocally between participants, thereby creating, precisely through this indistinctness, the tension required for erotic passion. Freud (1905) isolates three central obstacles to sexuality, namely shame, disgust, and morality. In an effort to sharpen Freud's metapsychology, I venture to claim that all three of these constitute specific effects of the more general phenomenon of *power disambiguation.* De-sexualization occurs when the *dynamics* of power falter into the *inertia* of sheer domination. When it becomes all too clear where the locus of power resides, we have the flattening of the erotic tension. It is at that point that shame, disgust, or morality set in. Wielding too much power over another who refuses to even feign the slightest resistance can lead to guilt and resentment (morality), shame in both parties, or simply disgust at the lowly position assumed by the victim. With this idea, we may posit a spectrum measuring a subject's degree of perversion. The resilience of a subject's sexual desire in the face of heightened power disambiguation constitutes the measure of his/her perversion. By contrast, the more readily de-sexualization sets in when confronted with the slightest power disambiguation gives us a measure of a subject's neurosis. When Freud claims that "neurosis is the negative of perversion," he gives expression to the inverse proportionality between the aforementioned tendencies. The films deal principally with the ambiguity of power in erotic relations and, moreover, with the advent of de-sexualization when power loses that sweet opacity that founds it as the principal aphrodisiac.[22] Moreover, the films reveal moments of de-sexualization where the dialectics of power come to a halt and something like total domination takes over. The scenes where Alma repeatedly slaps Elisabet in the face while the camera zooms in on the sadistic grimace of her face and where she threatens to burn her patient with boiling water testify to the triumph of a "pure culture of the death drive" (Freud, 1923) where aggression ceases to be *erotic* and enters the domain of the deathly.[23] Such moments of "instinctual defusion" where the death drive triumphs over life are marked by a peculiar materiality where the libidinal body becomes inert flesh. More specifically, de-sexualization disparages the gaze to the sheer materiality of the eye, something Bergman captures with a close-up of an eye's veins. The dimension of the invocatory undergoes a similar *fall* as we witness the triumph of undignified sounds (e.g. snoring, farts) in both films.

The opposition of faith and disbelief forms another essential axis of the films. Elisabeth does not believe in the semblances of language, truth, duty, and so on. Maternity was the last semblance, the last identity, she espoused and even there she rejected its duties. Alma, by contrast, believes in the fictions that weld together the fabric of social semblance. However, the development of the plot unfolds Alma's crisis of faith. This conflict concerning disbelief emerges when Alma asks Elisabet if she agrees with the nihilistic precepts of the book Alma was reading. By contrast to Elisabet, Alma resists slipping into the void of skepticism and faithlessness. To this end she makes use of the antiquated values of family, motherhood, and the blessings of work. Also, her idealization of art and artists such as Elisabet (whose name "Elisabet Vogler" she repeats with infantile fascination – confirming thereby her transference) functions as yet another shield against the abyss of total disbelief. Eventually, semblances no longer hold despite her desperate attempt to maintain appearances. The fiction of maternal love – the very foundation of Christian ideology – is the last one to fall as Alma is forced to recognize that her moralistic plea against Elisabet's failure as a mother is equally applicable to her. The more Alma tries to assert her faith the more she falls into faithlessness. All her weeping and self-torment is an index of her guilt for sinning against the semblances she continues to uphold hypocritically. Bergman is arguably staging here for us the crisis that led to his own decision to abandon faith. In his memoirs, he confesses that faithlessness liberated his spirit from the alienation of religious ideology by allowing him to re-appropriate as his own what was once projected beyond the celestial spheres: "Now that God is gone, I feel that *all this* is mine; *piety* toward life, *humility* before my meaningless fate, and love for the other children who are afraid, who are ill, who are cruel" (1990). The saga of Alma's fall into disbelief, her progressive killing of the social Other with its ideals, injunctions, and interdictions renders for us the idea that disbelief is the truth of faith. Elisabet's silence is an essential rhetorical (and therapeutic) device; she need not utter a single word to prompt Alma's spiritual demise. What Alma experiences is strictly personal; her spiritual crisis is immanent to her inner world. Faith deconstructs under its own spell rather than through the force of an external compulsion. What is the atheistic assault on faith in comparison to the assault that is faith itself?

Many scenes of *The Silence* involve subjects not speaking the same language. Anna's lover does not speak her language and Esther cannot find a common language with the butler. Interestingly, the lack of a common tongue not only does not stop Anna from endlessly chatting with her late night lover, it actually disinhibits her to confess her sororicidal wishes to him. There is a veritable crisis of language at work in the film underlined by Anna's avowal to her lover: "How nice that we cannot understand each other." This crisis is further highlighted by the important role marionettes (the quintessential silent dummies) play in the film. Furthermore, Elisabet is mute and, interestingly, her husband is blind, thereby closing off for good all means of communication as if to give concrete expression to the impossibility of the sexual rapport. The very title *The Silence* evokes the realm of the foreclosure of language. According to Sontag (1916), in *Persona*, language itself is put into question. She further argues that cinema itself is the home of those who do not trust language. *Persona* is thus, as Sontag aptly notes, a monologue rather than a dialogue. Through this artistic choice, Bergman shows that monologue is the truth of dialogue or, as Lacan puts it, all dialogue is but an exchange of two self-enclosed monologues. What we witness here is the crisis of language relegating subjects to the confines of ego-speech where connection to the other is reduced to an engagement that is strictly narcissistic. For Sontag, language is an instrument of fraud and cruelty. Likewise, for Lacan, it is the instrument of lying, of *jouissance*, and correlatively of misunderstanding. Sontag rightly explains that

Persona (we may add *The Silence*) shows the lack of an appropriate language. There is, she continues, only a language with lacunae where absences are more potent than words. What, Bergman pushes us to ask, is the non-sense outside language in comparison to the non-sense that is language?

As argued earlier, the theme of female homosexuality echoes the idea of narcissism, as does the theme of self-reflexiveness. Are these two films narcissistically closed upon themselves in an autoerotic self-consuming autophagia? Or could the specificity of *female* homosexuality point to a radical opening? This option remains available to us according to another psychoanalytic precept contradicting the previous linking of homosexuality and narcissism. For Lacan, heterosexuality and male homosexuality fail to reach the Other sex, namely woman. By contrast, the female homosexual is the only true heterosexual; she alone is interested in the Other of sex. The gay man as well as the straight man and woman care only for the man's phallus (the partner's phallus or his own) and are, as such, bound within phallic closure. Do the vicious dialectical reversals staged in the two films testify to the daunting narcissistic closure of *homo*sexuality or are they testament to the opening of the space of the feminine, of the Other, reached through the paradox of a female homosexuality that stands as the only viable harbinger of *hetero*sexuality?[24] How are we to understand the mad spiraling of a concept to its opposed "lower term"? Does the carnivalesque madness of dialectical–philosophical autophagia point towards narcissistic closure or does this particular form of self-reflexivity provide a means of reaching the Other? What kind of resolution or respite from conceptual autophagia did Bergman envisage in these films? How could an order be re-established where adulthood does not falter to infantilism, where manhood does not dwindle away, where power can hold a modicum of integrity, where truth does not disparage into lie, where beauty does not decay to the beastly, where innocence is not the mere underside of guilt, where identity is not the harbinger of disintegration, where Eden is not mere false paradise, where light is more than a deceitful mask cast upon obscurity, where reality can make a claim to the real, where the good does not sink to wicked lowliness, where love is not an outgrowth of hate, where faith is not a mere shroud cast upon cynical disbelief and where sense does not spiral into the madness of non-sense? Since semblance is also doomed to fade into the real, respite cannot be achieved through the hypocritical cloak of artful appearance. Bergman stages the choice between the madness of conceptual autophagia and a solution that would not rely on the falsity of semblance. What could such a solution be? Where can one find respite from the mad spiraling of the concept to its "lower term" without relying on deception? Cast psychoanalytically, can one avoid *erring* without paying the price of being *dupe*?[25] Is there a Bergmanian ethics/aesthetics that neither errs into *autophagia* nor remains fool to semblance? Can one remain open to the Other (the opposed "lower term") without deteriorating into insanity? Correlatively, is the only means to safeguard sanity through recourse to the closure of semblance (the falsity of the "higher" term)?

Answers to these questions may forever elude us and the strength of the films may consist precisely in maintaining equivocality in this regard and thereby retaining a tension akin to erotic ambiguity. Interesting here is Bergman's pre-occupation with Bach. While, at the level of content, *The Silence* is filled with references to the composer and his music, at the level of form, *Persona* is argu-ably structured as a fugue.[26] A fugue is also an ambiguous form; the word liter-ally means escape and yet every fugue ends with a return of the theme in the tonic key. Is a fugue thus a flight away from or a return home? Is the fugue the quintessential aesthetic form that eschews at once the artifice of semblance (as the anti-kitsch form *par excellence*) and the mad dwindling into autophagic self-consumption? With respect to the contradictions and paradoxical turns of perversion, Sergio Benvenuto (2016) speaks of a "baroque oxymoron." In exten-sion we could say that the unconscious is a veritably polyphonic or contrapuntal structure insofar as contradictory *voices* overlap and intermingle in a confusing display where one no longer knows who is master and who slave; as soon as one gets an inkling roles suddenly shift. Is the fugue the contrapuntal form that gives expression to conceptual autophagia irreducible to madness? Could the fugue be the veritable sinthome of the films, namely a means to restore order through an aesthetic organization of the real without paying homage to spurious/narcis-sistic semblance? If so, the self-reflexiveness of the films would paradoxically point to the rupturing of narcissistic closure and the consequent openness to otherness.

In the spirit of the fugue, let us conclude with a recapitulation in the tonic key bringing together the various voices in a final enquiry: do the endings of *Persona* and *The Silence* – insofar as they entail a *fugitive escape* from "Timoka" and the seaside as well as from the respective female partners and insofar as a return home is suggested – point towards a return to the realm of semblance and the closure of normality? Or do the films represent Bergman's baroque experimentation in *lesbian contrapuntal dialectics* treading the fine line that delicately eschews, on either side, the falsity of semblance as well as *carnivalesque* insanity, thereby opening the space of a paradoxical stability of the concept through philosophical autophagia?

Notes

1 Bergman wrote this as his acceptance speech for receiving the Dutch Erasmus Prize. He published it as a preface to *Persona*. The piece is reproduced in *Images: My Life in Film* (Bergman, 1990).

2 Hegel uses this term to designate the subject who cannot appreciate his/her complicity in the situation that he/she bemoans.

3 Sontag (2016), by contrast, considers the following polarities as central to *Persona*: violence and powerlessness, reason and unreason, language and silence, the intelligible and the unintelligible, mask and person, speech and silence, actor and soul.

4 Pierre Legendre coined this expression to denote the emotional transformation that arises when a subject, initially the child of his/her parents, assumes a parental role by becoming a parent for a new generation.

5 The original quotation from Brecht is the following: "What is the robbing of a bank compared to the founding of a bank?"

6 Lacan truthfully notes the paradox by which "virile display in human beings seem[s] feminine" (Lacan, 2006, p. 584).

7 The triumph of the feminine and the infantile over the masculine and the adult make it clear that *Persona* and *The Silence* take place in the dreamy state induced by transference. As Assoun (2007) put it best, transference involves the infantile and occurs in the feminine. Resistance to psychoanalysis is always resistance to transference, namely to the triumph of the infantile and the feminine where semblances fall. The love of semblance is another name for that most fundamental of passions Lacan (1998) christened as the passion of ignorance.

8 Interestingly, the decline of the phallic/patriarchal and the concomitant rise of the feminine is a common theme of contemporary psychoanalysis. Bergman's decision to centre these, and many other, films on female characters not only presciently heralds the theme of the ubiquity of the feminine in late modernity but prefigures (perhaps through influence) the work of Lars von Trier who, placing women as lead characters of his films, is also very fascinated with the upsurge of feminine *jouissance* in the face of phallic demise. He did after all make a film about Medea, that quintessential woman capable of an act totally unbound by maternal feeling.

9 Lacan (1998) coins the portmanteau word *jalouissance* combining the words *jalousie* (jealousy) and *jouissance* to denote the enjoyment derived from jealousy.

10 Allouch (2015) argues that for Lacan the transference is inverted when working with psychotic patients. Rather than occupy the position of *supposed subject of knowledge*, the analyst relinquishes this position to the patient. Indeed, the psychotic is bearer of a grand system of knowledge which he/she imparts to the clinician (should he/she have ears to hear). As a result, it is the clinician, rather than the patient, who is in transference love. Freud (1911) had presciently pointed in this direction when he claimed that the psychotic's knowledge mirrors his own libido theory.

11 Miller (2006) compellingly argues that reality TV robs our gaze of the power to shame insofar as we are pulled into perverse voyeuristic *jouissance*.

12 The 20th century bore witness to the way the semblance of art, formerly relying on the artifice of beauty, revealed itself as harbinger of the very real it sought to keep at bay. Modern art testifies indeed to the autophagic moment where beauty devours itself in an ominous display of the ugly.

13 The genius of David Lynch arguably consists of suggesting the gloom of the real within the interstice of semblance. The scenes of tranquil serenity in *Mulholland Drive* and *Blue Velvet* suggest an eerie "calm" before the storm more tempestuous than the storm itself.

14 This is the very reason for Lacan's rejection of the term "depth-psychology" as a rendition of psychoanalysis. For Lacan, the unconscious is not located *beneath* the surface; rather, it is a mere torsion *on* the surface. Likewise, the real is nothing more than a twist on the surface of semblance.

15 Her grimace is akin to that of Sygne de Coufontaine from Claudel's *La trilogie des Coufontaines*; it is more a *tic* on the face, a senseless bit of nervous *jouissance*, than a sign of recognition granted to the other.

16 The one thing we owe capitalism is indeed the fall of the suffocating semblances of feudalism, namely the burden of tradition misconceived, under oppressive Medieval ideology, as "nature," "divine right," and so on. Though one cannot deny the archaic mystifying tendencies of capitalism, one has to admit, with Marx, that capitalism has done much in the way of freeing thought from the burden of semblance.

17 There is an ancient Persian adage that states that this world is an old woman. The proverb means that all things of this world, as opposed to the perennial heavens, are destined to decay, as the splendor of a woman's youth will eventually give way to ugly decrepitude.

18 The tactile element (the boy touches the screen) adds something important to the Lacanian emphasis on the scopic. This is interestingly in line with Anzieu's (1995) work on the "skin-ego."

19 The kink in the Moebius strip embodies in the real of topology the self-reflexive turn by which humanity falls from grace into the destitution of a veritable *bite of consciousness*.

20 For Nietzsche, Christian love is a mere mask intended to hide hatred and *ressentiment* felt towards the Romans: "out of the trunk of that tree of revenge and hate, Jewish hate … grew forth something just as incomparable, a new love, the deepest and most sublime of all kinds of love … But by no means should one suppose it grew upwards as, say, the true negation of that thirst for revenge, as the opposite of Jewish hate! No, the reverse is the truth! This love grew forth out of it, as its crown" (Nietzsche, 1998, p. 17). Cast in Freudian terminology, Alma's love is but a reaction formation to the hate she harbors in the deep recesses of her soul and which she finally owns after the moment of dialectical reversal when reading the letter.

21 Is there anything more erotic than dialectics? Was Nietzsche (1999) not one thousand times right when he sacrilegiously christened Socrates (the eternal dialectician) as the "true eroticist"?

22 It is no wonder that the great pervert of international relations, Henry Kissinger (the deplorable winner of the peace prize), would coin the adage according to which "power is the greatest aphrodisiac." Where most neurotics would collapse under the weight of moral pressure, the great enthusiast of war retains his *erotic* investment in domination; the blood and cries of the innocent will not slacken the vigor of his zeal.

23 More subtly, when Alma tells Elisabet that she is "rotten" we enter again the domain of the overtly insulting and therefore verge on the de-sexualized. Insults and profanations offer a delicious spice to the exquisite delights of the forbidden fruit. However, when these break a certain threshold sexual tension is flattened, thereby paving the way to the triumph of the comic or the tragic. A joke testifies to this. A young woman tells her partner that she finds it kinky to be insulted during sex. In the midst of their next sexual encounter, he thus exclaims: "I shit on your father's grave." Of course, he missed the subtle mark of the sexual. If at that moment she did not burst out laughing (comedy) she would have fallen instead into tears or deep rage (tragedy). What was surely missed was the orgasm as she pulls her body away from the stunned boy leaving his sword unsheathed, hanging ridiculously in the stupefaction of man's ignorance of the feminine.

24 In this regard, Pierre Bruno (2010) makes the very perspicacious remark that female homosexuality involves the relation of the Other to the Other rather than of the same to the same.

25 I am playing with Lacan's adage according to which those who are not duped by sem blance are doomed to err ("the non-dupe err").

26 A detailed study of the fugue-like structure of *Persona* would take us beyond the scope of this chapter.

Bibliography

Allouch, J. (2015). "Psychotic Transference." In *Lacan on Madness: Madness, Yes You Can't*, edited by Patricia Gherovici and Manya Steinkoler. London: Routledge, pp. 86–94.

Anzieu, D. (1995). *Le Moi-Peau*. 2eme edition. Dunod.

Assoun, P-L. (2007). *Leçons psychanalytiques sur le transfert*. Economica.

Bakhtin, M. (1984). *Problems of Dostoevsky's Poetics*. Minneapolis: University of Minnesota Press.

Benvenuto, S. (2016). *What Are Perversions? Sexuality, Ethics, Psychoanalysis*. London: Karnac.

Bergman, I. (1990). *Images: My Life in Film*. With an Introduction by Woody Allen. Translated by Marianne Ruuth. New York: Arcade Publishing.

Bruno, P. (2010). *Lacan, passeur de Marx. L'invention du symptôme*. Editions érès. Point Hors Ligne.

Claudel, P. (1972). *L'Otage. Le Pain dur. Le Père humilié*. Paris: Gallimard.

Freud, S. (1905). "Three Essays on the Theory of Sexuality." In *The Standard Edition of the Complete Psychological Works of Sigmund Freud (SE) VII*. London: Hogarth Press, pp. 123–245.

Freud, S. (1911). "Psychoanalytic Notes on an Autobiographical Account of a Case of Paranoia (Dementia Paranoides)." In *SE XII*. London: Hogarth Press, pp. 1–82.

Freud, S. (1923). "The Ego and the Id." In *SE XIX*. London: Hogarth Press, pp. 1–66.

Freud, S. (1924)."The Dissolution of the Oedipus Complex." In *SE XIX*. London: Hogarth Press, pp. 171–179.

Freud, S. (1937). "Analysis Terminable and Interminable." In *SE XXIII*. London: Hogarth Press, pp. 209–253.

Jacquot, B. (1974). *La psychoanalyse 1 & 2*. https://m.youtube.com/watch?v=7NegXfypevU. Retrieved on January 26, 2022.

Kleist, H. "On the Marionette Theatre." Translated by Idris Parry. https://southerncrossreview.org/9/kleist.htm. Retrieved on January 26, 2022.

Kojève, A. (2014). *The Notion of Authority (A Brief Presentation)*. London and New York: Verso.

Lacan, J. (1977). *The Seminar of Jacques Lacan. Book XI. The Four Fundamental Concepts of Psychoanalysis (1963–64)*. New York and London: W. W. Norton & Company.

Lacan, J. (1986). *Le séminaire. Livre VII. L'éthique de la psychanalyse*. Paris: Le Seuil.

Lacan, J. (1988). *The Seminar of Jacques Lacan. Book II. The Ego in Freud's Theory and in the Technique of Psychoanalysis (1954–1955)*. Cambridge: Cambridge University Press.

Lacan, J. (1994). *Le séminaire. Livre IV. La relation d'objet*. Paris: Le Seuil.

Lacan, J. (1998). *The Seminar of Jacques Lacan. Book XX. Encore (1972–1973)*. New York and London: W.W Norton & Company.

Lacan, J. (1992). *The Seminar of Jacques Lacan. Book VII. The Ethics of Psychoanalysis (1959–1960)*. Edited by Miller, J-A. Translated by Porter, D. W.W. Norton & Company.

Lacan, J. (2004). *Le séminaire. Livre X. L'angoisse*. Paris: Le Seuil.

Lacan, J. (2006). *Écrits*. Translated by Bruce Fink in Collaboration With Héloïse Fink and Russell Grigg. New York: W. W. Norton & Company. (Page numbers refer to the French original displayed on the margin of the text).

Miller, J-A. (2006). "On Shame." In *Reflections on Seminar XVII. Jacques Lacan and the Other Side of Psychoanalysis*, edited by J. Clemens and R. Grigg. Durham and London: Duke University Press.

Mulvey, L. (1975)."Visual Pleasure and Narrative Cinema." Published in *Screen*.

Nietzsche, F. (1998). *On the Genealogy of Morality*. Indianapolis and Cambridge: Hacket Publishing Company.

Nietzsche, F. (1999). *The Birth of Tragedy and Other Writings*. Edited by R. Geuss and R. Speirs. Cambridge: Cambridge University Press.

Rilke, R. M. (2017). *The Duino Elegies*. London: Bibliotech Press.

Rosolato, G. (2002). *Le Sacrifice: Repères psychanalytiques*. Paris: Presses Universitaires de France.

Sontag, S. (2016). "Persona: Review." https://scrapsfromtheloft.com/2016/10/16/persona -review-susan-sontag/.

Žižek, S. (2009). *Organs Without Bodies. On Deleuze and Consequences*. New York and London: Routledge.

Chapter 9

The Father(s) in *Moses and Monotheism* and *Fanny and Alexander*

A Closer Look at Isak Jacobi, the Jewish Magical Savior

Elisabeth Punzi

In *Moses and Monotheism* (1939), Sigmund Freud reflects on myths about male heroes and how these myths tend to portray parents that are infertile or sexually abstinent. Usually, the boy threatens the father figure, is displaced, saved by people of lower descent, and later is reunited with his family of origin. Often the child is saved through being hidden in a chest. Revenge and the question of the identity of the father are constant themes. The myth comprises oedipal themes but is more than that since topics such as displacement, rescue, and the question of the identity of the father are central to the myth about the male hero.

Moreover, Freud investigates anti-Semitism and how the characteristics of the Jewish people developed. Is there something essentially Jewish that is inherited throughout the generations? He writes that the prohibition to portray God has supported critical and symbolic thinking, and submits that the idea of being God's chosen people has invoked a sense of pride and a tendency to strive toward improvement. Freud also suggests that Moses was Egyptian. Thereby the origin of the Jewish people is questioned, just as the identity of the father is questioned. He also presents the idea that Jews/Israelites murdered Moses. The crime became repressed, but returns as a sense of guilt. This theme has been thoroughly investigated, for example by Yerushalmi (1991), but is not in focus here. Moreover, Freud writes that Jewish history is known for its dualities, and for prohibiting magical sentiments and mysticism.

Mystical traditions, however, exist in the Jewish as well as in the psychoanalytic heritage (Berke & Schneider, 2006). Freud was rooted in a Jewish mystical tradition which influenced him and his theories. This does not mean that psychoanalysis is a mystical tradition. It means, however, that cultural heritage and traditions cannot be ignored when understanding individuals, for example, Freud, or ideas and disciplines, for example, psychoanalysis. In the Jewish tradition there are various forms of dualistic thinking, including the idea that within human beings there is an internal conflict between good and evil inclinations (Towers, 2018), an idea that also is central to psychoanalysis (Aronson, 2010). The evil inclination is called Yetzer Hara. It should, however, be noted that Yetzer Hara is not evil in itself. Yetzer Hara seeks pleasure, and the pleasure seeking may lead to evil deeds. Therefore, inclinations and strivings for pleasure need to be controlled

DOI: 10.4324/9781003200246-10

and handled so that their forces can be used for benevolent, productive means. The animal soul is another mystical Jewish concept, derived from Kabbalistic ideas. The animal soul is selfish and connected to physical pleasures, but it also provides energy. The evil inclination exists alongside the good inclination, called Yetzer Tov, and the animal soul exists alongside the Godly soul. They are even intermingled, just as libidinal and aggressive strivings may be intermingled, and what is good may originate in the evil (Berke & Schneider, 2006). Moreover, the heritage of Midrash, a form of Jewish storytelling in which critical thinking and acknowledgment of narrative gaps and how these may be addressed, has become inscribed in psychoanalysis (Cushman, 2010). When Freud wrote *Moses and Monotheism*, he did not present his ideas as the truth, but engaged in story telling. Another part of Jewish heritage that can be traced in psychoanalysis is the interest in contradictions, multiple truths, and the idea that there are hidden meanings which demand interpretation to be understood (Cushman, 2010).

This chapter focuses on Isak Jacobi, the Jewish character in *Fanny and Alexander*, played by the Jewish actor Erland Josephson (1923–2012), who had an almost lifelong collaboration and friendship with Bergman. Isak is an antique dealer, a banker, and most importantly, a magician with supernatural powers. I strive to acknowledge contradictions and hidden meanings connected to Isak Jacobi. I also strive to understand *Fanny and Alexander* as a myth about the male hero, as such myths are presented in *Moses and Monotheism*. I do not suggest that I am able to present the truth about Freud, Bergman, *Moses and Monotheism*, or *Fanny and Alexander*. I do, however, suggest that my interpretation illuminates how, in these works, Freud and Bergman wrestled with God, religious heritage, the role of the father(s), mysticism, and mythologies. I will begin the chapter with presenting the movie *Fanny and Alexander*.

Thereafter I describe how Isak saves Fanny and Alexander, and how Alexander transgresses the borders of reality together with Ismael, one of Isak's nephews. Finally, I will reflect on how *Fanny and Alexander* can be understood as a myth about the male hero and his father figure(s).

Fanny and Alexander

Fanny and Alexander was released in 1982 and received mixed reviews. Some sensed it was sentimental or superficial, whereas others praised its richness and multilayered allegorical themes (Bundtzen, 1987). The movie exists in several versions. This chapter concerns the longer version, which was broadcasted as a series on Swedish national television.

Fanny and Alexander is centered on the well-to-do Ekdahl family, headed by the matriarch Helena. Her sons, Oscar, Carl, and Gustav, and their families, are central to the town of Uppsala where they live, and where Bergman himself was born. Oscar and his wife Emelie run a theater, Carl is a professor at Uppsala university (it should be noted that Uppsala is an important university town in Sweden), and Gustav is a restaurateur and business man. This means that through

Oscar and Emelie, the family is connected to imagination and creativity, through Carl to academia, and through Gustav to money, enjoyment, and desire. They are, however, not connected to the power of religion. Not yet …

The story is told from many perspectives but mainly from the perspective of Alexander, the son of Oscar and Emelie. Alexander is a child with a rich imagination, and he embodies parts of Bergman's own childhood experiences and views of life (Koskinen & Rohdin, 2005). The first part of the movie portrays the Christmas celebration at Helena's large apartment. The apartment contains numerous rooms, furniture, objects, draperies, and individuals, not least Isak who once was Helena's lover, and now is a close friend to the family. He celebrates Christmas with the Ekdahl family, wearing his kippah, surrounded by pork food and a decorated pig's head – a traditional decoration at a Swedish Christmas dinner table.

In the second part of the movie, Oscar dies. But throughout the movie, he returns as a ghost. Throughout the movies, Alexander challenges his father – he becomes upset when Oscar shows himself, and he asks Oscar to leave him alone. The opulence and the liberated tone in the first part of the movie are replaced by grief and Emelie's self-examination. About one year after the death of Oscar, Emelie marries Vergérus, who is a Bishop in Uppsala. Together with her children, she moves to the vicarage. Vergérus is cold-hearted, punishing, and violent. He terrorizes his new family and exposes Alexander to severe emotional and physical abuse, and humiliation. It should be noted that the bishop of Uppsala is also the arch bishop of Sweden. Moreover, Uppsala Cathedral is infamous for its "Jews' sow," a sculpture from the 14th-century depicting Jews suckling a sow. Such sculptures were not uncommon in Europe, and the abusive German word for "Jews' sow," "Judensau" was used in Freud's days towards Jewish persons (Richards, 2014). The sculpture is clearly anti-Semitic. To this day it has not been removed, despite protests against it. Through involving Vergérus in the drama, Bergman explicitly and implicitly incorporates references to religious power and its darker aspects.

In contrast to Helena's apartment and its inclusive atmosphere, the vicarage is cold, isolated, and austere. Vergérus lives there together with his mother, his sister Henrietta, a disabled aunt named Elsa, and some servants. Vergérus subjugates Emelie, mistreats the children, imprisons them, and is sadistic toward Alexander. His family and the servants are either part of the sadistic enactments or complicit.

The Rescue of the Children

The extended Ekdahl family understands what goes on. One day, Isak shows up at the vicarage. He encounters Henrietta, the bishop's sister, and says that he wants to see Vergérus. She refuses and tells him that he is unpleasant and that she has neither time nor inclination to talk to him. Isak reveals that the bishop is in a pecuniary predicament and has tried to borrow money, and has also offered Isak to buy furniture from the vicarage, including a coffer that Isak is there to buy. When Isak says that he is prepared to offer almost any price, Henrietta's attitude changes. She brings Vergérus, who wants to sell the coffer. When Isak for a moment is left alone, he places the children in the coffer. After the financial transaction Vergérus erupts in anti-Semitic tirades. He calls Isak a damn filthy Jewish swine and abuses him physically. Isak endures and when once again left alone he cries to God and we can see a sharp light. Through Isak's magical power, Vergérus cannot see the children in the coffer but sees them in another room. Thereby Isak, perhaps in collaboration with God, saves the children.

Throughout this scene, Isak acts out the stereotypical role of an ingratiating and subservient Jew, preoccupied with money. Most importantly, the scene shows the deeply racist attitudes of Vergérus and Henrietta. It seems as if Isak, through courageously acting out the anti-Semitic stereotype, makes the bishop lose his temper, his guard, and his ability to judge how to handle the situation. Thereby, the children can be saved. Bergman shows that Vergérus and Henrietta are the ones who are obsessed with money. He also shows that Isak's real power is magical.

Isak's assistants carry the coffer with the children to Isak's home. There, a series of magical and non-magical events take place. The events are transformative for Alexander and also for the bishop and his cold-hearted family. Thanks to Isak and his nephews, the children are united with the large Ekdahl family by the end of the film.

Isak Jacobi

Isak is introduced 16 minutes into the movie. The scene portrays him getting dressed, assisted by his nephew Aron, leaving his home to celebrate Christmas with the Ekdahl family. Isak and Aron speak in Yiddish. Thereby, they are established as persons who transgress borders and belong to more than one world. Isak and Helena have been lovers. This means that there have been other forms of transgressions.

As a character, Isak has been understood from many perspectives. While some see Isak as representing and reproducing anti-Semitic stereotypes, others see him as representing wisdom, love, and goodness (Gentele, 2012; Josefsson, 2012; Zern, 1993).

Isak is an antique dealer, a banker, a lover, a magician, and a savior. As an antique dealer he is connected to materiality but also to ancient treasures, narratives, and heritages. As a banker, he represents the productivity and the capacity to handle symbolic values which, in *Moses and Monotheism*, Freud described as clearly positive Jewish characteristics. Simultaneously, it cannot be denied that the stereotypical image of the Jews as preoccupied with money, and as usurers, is invoked. How can this be understood?

In the first part of the film, at night after the Christmas celebration, Helena and Isak sit down and talk, alone. Helena talks about her children, Isak listens and sometimes nods. Helena describes Oscar as a kind and loving man, but somewhat weak. Whereas Gustav and Carl were provided with too much desire and lust,

Oscar had too little, she says. Moreover, Carl has difficulties with alcohol, relationships, and money. Helena shares that he borrows money from her and says that Isak should never lend Carl any money, and asks Isak if he knows anything about Carl's finances. Isak denies knowing anything. However, in another scene it is revealed that Carl has borrowed money from Isak. Hereby, Isak is for a moment portrayed as unreliable, and perhaps greedy, characteristics that are traditional anti-Semitic stereotypes.

One may wonder why Bergman shows Isak as a usurer who withholds the truth from Helena. As a young man, Bergman had Nazi sympathies, described in his autobiography *Laterna Magica* (1987). From 1934, he studied in Germany and witnessed a Nazi party demonstration in Weimar (Ohlin, 2009). He was sixteen years old and swept along by the atmosphere. Ohlin examines "Bergman's Nazi past," and finds that while being swept along, the young Bergman simultaneously noted the Nazi movement's absurdities. During his life he never expressed contempt for the Jews, and seem to have dramatized and exaggerated these parts of his past. Ohlin concludes that Bergman became intrigued by the collapse of society, and by evilness itself, which sparked a striving to use art to probe ethical standards that confront Nazism and fascism, in all their forms. Gitta Sereny, renowned journalist and author, similarly and explicitly, had a mission to comprehend, present, and counteract evil. As a child, Sereny (2001) was also swept along during a Nazi demonstration. With this first-hand experience, she knew how easy it was to be lured, and this sparked her interest in understanding and counteracting evil (ibid.). It should be noted that Bergman in his movies does not portray Christianity benevolently, whereas Jewish characters are often positively presented (Zern, 1993). In *Fanny and Alexander*, this is pushed to the very limit. While Freud presents the Jewish people as of lower descent in *Moses and Monotheism* (1939–1964), in *Fanny and Alexander* the Jews are the Noble ones and the Christians are the abject. Isak is included in the Ekdahl family. Vergérus remains an evil outsider (Zern, 1993).

Vergérus represents wickedness underneath a polished and stable surface, whereas Isak represents humanity and kindness. I suggest that when Bergman shows Isak as somewhat careless with the truth, he is doing this in order to present Isak as a complex human being. As with anyone, Isak has less appealing characteristics alongside positive ones. As human beings we all have our struggles, and we cannot always resist our evil inclinations: the Yetzer hara (Towers, 2018). So, when Bergman reveals Isak as a liar, he makes Isak fully human and thereby more credible. Had he been all-good, the movie would have been too sentimental, as some critics (in my opinion wrongly) perceive it. Moreover, Bergman shows the double standard of the Swedish society (and of course other societies as well). *Fanny and Alexander* unfolds between 1907 and 1909. By this time in Sweden, Jewish people were often perceived and portrayed as greedy and obsessed with money. Simultaneously, Jews were expected to contribute to financial development and money lending, and were included in Swedish society if they accepted this role (Bredefeldt, 2011). Bergman also shows how the Swedish clergy were particularly hostile to Jews who established themselves in Sweden during the 18th and 19th century (ibid.).

It should be noted that the preoccupation with money is central to more or less all the adult characters in *Fanny and Alexander*. The movie is centered on affluent people who hold positions of power, and who are careless with the truth and often with money. In the midst of this, Isak is kind, calm, and wise, and harbors unique magical powers that he uses to save the children.

From the vicarage, the children are brought to Isak's antique shop, which is also his home. In this labyrinthic place, cluttered with antique objects, Isak lives with his nephews, Aron and Ismael. Bergman's (1983) manuscript explains that Isak never sells anything. The objects are just there; frightening, overwhelming, mysterious, but also beautiful, meaningful, and exciting. Isak and Aron tell the children about Ismael, who may be awake and singing at night, and who is ill. Therefore, the door to his room must always be closed. A bedroom has been prepared for Fanny and Alexander. Isak and Aron help the children to bed and Isak reads to them.

After the rescue of the children, Carl and Gustav try to bargain with Vergérus to make him accept a divorce so that Emelie and the children can be free. Vergérus refuses and underlines that he is the stepfather and accordingly the legal guardian of the children. The scene shows that the bishop's financial situation is deplorable and his indebtedness have been acquired by Gustaf. Thereby, the depth of the double standards of Vergérus are revealed. This sharpens the image of the bishop as the one who is greedy and untrustworthy. Through projection, his own greediness has been transferred to Jews in general, and to Isak specifically.

In 1986, Erland Josephson, who played Isak, published a fictional book named *Loppans kvällsvard* (The flea's supper) (Josephson, 1986). The blurb says that it is a book about the roles we all have to play when we express ourselves, and about truth and lies. The lyrical self, Gabriel, is an aging actor who in his last role portrayed an old Jewish man in a movie directed by an assimilated Jewish man. As much as about roles, the book is (according to me) about Jewish identity and the blurred boundaries of characteristics, stereotypes, and anti-Semitism. When Gabriel was young, he flirted with fascism and anti-Semitism. Later he realized that he had Jewish ancestors. When playing the role, he embraces his Jewish heritage. Or does he? Josephson directly and indirectly poses a number of questions. Has Gabriel appropriated a Jewish identity in order to gloss over his fascist and anti-Semitic past? The thought of glossing over past flirtations with fascism, Nazism, and anti-Semitism could be an allusion to Bergman. Is Gabriel's portrayal of the old Jewish man empathic, or does he exaggerate Jewish characteristics to such an extent that it becomes an anti-Semitic stereotype? Does Jewish heritage permit such a portrayal, and can characteristics be equated with stereotypes and racism? Should traditional Jewish characteristics be wiped out in order not to arouse any references to anti-Semitism? Josephson gives no answers. Rather, he shows that these questions cannot be avoided. To avoid Jewish characteristics would be a form of exclusion, to portray them is to run the risk of invoking anti-Semitism. It is a problem with no solution, a question with no answer.

It is difficult to read *Loppans kvällsvard* without reference to Josephson's role in *Fanny and Alexander*. Josephson seems to ponder Isak Jacobi's position in the movie, his own portrayal of Isak, and Bergman's approach to the Jewish people and his own past. In many movies Josephson portrayed Bergman's alter ego (Gentele, 2012). In *Loppans kvällsvard*, he questions all identities and simultaneously portrays and dissolves the boundaries between them. Similarly, Isak's nephew Ismael dissolves the boundaries between identities, time, and space and thereby conquers Vergérus. So, let's return to Isak's home, the sleeping children, and Ismael who is often awake at night.

Encountering Ismael

Alexander wakes up in the middle of the night. He needs to find a bathroom and leaves the bedroom. He sees objects that are moving, in the master bedroom he sees Isak and Aron sleeping, and suddenly he is lost in the labyrinth of rooms, floors, stairs, and corridors. He encounters Oscar who sighs and says that he cannot leave them. Alexander asks Oscar to ask God to kill the bishop. The next scene portrays a course of events at the vicarage. Emily gives Vergérus sleeping pills while he looks after his aunt. Vergérus admits to Emily that he is afraid of Alexander.

Then the camera returns to Alexander who sees a door opening and hears a voice saying, "It is God behind the door." Alexander asks God to show himself. "No living being may see God's face," the voice responds, but thereafter says, "Now you will see me." The walls and cupboards start shaking and God is suddenly seen, wearing sandals and a red robe, notably similar to both Michelangelo's Moses and to Sigmund Freud. But God falls to the floor. He is just a large doll, created and handled by Aron, who is a puppeteer. Aron and Alexander hear Ismael singing. Aron tells Alexander that Ismael cannot stand human beings, and when he is furious, he is dangerous. Aron also says that nothing happens by chance, nothing is meaningless, and many things cannot be explained. He shows Alexander an ancient mummy that breaths and glows and says that the inexplicable makes people angry. Then he uses his hand to make the mummy turn its head. We then see Elsa, Vergérus' aunt, in bed, turning her head. But we are soon back with Aron and Alexander. Aron continues talking to Alexander, as if he is educating him, and says that everything is alive. Everything is God or God's thought, not only the good but also the cruel, the evil. And then they go to Ismael to serve him breakfast. Back at the vicarage we see Vergérus waking up, feeling bad, and Emile tells him that she gave him sleeping pills.

Ismael asks Aron to leave. He tells Alexander, "I am considered dangerous," and asks Alexander to write his name on a piece of paper. Alexander writes and the text says "Ismael Retzinsky." "Perhaps we are the same, perhaps we have no boundaries," Ismael says and continues; "You carry terrible thoughts, both painful and alluring. The evil thought can travel." Ismael also explains that Alex now is talking through Ismael.

Thereafter, we see Elsa reaching for a kerosene lamp, pushing it to the floor. A fire breaks out. "Don't hesitate," Ismael says to Alexander. While Ismael tells Alexander what is happening, we see the burning Elsa running from her room. Alexander wants to avoid everything but Ismael tells him not to be afraid, "I am with you." Elsa sets fire to Vergérus and the vicarage is burning.

Ismael is an enigmatic character, played by female actor Stina Ekblad which accentuates the transgressive element of the scene. Ismael continues the mystical interventions that were initiated by Isak. Ismael can also be understood as representing the shadow side of human nature, the evil force that exists in all of us, with all its desires (Berke & Schneider, 2006). One can see Ismael as Alexander's animal soul. It is also possible to understand the events as portraying magical forces that intervene and change the course of the story. If we adapt to this interpretation, we may see the scene as an acknowledgment of magic and mysticism. Bergman most likely understood that some critics and viewers would perceive this as a shortcoming (Bundtzen, 1987). I believe that he did not mind. After all, his autobiography was called *Laterna Magica* (Bergman, 1987).

Fanny and Alexander, the Myth and the Father

Fanny and Alexander is a story about a young boy who is taken from his family, defeats a father figure, is rescued and reunited with his family of origin. This is in line with Freud's (1939) presentation of the myth of the hero as a boy.

Both Bergman and Freud struggle with their father figure(s), including God, and place psychological emphasis on the father, sometimes to the extent that the mother – and the relationship to her – is neglected (Whitebook, 2017). It should be noted that even though this specific text concerns father figures, relationships to the mother and to mother figures are equally important. Yerushalmi (1991) describes *Moses and Monotheism* (1939) as a form of reconciliation between Freud and his father, Jakob, since Freud – through engaging with Moses, Judaism, and Jewish identity – follows the suggestion from his father to return to the Bible. Yerushalmi refers here to an inscription in Hebrew in an old family Bible that Jakob restored and gave to Freud on his thirty-fifth birthday.

Freud seemed assured that Jakob was his father. As a young boy, however, Freud had fantasized about another father – a more heroic father, like Hannibal – who did not have to endure anti-Semitic threats and abuse. When anti-Semitism increased, Freud's identification with his Jewish heritage increased, and he openly came to identify as Jewish. To this, we can add that we all struggle with our identities and with coming to terms with our heritage and our relationships to members of our family. Freud repeatedly investigated how we as human beings are involved in dramas and complexes with our close family members. The professor was, however, not always right, as Hilda Doolittle – poet and one of Freud's analysands – wrote (H.D., 1956). Of course, he was not always right. No human being is always right. Specifically, when it came to femininity, the psychology of women, and the development of girls, Freud lacked the capacity to understand; something he admitted himself (Freud,1925; Whitebook, 2017). This should, however, not obscure his insights regarding the position of the father(s) and the family as a system of explicit and implicit relationships. Despite his shortcomings, Freud was able to illuminate the family dramas, complexities, and failures with which every human being has to live, manage, and perhaps overcome. We are murderous, envious and demanding, and unfortunately, we never forget. Even if we think we have forgotten our destructive inclinations and the wrongdoings of ourselves and others, our super-egos, bodies, and mood states remind us of them (Sletvold, 2013). The superego is formed through identification with others, those who are close to us, but also from the heritage and culture in which we live. Christian heritage positions itself as centered on forgiveness and turning the other cheek, so to speak. The family drama of Jesus is modest: Jesus is the son, the only son. Christianity is a son–religion, and the son is presented as goodness personified. The Jewish heritage is a father–religion with roots in biblical narratives that involve patricide, fratricide, betrayal, and revenge – good and evil exist everywhere. Moreover, Freud was firmly rooted in the ideal of Bildung, with a lifelong interest and deep knowledge in mythology, specifically Greek mythology, and he knew both Latin and ancient Greek (Richards, 2014). The stories from the Torah as well as the stories from Greek mythology comprise several murderous, peccable, and revengeful themes. An obvious example is Abraham, who is prepared to murder his own son, if God wants him to do so. For Freud, it was not strange or scandalous to acknowledge and investigate the evil inclinations, violence, envy, and intrigues that take place between siblings, children, parents, caretakers, and the extended family. For despite the widespread idea that Freud was an advocate for the bourgeoise nuclear family, he was open for various forms of living together. He for example encouraged H.D. to live her life as a bisexual woman, together with men and women who had various gender expressions and sexualities (H.D., 1956; Friedman, 2002). He also lived his own life in various forms of extended families (Molnar, 2015; Whitebook, 2017).

Moses and Monotheism is a multilayered text. *Fanny and Alexander* is a multilayered movie. The text has sometimes been dismissed, as if it was unworthy, as below Freud's level. Likewise, the movie has been dismissed as superficial, below Bergman's level. In these two creations realism, mysticism, religion, imagination, and mythology are intermingled. They need interpretation. As both Judaism and psychoanalysis tell us, there are many layers that need to be understood. Topics that are concealed or implicit may be equally – or even more important – than explicit ones.

For example, there is a concealed Freud (Berke & Schneider, 2006). It is well known that Freud wanted to prove psychoanalysis as a real science, and made great attempts to shield psychoanalysis from being the target of anti-Semitism. Berke (2015) argues that Freud's Kabbalistic and Chassidic heritage – including their mystical elements, as well as the connections between psychoanalysis and

Jewish traditions – are profound. Freud was a target of anti-Semitism and therefore carefully contemplated what should and should not be revealed. Given the extreme anti-Semitism of his time, Freud's decision to conceal his Jewish heritage (Gilman, 1993) and the connections to mysticism is understandable, not least since connections to Jewish mysticism could invoke the anti-Semitic stereotype of the Jew as a quack and a fraud (Gilman, 1991).

But to others, mysticism has positive connotations. To H.D., mysticism was a part of life. In *Tribute to Freud* (1956), she describes how Freud took mysticism, religion, and mythology seriously, even if he did not always agree with her ideas about mysticism and magic. In *The Master* (1983), H.D. writes that Freud held mysteries, and she describes his writings as sacred. In *Fanny and Alexander*, Bergman also takes mysticism and magic seriously. When Isak rescues the children, time and space are transgressed. Thereby mysticism and magic become natural parts of the story. And throughout the movie, Oscar transgresses time and space as well as physical boundaries when he returns as a ghost.

It should be noted that Oscar's wife, Emilie, had affairs with other men. Oscar is not the biological father of the children. This is explicitly stated both in the movie and in the book (Bergman, 1983). Oscar permitted her affairs and was a true father to the children. He clearly loved them. Indeed, he loved them so much that he could not let go of them, his soul returned.

A family is more than biological kinship, a father is more than the biological connection. The position(s) of the father(s) in *Fanny and Alexander* resemble the position(s) of the father(s) in *Moses and Monotheism* (Freud, 1939). There are various father figures and various symbolic fathers, including God himself. In *Fanny and Alexander* and in *Moses and Monotheism* some father figures are defeated or even killed, while others are loved and identified with.

I want to acknowledge that Helena and Isak had been lovers. Oscar was the oldest son. In the book that accompanies the film, Bergman (1983) reveals that Helena, before she was married, had the name Mandelbaum. This is a Jewish name. Was she closer to Isak than what was disclosed? Could Isak be the father of Oscar? When the children are reunited with their family of origin, the family includes Isak and Oscar's ghost. A family is not an unambiguous or unified entity, something Freud makes clear in *Moses and Monotheism* (1939), sometimes the father is the biological father, sometimes he is not. Freud also asks if there is a Jewish essence that mysteriously is inherited from generation to generation? Such a question is not easily answered. As Josephson (1986) describes, characteristics, stereotypes, and racism are close to each other. What even is an essence? Freud was not sure himself. In the preface to the Hebrew translation of *Totem and Taboo*, Freud asks himself what is there left of him that is Jewish? He responds to his own question with the following words: "A very great deal, probably its very essence" (Freud, 1913).

In *Fanny and Alexander*, Bergman provides a possible answer to the question of identity and essence, through showing that biological essence and biological kinships may not be the most important. What is important for Alexander is to challenge his father figure(s), as well as his origin and himself; to believe in magic, to find his own way – with the support of others and while supporting others – and to return to his family of origin. To return to the family of origin is to return to those who love you, and perhaps to return to your very essence.

Bibliography

Aronson, S. (2010). "The Problem of Desire: Psychoanalysis as a Jewish Wisdom Tradition." In *Answering a Question With a Question. Contemporary Psychoanalysis and Jewish Thought*, edited by Lewis Aron and Libby Henik. Brighton: Academic Studies Press, pp.313–326.

Bergman, I. (1983). *Fanny and Alexander*. Stockholm: Norstedts.

Bergman, I. (1987). *Laterna Magica*. Stockholm: Norstedts.

Berke, J. H. (2015). *The Hidden Freud: His Hassidic Roots*. London: Karnac.

Berke, J. H., and Schneider, S. (2006). "The Self and the Soul." *Mental Health, Religion & Culture*, 9: 333–354.

Bredefeldt, R. (2011). *De Svenska judarna. 1782–1930. Ekonomiska strategier, självuppfattning och assimilering [The Swedish Jews: Financial Strategies, Self-Conceptualization and Assimilation]*. Uppsala: Hugo Valentin-centrum.

Bundtzen, L. (1987). "Bergman's 'Fanny and Alexander': Family Romance or Artistic Allegory?" *Criticism*, 29: 89–117.

Cushman, P. (2010). "A Burning World, an Absent God: Midrash, Hermeneutics, and Relational Psychoanalysis." In *Answering a Question With a Question: Contemporary Psychoanalysis and Jewish Thought*, edited by Lewis Aron and Libby Henik. Brighton: Academic Studies Press, pp. 369–404.

Freud, S. (1913). "Totem and Taboo." In *The Standard Edition of the Complete Psychological Works of Sigmund Freud (SE)* XIII. London: Hogarth Press, pp. 1–255.

Freud, S. (1925). "Some Psychical Consequences of the Anatomical Distinction Between the Sexes." In *SE XIX*. London: Hogarth Press, pp. 241–258.

Freud, S. (1939). "Moses and Monotheism." In *SE XXIII*. London: Hogarth Press, pp. 17–55.

Friedman, S. S. (2002). *Analyzing Freud: Letters of H.D., Bryher, and Their Circle*. New York: New Directions.

Gentele, J. (2012). "Josephson i filmen. [Josephson in the Movies]." *Svenska Dagbladet*. Retrieved December 13, 2021. https://www.svd.se/josephson-i-filmen.

Gilman, S. (1991). *The Jew's Body*. New York: Routledge.

Gilman, S. (1993). *Freud, Race and Gender*. Princeton, NJ: Princeton University Press.

H.D. (1956). *Tribute to Freud*. New York: New Directions.

H.D. (1983). "The Master." In *H.D. Collected Poems. 1912–1944*, edited by Louis L. Martz. New York: New Directions, pp. 451–461.

Josefsson, E. (2012). "Sprituell resonör har gått ur tiden. [Witty Arguer Passes Away]." *Göteborg-Posten*. Retrieved December 13, 2021. https://www.gp.se/kultur/kultur/spirituell-reson%C3%B6r-har-g%C3%A5tt-ur-tiden-1.699056.

Josephson, E. (1986). *Loppans kvällsvard [The Flea's Supper]*. Stockholm: Brombergs.

Koskinen, M., and Rohdin, M. (2005). *Fanny och Alexander. Ur Ingmar Bergmans arkiv och hemliga gömmor|Fanny and Alexander: From Ingmar Bergman's Archives and Hiding-Places]*. Stockholm: Wahlström & Widstrand.

Molnar, Michael. 2015. *Looking through Freud's photos*. London: Karnac Books.

Ohlin, P. (2009). "Bergman's Nazi Past." *Scandinavian Studies*, 84: 437–474.

Richards, A. D. (2014). "Freud's Jewish Identity and Psychoanalysis as a Science." *Journal of the American Psychoanalytic Association*, 62: 987–1003.

Sereny, G. (2001). *The German Trauma: Experiences and Reflections, 1938–2001*. London: Penguin.

Sletvold, J. (2013). "The Ego and the Id Revisited: Freud and Damasio on the Body Ego/Self." *The International Journal of Psychoanalysis*, 94: 1019–1032.

Towers, S. (2018). "The Rabbis, Gender, and the Yetzer Hara: The Origins and Development of the Evil Inclination." *Women in Judaism*, 15: 1–20.

Whitebook, J. (2017). *Freud: An Intellectual Biography*. Cambridge: Cambridge University Press.

Yerushalmi, Y. H. (1991). *Freud's Moses: Judaism Terminable and Interminable*. New Haven: Yale University Press.

Zern, L. (1993). *Se Bergman [See Bergman]*. Stockholm: Natur & Kultur.

Chapter 10

Prolegomena to *Persona*

As Existential Psychoanalysis

Walter A. Davis

for Bibi Andersson

Once and Again: Bergman and Existentialism

There was a time when meadow, grove, and stream did seem appareled in celestial light … and then a time when existentialism was all the rage and Ingmar Bergman, concurrently, esteemed as the world's greatest filmmaker. Now both have been relegated to the dust bin of history: existentialism reduced to a few faddish memes about angst, the absurd, and the intense inane; Bergman fast fading as a bad dream, consigned to the dust bin of Hobbesian memory as decaying sense.[1]

There's a justice to this. We deserve to lose what we fail to comprehend. And with that recognition, a chance to advance a rigorous concept of existence and to restore Bergman's *Persona* (1966) to its place as (arguably) the greatest film ever made. And in *Persona* a further boon: a fusion of existentialism and psychoanalysis as the framework required for an in-depth understanding of human drama, in art and in life. For Drama is the being of the subject, awake and asleep; these the necessarily interconnected ways that the activity of the Unconscious subjects us – in anxiety – to inner conflicts that we cannot escape.

Cinema for Bergman: The Fusion of Dream and Reality

Thus cinema is that art form uniquely suited to dramatizing the ways in which dream and reality flow into and out of one another. In the projection of traumatic inner conflict, symptoms, fantasy, and desire, the ineluctable modality of the cinema, dream, and reality rub against one another, as they do throughout each day's long journey into night; the stream of consciousness ruptured repeatedly by suppressed conflicts projected, denied, and preserved as residues we take with us into that private theater of dream where the psyche suffers its buried life. Cinema offers a unique way of apprehending this drama, thanks to the ways it can deploy – and oppose – language and image as distinct modes of cognition and the primary dialectic whereby Bergman probes the psyche.[2]

DOI: 10.4324/9781003200246-11

Interpretive Method

The act of interpretation is an attempt to apprehend the unity of a work's structure and thereby the dynamic, organic function of every cinematic and psychological principle that enters into its construction. Several mutually reinforcing structures can be established in *Persona*. Foremost among them, that of a five act psycho-drama (identified by titles and subtitles in what follows), requiring for its understanding some of the now standard categories of recent Lacanian film theory (Gaze and Voice, the *object a*, Anxiety, the Real, *Das Ding*, Desire, feminine *jouissance*, subjective destitution) supplemented by concepts central to a distinct theory of the psyche that I've developed over the years.[3] I introduce them here in general terms, *Persona* as drama providing their concretization.

Toward Existence

Two Basic Contrasts

Ego – A false identity based on the defenses that protect us from the (repressed) conflicts of our inner world.

Psyche – The core conflicts defining the anguish of one's relationship to oneself.

Emotion – The ways of feeling whereby one discharges threats to the ego.

Affect – The burden and torment of an assault within the psyche threatening one's ability to go on being.

The Dynamics of Self-Reference

Subject as who/why – That "I am" (beyond all *cogitos*) brought into being through the traumatic experience of humiliation and cruelty. As who/why one is living out two questions: who am I to be so vulnerable that the other has the power to destroy me? Why would anyone attempt to do that to another?

Subjectivity – The "I am" felt and experienced as the agent underlying the stream of consciousness in its connection to the Unconscious as the force that ruptures that stream.

Experience – (a difference that makes a difference) is the dynamic dialectical connection between being-in-the-world as engagement with what's going on within the psyche.

Inwardness – That ongoing meditation on one's existence sustained as sufferance, memory, and reflection on those experiences with which one can never really be done because they engage one's deepest conflicts.

The Primacy and Depth of Inner Conflict

Core Conflicts – Those conflicts in which Love and Hate toward the other and toward oneself are fused. This is how the psyche experiences the persistence of its origin: the imposition of the m/other's conscious and unconscious conflicts as demands for self-sacrifice as the price of love, as such core conflicts form the basis of how one acts in all complex relations with others.

Sexuality – Core conflicts expressed as bodily clash of eros and trauma in an inescapable drama experienced with immediacy. Sexuality thus not one of the things we do, but who we are. Spinoza's unity of Mind and Body thereby rethought and concretized. For mind read *psyche*. For body read *sexuality*.

Eros and Thanatos: Psyche vs. Super-ego – The ultimate terms of the inner drama that defines the psyche as the process whereby we either capitulate to soul–murder (becoming ego, "I," as death-in-life) or risk our being through actions aimed at engaging and reversing the power/voice of the other planted in us.

Drama as Existentializing Process

Existence – The very being of a psyche once stripped of all defenses, burdened with its core conflicts in the necessity of finding the agency and actions required to engage them. Existence is psyche at issue and at risk with no essence or guarantees (in the order of nature or of culture) to which one can appeal for deliverance from an absolute responsibility. Existentialism is not a humanism. We only exist when all the old meanings and guarantees have been, with the ego, consigned to the flames.

Drama – Psyche and existence fused in irreversible developments. I am who I become through the agency I attain by the actions I perform whenever my core conflicts are engaged. Taking action within, as the only way to sustain external action as a deepening crucible of conflict, crisis – and change.

Anxiety – The affect revealing that a traumatic conflict has erupted, as well as the dynamic whereby it is sustained. Persistence in anxiety is the process whereby a subject earns dramatic agency in an existence projected beyond the limits of ego, symptom, fantasy, and desire. Anxiety as an assault from within that is first experienced as a visceral mania threatening psychic dissolution. As such, anxiety is the origin and driving force in all feelings, both in those primary affects (dread, melancholia, love …) whereby we sustain the possibility of affective self-mediation and in those emotions (pity, fear, apathy …) through which we extinguish it. This is another way of saying how deep and dark *Persona* is, how easy and safe it is to reduce its action or plot to more manageable (literalizing) parameters, and why its understanding requires a consecutive scene-by-scene analysis explaining each fundamental psychological change.[4]

Prologue: In Dreams Begin Responsibilities

Persona begins with a montage of traumatic images – fragmentation, regression, manic movement – in discontinuous leaps; a psyche threatened with dissolution seeking some way to stop the chaotic flow. "The impatience of the film to begin," according to Bergman (Shargel, 2007, p. 86), to find some way to stem a tormented self-fragmenting; some central scene where one might coalesce as a subject in the anxiety of an impossible desire from which, nonetheless, some dramatic narrative might emerge. This is not dream as wish fulfillment, but rather dream as the psyche's representation of its inner constitution;[5] the anguish of a self-persecutory condition. There is no censor here. No displacement. Desire and anxiety are fused in a traumatic search for some rudimentary coherence of psyche; some way to go back from the adult you are to the age you were when some wound changed everything (that age itself a displacement of a prior wound more deeply repressed). Such dreams, in creative regression, ransack the past, seeking to return to where the psyche is blocked, and thus within the montage, images recapitulate Bergman's career as a filmmaker – failures recalled to be cast aside in quest for a deeper, darker probing of death–work within the psyche. Thereby, the first unity: that of place. A morgue and a procession of the dead laid out on slabs. Among them, apparently, a pubescent boy under a sheet. But no, we learn he is the dreamer, awakened. Soon to seek to touch the face of a woman separated from him by some transparent pane, he moves his hand all over, as if to caress that face or trace its image as it dissolves into the face of another woman, her face soon dissolving back into the first, now out of focus, blurred, her eyes then shut, like those of the dead – and out of that the title and the credits, intervening among them further images, some seen before, others new.[6]

Four images singled out define a structure. The very first image – excised from the American release – an erect penis, as if to signify that all will take place under the sign of the phallic signifier; or the desire for the same. From hectic fragmentation ensuing, to the first coalescence, among the dead – an older woman on a slab, seen upside down; her eyes suddenly snap open, staring at us. The third, a boy awakened by the sound of a phone and unable to sleep again, sitting, facing us, reaching out his hand as if to touch us; this same image is then seen from behind, the hand now extended toward the face of a woman, whose face covers the entire movie screen, from which he (like us) is separated by some barrier, with the image receding the more ardently he reaches out toward it.

The fourth image is included with the credits: an image that could only appear once the film has begun, slipped in between the names of Bibi Andersson and Liv Ullmann – a woman's lips, turned sideways – mouth that would speak, kiss, imaged as vaginal antithesis to the initial phallic signifier … or rendered a mute medusa, anxiety in its pure state threatening to engulf the psyche, and as such something you can only let yourself see in a flash set between the two actresses cast as protagonists in some oneiric attempt to split the good mother from the bad, thereby securing at least the possibility of the love you were denied.

Act One: The Ego and the Psyche

Cast of Characters

Alma – A (psychiatric) nurse, helper of troubled souls; a woman possessed of an identity firmly rooted in normalcy. Her life mapped out: the stable fiancé, the future as wife and mother. Two signs alone betray something else beneath the surface: her hands behind her back tightly knotted while briefed on a patient, and a tic (a symptom), the unconscious habit of smoothing back and in place the hair on her forehead, as she does just before she enters the room where that patient lies.

Elisabet – An actress suffering a prolonged depression, silent as the grave. Its onset: three months before, during a performance of *Elektra* she stopped, silent and motionless for over a minute before continuing. Afterword, she confessed a sudden desire to laughter. And yet the voice-over providing this information is accompanied by an image revealing the terror, suffering, panic, and rage Elisabet felt before seizing on laughter as a way out (thereby introduced along with this character, the difference between word and image as ways of representing the psyche).

The contrast joined. Alma offers Elisabet the sedation of a radio play. A soap opera full of trite dialogue – a woman begging forgiveness, asking for love. Elisabet, in rage, shuts off the radio; then affecting great suffering, grabs Alma's hand, seeking comfort. Alma, in reply, offers banal words about her respect for art and actors, leaving Elisabet alone but with music now playing on the radio – the slow movement from Bach's E major violin concerto.

Inwardness: The Face

Words appall and enrage Elisabet. Music taps into something deeper, and with it one of cinemas defining powers – the close-up. For seventy seconds, ever closer, the camera studies this face as day passes into twilight, then night. Image without word, soliciting something deeper in us. This is a moment out of time, a singular beauty suggesting a psychological depth we alone can constitute, by projecting our psyche into hers.

A woman's face. *Mona Lisa* – enigma and threat. *Girl with a Pearl Earring* – sexuality at the moment of its astonished birth and violation, seized by a gaze of male desire. Elisabet – beauty as an infinite depth of suffering, plumbed in the sublime pleasure of holding a beautiful woman captive to every pulse and tangle of desire. For this is a face you can lose yourself in, as Bergman did, his camera a caress; his own inwardness torn open by some lure of the eternal feminine, deepening as light passes to twilight, then night.

This, the camera affirms, is not a role but rather what Elisabet feels when alone, who she is as she opens herself to Bach, what she feels in an inwardness penetrated by the camera (as you would, as lover, her body). To drown in an eternal silence. Not Elisabet as we first meet her – face caked thick with makeup, a histrionic *Elektra* in tragic mask under the hot lights, acting a role, performing emotions – but Elisabet in deepest subjectivity, delivered over to us, a psyche plumbed by losing yourself in her face.

Or this the moment in which inwardness as depth of feeling is asserted, so that it can later be questioned. The camera eye moves ever further into this face, as if certain to find an answer to the question a man asks of a beautiful face, especially when privileged to view it in the solitude of her intimate communing with herself. What is she thinking? What does a woman want? Who is she in her inviolable privacy – and why is it then that I most desire her? What is her secret? What the truth of femininity reveals when there is no mask or masquerade, and I am free to plunge ever deeper into that face, aided as prompter to her response, my bewitchment, the Bach slow movement – at twilight, with the shift to the minor key as darkness first encroaches. This was the first film Liv Ullmann made with Bergman. "He moved his camera so close to my face," she said, "that most of the time I thought I was acting only for him."[7] Which, of course, is prescient and true – as evident here in an image that passes from sadness to some inconsolable grief as she turns away; a shadow now in profile as she covers her face with her hands ... Or was all that depth merely our projection, aided by Bergman's direction, Sven Nykvist's lighting and Ullmann's ability to hold a pose without letting feelings intervene?

The myriad questions we bring to the endless fascinations of this face become, as we lose her to darkness, the tug of something profound in the heart; the final hook luring you as surely as the Siren's would, through the deep solitude of an unappeasable suffering. For what better lure to snare the deepest desire? To be the one who gives the other what she lacks, through love – an Orpheus come to make her whole and well again, as only your love can.[8]

And for the female viewer, perhaps the seductions of an equally troubled passage – the lure of being so idolized, so caught up, so mastered by the brute blood of the mesmerized male gaze, arrested by the power of Beauty. As if it, too, were not a mask in which beautiful women perish, each alone, unable to communicate an inwardness antithetical to the needs and demands projected?

Catechism: The Restless Sleeper

We pass, with relief and rue, to Alma, like the boy in the morgue – a restless sleeper – on whom Elisabet's face has also made an impression. Something anxious opened up in her by Elisabet, awakened to that which begins as a probing inner monologue: "It's funny, you can go about as you please ... do almost anything ..." abruptly arrested by a catechism proclaiming her complete adaptation to normalcy; an ego restored by reciting its articles of faith, soothing as surely as the lotion auto-erotically applied to her body. "It's a safe feeling." Repressions restored, rest, save for a question taken with her into sleep – "I wonder what's really wrong with her" – and a name, "Elisabet Vogler," spoken in darkness, in incantation, like a voice calling to Alma from deep within.

Cut back to Elisabet, for whom Bach has not provided passage into sleep that knits up the raveled sleeve of care. Elisabet is restless, pacing, her shadow on the wall huge, looming over her; light from a TV; language – a reporter's voice, objective, dispassionate, droning on with statistics, a body count as accompaniment to the Artaudian image: a Buddhist monk immolating himself to protest the

Vietnam war, in disciplined suffering "still signaling through the flames."[9] That image registered in Elisabet's face, her eyes in close-up, registering horror, backing her into a corner, mouth wide open in a silent howl. It's as if the suffering seen previously on her face was a mask, a role, and this the real thing. A psyche ruptured from within by the traumatic force of a true image, which she must take into herself, or falsify the ethical choice informing her silence – to internalize suffering, its acolyte in duty sustained until she's reached its limit, thereby realizing what Bergman stated as his goal in the film.

A Letter from Home

But only artists and saints believe in such suffering. We return to its proximate cause: a letter from Elisabet's husband read to her by Alma, impassively, without comprehension. His words (reminiscent of that radio soap opera) passive–aggressive, manipulative, and sentimental, proclaiming the truth of an evident falsehood: "You have taught me we must look upon each other as two anxious children." Elisabet's words quoted back to her, her cry of desperation transformed into a testament of marital fidelity in order to deny another image: Elisabet (in sexual hunger, and in rage) grabbing him by the belt – just as she now grabs and crumbles the letter – and with it, later after a long pause, his final ploy – a photo of their son she tore in two. She will be true, in silence and isolation, to another suffering.

Psychiatric Diagnosis

Which must be diagnosed after all is not the role of psychiatry to set our minds at rest through analytic mastery of the causes and cures for neurotic misery?

And so, equally cryptic and cruel, an analysis of the shrink's analysis of Elisabet. A contradiction defines it as classic countertransference revenge: a frustrated analyst invoking a rich existential problematic, only to reduce it, and Elisabet, to self-indulgent role playing. "The dream of being" (for which read *existential authenticity*) invoked, then mocked, to proclaim a void where one hoped to find a subject. The one authentic desire: extinction. One's true face, a grimace. And all roles – especially motherhood – a torment for anyone capable of self-contempt. All this insight then disavowed, blown away by the assertion that it, too, is a role – with boredom the sole cause and source of change.

An ironic shrink, post-modern before the fact. Authenticity, a word. Anxiety, a delusion. In the strength of will Alma intuited in Elisabet, the shrink sees only bad acting, the folly and fraud of inwardness. So simple Elisabet's malaise, the only cure warranted – a month in the country.

But as we depart for some pastoral comedy of the cure, a pause to offer a different diagnosis; and as its complement, a psychological portrait of Alma.

Elisabet – I am, as existentialized subject, an absolute break with everything I've been as an artist and as a person; a self-consciousness sustained by a single awareness. Suffering is the primary reality, internalizing the trauma of the real is my project. Suffering engages psyche in the one true dialectic – with the violence of the world sounding a call to what's buried within but accessible only through a Heideggerian silent waiting, attuned by melancholia. Silence as ethical act.[10] An ethic of abjection and thereby a recovery of all she experienced that night on stage before the flight into laughter. Silence sustaining what is not a role but – in Hegelese, the very labor of the negative – an overture perhaps to suicidal despair, but in a rage against all lies, all fake emotions. In their place a new desire: to live out the recognition that for her there is no other anymore, only a solitude from which perhaps one can never return, or self-contempt if pulled back into life by the persistence of old habits and needs. Against that threat, an art of suffering nurtured through images of abjection (a monk on TV, later a photo from the Warsaw ghetto). Silence the only way to stay attuned to what spoken words destroy; fragmentation and self-dissolution – inner death – the risk one must run in order to exist.

Alma – Initially, an ego identity tightly bound to defenses proclaimed in catechistic affirmation; a babble of adaptational verities, everything in order within; psyche a matter of repeatable words, the future thereby mapped; everything within that might disrupt the defense ego banished, everything without that might have threatened it (such as art) contained through condescending truisms. As capstone, one's goodness assured by one's vocation: one's role as nurse and nurturer, health personified. In process, an ego disrupted by the stirring of desires buried deep within, defenses now asserted under a strain, anxiety nibbling away at all her beliefs. And in the other now, not safety, but the promise of some hidden treasure (*agalma*), and thereby a chance to recover all that she's split off and repressed in herself; compelled to speak in an attempt to fathom desires she would disavow were it not for Elisabet, this silent other unique to her, in whom she sees her chance to share things she's never been able to put into words.

Act Two: The Drama of Desire

In the Country: The Health Cure

For the filmmaker, too, a chance to begin again, returning to the image that gave birth to the work. Two women at a table outdoors, humming as they clean mushrooms. One gently takes the other's hand, tenderly held in overture to intimacy from which the other quickly withdraws. Yet she remains so haunted by this gesture that by evening it will birthe a tidal wave of self-disclosure. To which we add the ironic fact: Elisabet is the one who reaches out to take the other's hand, in thanksgiving for nurturing, in recognition of a need for intimacy … as a ploy to draw the other into her web? Or all of the above …

Something has changed in Alma, too, her fascination with Elisabet having given birth to an unexpected choice of reading material: some pop–existential tome about forlornness and terror, a passage from which she reads to Elisabet, asking her opinion. To Elisabet's nod of assent, Alma's vigorous denial – in perfect illustration of Freud's theory of negation as a sign of disavowed desires.

The Perfect Analytic Session: Feminine Jouissance and the Subject Supposed to Know

Which brings us to evening and within a confessional tale – seven of the most erotic minutes in the history of cinema. Also the perfect analytic session. In Lacanese, Elisabet – as subject supposed to know – sits in sublime sphinx-like silence, drawing forth from Alma one confession after another, each delving deeper toward recovery of desire.

Self-revelation in stages: first, free associative babble of ego identities ruptured by eruptions of recognitions that Alma's life has been that of a sleepwalker. Then, the one event that might have been real: a five-year affair with a married man, acknowledged as a dime store novel – his boredom, her disposability. Except for the suffering, "that was real." Yet unlike Elisabet's suffering, meaningless, save as spur for a gallop into normalcy. Against which memory re-awakened returns in creative regression to that one closely kept secret, that close pent-up guilt, never before revealed to another.

And so seven minutes of untrammeled eroticism, evoked then analyzed: a drowsy noon on a sunny beach on a deserted island. A vacation within a vacation, far from one's normal life – and one's intended. A moment, as it were, outside time. Sunbathing nude beside another woman, a stranger. Suddenly, as if materialization of fantasy, two boys appear on the rocks above, voyeurs to your companion's display of a brazen female nudity, turning over, as if in answer to their desire, while you remain frozen, bare bottom up. Yet somehow calm. And mesmerized by Katarina beside you "with her little breasts and thick thighs and great bush of hair." One of the boys approaches, squatting down beside her. You find yourself "all wet," yet still guarded, your hat over your face. Motionless you lay as they begin to fuck. But watching, stirred by the sexual proficiency of an experienced woman, using the man, a boy, for some perverse pleasure, her expert hands holding him "round his thin, hard bottom," laughing, muttering in his ear – then again sudden, grotesque, the sight of his "red face, sort of swollen" next to yours, and the words suddenly coming out of you, words you could never imagine saying, "Why not come to me, too?" Which he does, so encouraged by Katarina. Roughly he falls on you, painfully grabbing your breast, yet sudden, immediate your orgasm, stronger than ever before and again in hot quick pursuit his cum shooting into you, that, too, something you've never felt before – and now the miracle of your cumming, over and over, as if it would never end – this ravishment of flesh incarnate as an excess without limit or goal other than its own persistence, cleansing consciousness of every lie and inhibition. And with it, transformation. Katrina now the one watching yet participant, too, almost as if she's the one doing it to you, "holding her hand round his balls from behind." After which she services the other boy orally, your partner so excited by that sight you must have at it again "fast ... and as good ... as the first time," and with desire still randy in you that night, doing it with your fiancé, "better than ever before or since." No wonder. After all, Alma spent the afternoon in congress with a god.

A tale told – challenging the privilege thus far accorded image over word – and for the viewer a new experience: from words to create the image, voyeurism replaced by the projection of things far deeper in your psyche and thereby a chance to recover what porn takes away in its repetitive, joyless, and sweaty grinding away of mechanical couples. Here instead a true erotics, substituting for masturbatory self-indulgence, perilous possibilities and discoveries – even perhaps your own sexuality, like Alma's, something lost you might try to recover.

A tale told in a voice of "shameful lust" (Bergman's term of amazement for what Bibi Andersson here realizes), a great actress in this the deepest reach of her greatest performance, realizing an art that strips away all personae, revealing a psyche one with its words in naked self-revelation. Alma's psyche revealed at the very quick of any possible identity, in the drama of sexuality as the very pulse and determination of who we are: fantasy, desire, inner conflict, anxiety, and action here converging in bodily incarnation.

Therefore, for the analyst listening (Elisabet, Freud, Winnicott, Lacan), all that's needed to produce an in-depth interpretation, grounded in transference, knowledge of this above all. Alma's breathless narrative is the unbidden tendering of a free gift. One's secret – and in it one's subjectivity – open, vulnerable, delivered into another's hands as overture to love; recognition, in trust that the other would never appropriate it for any other purpose.

Also unknown to Alma is all she's revealed: the defining dynamics of feminine *jouissance* here expressed with utter lucidity – unbound excess, insatiability, an erotic power sustained in multiple orgasms. No end to this, this drenching in a flesh where lust triumphs over all defenses and anxieties. Inhibition, prohibition, shame (and its attendant affects) now spur to all identity obliterated in delirium, a ravaged affliction of flesh consumed in the phoenix of its burning.

Desire here is also experienced in a new freedom; a desire not triggered by a man but by another woman's boldness in foreplay, releasing Alma from all inner restraint. From this flows confirmation of a woman's power to reduce the male to something ugly, *de trop*, thing-like, and with nausea the goad to an impersonal and defiant sexual demand. Sex without tenderness, pain welcomed, part of the thrill of rutting, in orgasms immediate, intense, liberating a power beyond the phallus and all the restrictions that the typical male imposes, so that fucking will be the proof – to the fantasy witnesses and secret sharers, the other males in the room, watching – of a cock-crowing identity women must serve, doing whatever they must in bed to prop up the delusions – and disgusts – men require.

Over against that regime of pleasure as discharge of contempt, in feminine jouissance ravishment of multiple orgasms, radiating through the entire body, like some great river god in the blood, drenching psyche in an incarnate unity of flesh, in lust triumphant over all defenses and anxieties. For that's what lust is: a paroxysm of the psyche in contempt for all restraints, restrictions, prohibitions, and inhibitions, with shame the spice to an awe of astonished flesh, in pride of a liberation in an expenditure without reserve.

And for the Viewer, the Audience

For the Man – in anguish and protested, realization perhaps of why men hate and fear women, and why men invented morality – to impose their sexual limits on a superior power.

For the Woman – remorse of loss; possibility of liberation?

For the Analyst – knowledge that can be formulated in logical terms,[11] while exposing the contradictions and limits of the conceptual order; solid evidence here supplied in perceptual satisfaction of the Kantian requirement, a concept given in experience: woman as the *non-all*, without essence or limit, and with nothing intervening to inhibit the progressive unfolding of incarnate signifiers. No eternal feminine mystery to lurk in hiding, only this: sexuality as body/soul in fusion, flesh fully alive, desire become drive, still signaling through the flames of libidinal excess.

And for Alma – in her conscious mind, the split between her ego and her psyche no longer something she might repair; rather, what she must sustain in the annihilation of the former by the latter. That imperative delivered over to panic anxiety the moment her story ends and she finds herself caught again in the contradiction of being two people, one the bad conscience and super-ego attacking the other for desires that threaten its hegemony. Over against that a reaching out to Elisabet, sharing a fantasy first formed when looking in a mirror after viewing one of Elisabet's films: "I think I could turn myself into you. If I really tried. I mean inside. Don't you think so?" – an unanswered question and hot desire she will take with her into sleep … first in a moment's sleep, like a daydream, hallucinating, Elisabet breaks her silence with words of solicitation which, snapping back awake, Alma repeats, as prologue to the pivotal scene in the film.

The Double Dream of Eros

A dream defined by two central images. Initially, a fetal sleeper dreaming that the other woman visits her in the night. Rising, she goes to her, nestling her head in the arms of a maternal figure who comforts – becoming the woman who will enable you to see yourself as you really are. Positioning Alma as if for a photo, the two women face the camera, the audience, directly. Elisabet's look – eyes wide open, serene, sphinx-like, *Mona Lisa* enigmatic in half smiling certitude – bidding Alma observe the mystery of her being (i.e., "What we women have always known in our freedom from men and their world"). The symptom – that tic of Alma's – transformed by Elisabet's holding Alma's hair back, forehead fully visible now in a self-knowledge reflected in Alma's face, as Eros realized. Provocative, desiring, aroused, head angled backward, about to swoon, nostrils flared, eyes half closed, mouth full, moist, opening – that lost *jouissance* she hoped to reclaim here figured forth.

From the timeless purity of this image we pass to desire, the image in motion, as Alma's eyes close, her face that of a young girl, head descending toward Elisabet's shoulder. Her hand (in a brief, blurred shot) draws Elisabet's hair back over Elisabet's face, and in reciprocal gesture Elisabet, with Alma now the cause, eyes closed, lowers her head to the back of Alma's neck – that supreme erotic zone – to kiss, to suck, to bite, to ravish or ravage, in keeping with a scene replete with cinematic allusions to Murnau's *Nosferatu*. The pervading atmosphere, perhaps the Freudian navel and hidden center of the dream, that elusive "it" that escapes the dreamer (along with something else censored here, only to emerge near the end of the film) in premonition of what such utter opening of oneself to another will bring.

For this is the beauty and profundity of such a dream: a fusion of Eros and Thanatos apprehended at the very quick of the psyche in its descent into the profoundest sleep, in erotic abandonment and assertion of a Drive beckoning from beyond all petty discharge in service to the pleasure principle. This is the bliss of one caught in the toils of dreaming – a perfect union, communication, communion, never suspecting the forces within to which the dark god will deliver her.[12]

Act Three: The Drama of Humiliation

The Letter Killeth

A missive composed with a smirk to an imperious analyst reaches its true destination in the one who will not be able to resist the temptation to read it, finding there not a hoped-for recognition, but rather humiliation. Humiliation: to tender your most intimate, private, traumatic, and erotic experiences to another – as a free gift – and find yourself dismissed as an adolescent with a crush. A pathetic object studied, consumed then discarded; your most traumatic experience mocked as trivial and boring.

Such is the purpose of the letter Elisabet pens. In service to the most destructive form of psychological cruelty. The openness and vulnerability of another seized upon, as the chance to deliver a wound so crushing that self-contempt becomes the only self-reference. A feeling of worthlessness you can't exorcise no matter how decent or self-sacrificial your deeds.

Humiliation, however, is also transformative. Giving birth to the experience of subject as who/why, an existentialized being defined by two questions that constitute the very basis for one's persistence as a subject: (1) Who am I to be so vulnerable in my being that humiliation has the power to destroy any self-worth? (2) Why, knowing that, would one human being try to wound another that way? No essential humanity, no ego identity protects one from the tragic primacy of these questions. And no way for a humiliated subject not to undergo a radical affective change in one's self-reference.

This is what happens within Alma as she reads the letter, and immediately thereafter in the frozen shot of her standing in some forest clearing posed before her image reflected in a pool of water at her feet; a doubling suggesting the prospect of an infinite depth. A woman in a black raincoat, the image thereby sharpened, light caught and reflected in a shimmering of waters, transforming the head reflected there into pure light. An image held still in a moment of timeless contemplation, a subjectivity absorbed with the discovery of an unknown depth within; in deliberate pause, contemplating what she must do, not yet knowing that psychological cruelty can only be answered by an equal or greater cruelty, the drama between the two women having passed beyond humanistic coordinates into a Sartrean dialectic in which subjects only preserve their freedom by turning the other into a thing.

For Elisabet, too, a change, though of a lesser order. Her sublime solitude shattered by that need which, as artist, she can't resist – the chance to study another human being; their emotions, the laboratory offering its life's blood as food for one's future art. This perhaps a defensive retreat from feelings Alma has reawakened in her, cruelty the great exorcist of all that would make us weak. And in cruelty, assurance of continued dominance, blind to what she's unleashed in Alma.

Revenge: The Cut Glass

Alma's point of no return. A radical choice preceded by cold deliberation, reflected in Alma's face as she decides to leave cut glass on the ground for Elisabet to step on. A hideous silence then broken by a cry of pain. Drawing a curtain, Alma looks out to witness her handiwork. With that a violent cut in which the projector snaps, the film burns up, that image eating a hole in the middle of her face; all this the cinematic correlative, Bergman said, for what's happened in Alma. And in him. Unable to go on, the filmmaker and boy dreamer about to learn more about the good mother than he bargained for, caught in a nightmare from which he'd awake or dream anew toward some solution attempted by regressing back to the beginning – montage of fractured fragments, some old, some new, recomposed (sheep eyes now human, the veins in close-up, mapping some interior landscape) as if thereby to return to the scene of origin, pretending nothing has happened. In Žižek, is this not how the ego operates each time it must through displacement and denial, treating a traumatic break within by acting as if restoration were some quasi-automatic, guaranteed process?

And physical violence – a momentary loss of control. As in the popular, noxious phrase, "I just had to get my anger out," as if thereby returning to the pristine integrity of the ego by discharging some foreign substance – with the actual truth thus concealed, namely, physical cruelty the first step in that fascism of the heart that is at the root of all domestic violence – in its quest for a way to deliver a truly destructive wound and thus bound from the first blow to psychological cruelty as the only road to victory. In service to this inner necessity: to inflict on the other what will otherwise turn back inward as impotent rage, threatening a psychotic unraveling. Thus do we destroy one another in order to delay our own self-destruction.

And this the inner condition behind what is now a demand: that Elisabet speak, offering an explanation of her cruelty that will satisfy the ego, enabling Alma to resume the mask. Alma thus demands of Elisabet what she can't find in herself. For it is within, that Why finds no answer. Except this: cruelty is more primary than any of the ways we try to control or explain it.

Leaving only one possible self-mediation: to enter fully into a Strindbergian battle to the death. For words fail. Even, especially, the most heartfelt expression of having been violated. Caviar to the smile and mask of a superior consciousness and master of passive aggression, knowing that silence is the way to drive the other person crazy – which may now be Elisabet's motive as actress, coldly studying for future use each stage in Alma's psychological collapse. The ensuing sequence of psycho-physical actions shows Bergman a master of naturalistic representation: Alma in her panic striking out; Elisabet striking back; Alma spitting in her face; Elisabet bloodying Alma's nose; Alma in a rage about to throw a pot of boiling water in Elisabet's face. Momentary tearing away of the mask, Elisabet crying out "No, don't hurt me." Alma in triumph, crowing, "I scared you." Elisabet, after a long pause, in charge again, secure in that smug smile and that hideous silent laugh, reducing Alma again to panic anxiety, alone in her room, struggling to recompose her face. Returning to the scene, played by both initially as if nothing happened, but with Alma eaten up within by a last ditch effort of the ego to resume control. Through a rhetorical question – is it not better to embrace a tissue of self-protective lies, thereby escaping the torment of psychological honesty? – Elisabet's refusal to reply drives Alma into a super-egoic rage, the high horse of moral and psychological judgment charging the other with what festers within.

On the Beach: Psyche as Anguish

And that must come out, and does, in the scene that marks the turning point in the drama, Alma's pursuit of Elisabet across a rocky beach, a scene that begins in actual pursuit and ends in hallucination and psychological fragmentation as transition to the dream states that will now drive the action. In Alma, anxiety assumes command and with it the collapse of fantasy and desire before the trauma of the Real; in it an experience of psyche at ground zero, trembling before the abyss that's opened within.

Alma's "Forgive me" is the plea of an ego wedded to the defense known as undoing, that being her quest as she pursues Elisabet, in panic repeating those words, willing to assume all blame, hoping as Catholics once did that confession cleanses us of our deeds. Anxiety knows better, increasing the desperation of Alma's pursuit. Her cry, "I'm here to help you," the invocation of a vocational ego identity that no longer exists, any remnant of it unraveling in furious and vain effort to form sentences she can't complete: "I was …" "It seemed …" "I … I …

I ... I ..." becoming "it." In recoil a fantasy of merger, "I–you–forgive ..." "I ..." at which Elisabeth turns back and stares, unmoved, refusing any response. Then she's gone, and Alma still pursuing, caught in the toils of an impotent rage, "You ... You ..." that can't be discharged, only reiterated in subjective destitution; a psyche hanging on by the thread of a hollow negativity, "I won't ... I won't ..." – words that no longer have an object, only the abjection of one who throws herself to the stony ground, weeping.

Four shots of Alma seated among the rocks follow, the last a long-held medium shot echoing the long close-up of Elisabet in the hospital, but no Bach for accompaniment here. No beautiful face, suggesting an infinite depth. Instead, a face set in stone – cold and hard as the rocks that surround her (almost as if she's emerging out of them). Anxiety has hollowed her out from within, affecting the greatest transformation. From panic flight to the existential dread of assuming absolute responsibility for an existence bereft of ego, fantasy, and desire. Trauma has worked in her to another end. In Lacanese, the question asked the other, *"Che vuoi?"* "What am I for you? What do you want from me?" is here answered: Nothing. The greatest inner torment thus resolved. The threat of engulfment – of losing oneself in the other, in the ever failed quest to fulfill the other's desire – has become a murderous project. To act in a way that will expose the truth of the other, her psyche stripped of all its illusions, reduced to a condition of inner suffering that will mirror yours. An abject subject, still longing to regain the other at whatever cost, has become a tragic agent, dedicated to a cruelty with a single purpose: to tear off all of Elisabeth's masks.

Act Four: The Drama of Cruelty

No Limit to Suffering

To set the scene for that final act, an interlude picturing each woman alone, in bed, communing with her innermost self – one by looking at a photo, the other through troubled sleep, perchance to dream.

Elisabet, initially the far stronger psyche, seeks return to an earlier state, when internalized suffering defined her. Her aid to reflection: the terrified face of a young boy and others arrested by Nazi soldiers; this boy, a stand-in for the photo of her son that she tore in two. Her action now: calm, contemplative, propping the photo up under a lamp, as she lowers her head to a pillow to read this bedtime story. Told through a series of close-ups – from the boy to other terrified faces, from them to the Nazis pointing their guns, then back to that poor boy, hands raised in submission, eyes transfixed in terror – we the viewer are positioned so that we see what Elisabet sees, sharing her eyes, and thereby participants to the quest that informs her action. Is there a way from cruelty back to compassion? A place beyond anxiety where loss can be mourned purely, in some stasis or intermittency of a heart tuned thereby to that limit of suffering that renews, or that deadlock in which we perish, each alone?[13]

In another bedroom, another ravaged subject experiences what is for her the only possible answer. Alma, the restless sleeper, becomes the tormented one. Thrusting her body upward in sleep as if in some tortured coitus, her head shakes back and forth in frenetic motion, her face prematurely aged so that now you see it as the eyes snap open – her face so like that woman in the morgue. Alma, a sleepwalker among the dead, self-summoned to soul-murder; now the mission of a psyche that would know itself by stripping away everything, masking the inner death that defines both women. And the radio that brought Elisabet Bach, now brings only a soap opera and a voice calling "Elisabet."

Once upon a time Alma dreamed she could turn herself into Elisabet inside, despite the contradiction of knowing Elisabet the far greater, larger soul. Now she knows a truth beyond romantic doubling. Her own undiscovered country within, pursued in depth, offers the way to unearth Elisabet's secrets. Alma as psychoanalyst will, in knowing another, come to the most traumatic knowledge of herself. And as actress she will do so by moving freely between reality and dream states, projection of the latter the way to uncover what hides beneath the surface of the former.

First, in the face she will anatomize. So intimate her gaze, so close to Alma's face, to a face she might kiss or caress, but with all care now given to the perception of its flaws. Offering us, too, what we failed to detect when mesmerized: an ugly swollen mouth, a lined forehead, a scar usually concealed by makeup. A face no longer prepared to meet the faces that you meet, but slack, unguarded – summoned by a voice Alma answers with the most revealing line in the film: "I'll find out what he wants from us."

The Woe That Is in Marriage

And as she goes to him, Elisabet joins as hallucinated presence, her eyes snapping open, compelled to witness in some shared dream play the truth of a marriage enacted, of woman's state under the phallic signifier, with sex the ritual propping up male identity with a tissue of lies lived in the body, until the cost of sexual catechism collapses in the panic anxiety of truth. The woe that is in marriage epiphanized in an expressionist dream set in some crown of thorns forest, filmed without depth or perspective, the three characters pushed close to the picture frame, the screen.[14] Alma, the actress living the scene; Elisabet, the audience to this reply, to a letter she once penned. But this one is written on the body, and is thus both revenge and self-torment. Alma, as dreamer and artist, proclaiming in reply to her own earlier dream of erotic union: *you entered my sleep, now I'll ravage yours, dreaming our way together into the heart of cruelty.* By distilling the psycho-sexual truth of a marriage expressed in its essential stages; the husband's overweening need, peremptory, pathetic; the woman, an interchangeable prop. The cry, "Elisabet," not a name but a summons to wifely duty. Alma initially shocked, shielded by the negative – "I'm not your wife" – then overcome by *faux* empathy, playing her part as he writes it, hypnotized by a parade of manipulative

lies, compelled by the spell of love's old sweet refrain, to another ritualistic performance of bad sex, echoing his lies with her own catechism, his proclamation
of tender feelings, capped by the obligatory line, "I live for your tenderness" as
prelude to the incorporate conclusion. His hands touch her face (placed there in
fantasy by Elisabet), transforming Alma's expression to one of trust and unconditional love. This offering her face's contribution to the coital culmination, its
brevity capped by the question that has been its purpose and sole significance – "Is
it good with me?" – her cue to fulsome performance of the line that he (and the
ghostly presence, the other men, watching) must hear:"You're a wonderful lover,
darling." Words doubtless evermore the prologue to his sleep, beside a consciousness wide awake; the truth of phallic *jouissance* grinding away in a sexual panic
that can no longer be contained – another thrashing about of the head, ratcheting
words from a psyche dissolving in self-recrimination, assaulted by truth. With
the husband's consoling mutter of meaningless words, Alma's head turns away,
to gaze coldly at Elisabet's face, contorted in pain, humiliated, as Alma once was
by Elisabet's words. But with this crowning touch: she did it by appropriating
Elisabet's art – a consummate actress in a role played in Brechtian relish – to
expose it and be done with it, leaving her audience with the superior smirk of
a Sartrean freedom, imagining the churning away of the words she's carved in
Elisabet's mind. Words something like this: *see how easy it is to fit myself into
you and how quickly I outgrow the role. But wait, the play's not over. Now look
at what I'm going to show you.*

Motherhood Exposed

For there's another role defining womanliness as masquerade, and its deconstruction, the chance for cruelty to craft its masterpiece, tearing to shreds the one illusion Elisabet has retained in order to deny her inability to love. A myth cherished
– to make up for the failure of the sexual relationship perhaps – and clung to as
proof of an essence and identity that can't be lost: motherhood, where biology
and psyche become one in bonds of love assured;[15] this gift of the natural order
providing proof of something stronger than any psychological disorder.

Which is why (in thrall also to that dream) we find it so easy to picture Elisabet
seated at a table, one hand folded over the picture of her little boy, the two pieces
joined – as Alma finds her the next day – a passive victim unable to fight back or
intervene to protest the revelation visited upon her. But only if Alma's equal to an
even greater act of artistic imagination than in the previous scene – to reveal the
psychological truth within the few facts in her possession by delving deeper into
her own psyche than she ever has. Perhaps that abortion wasn't in service to practical egoic exigencies. Perhaps deeper motives made it the only possible choice.
In knowing Elisabet, Alma will know herself – but only if she can summon the
requisite psychological cruelty.

And thus a tale shown twice, so that we can gauge its effect on both subjects: a double exposure. Elisabet's face – seen as the truth of Alma's imaginary

reconstruction – descends upon her. That face in which we once drowned, solicited by beauty; that enigmatic look casting the lure of something secret within, transformed, peeled back the way a face becomes a rubber mask during an autopsy, so that the inner truth can be laid bare, step by step, affect consumed by affect. What's deepest within – pain, grief, guilt, sadness – each in turn gives way to the only suffering that's true: the suffering of who you are. Not a suffering theatricalized, externalized, or triggered in response to political events as testimony to the empathy of great artists. No, that way one will never attain Bergman's artistic goal: to find the limit of suffering. To attain it you must move in a completely different medium. Of what one suffers when one suffers oneself, without mask, displacement, distance, mitigation, delay. There's an attic-justice to it – this Godot arrival of a self-recognition from which there will be no escape. Justice is the return of the projections, your own cruelty come back upon you. In pain, Elisabet closes her eyes and turns away. She then turns back compelled to hear, her head bowed in grief but with no reprieve from what's revealed when she looks up – a face shown but for a second so that we can glimpse, in some recoil of nausea, a coming attraction of what will later become, in a prolonged shot, a permanent, traumatic register of memory – a rictus of suffering, a face transformed into a grimace, some terrible melting of the features to figure forth (as in Dante) some infernal condition of the soul.

From which we pass, seeking release, to the face of Alma, only to discover there mirrored the motive that will complete the picture … Alma's face, so varied, capable of so many different emotional expressions in the course of the film (Bibi Andersson's master class in an actor's emotional range and readiness) is now a face self-reified, carved in cruelty. And the proof – the absence of any change in it as she speaks – destroying Elisabet with a malicious Iago-like coldness. And what increases that horror: the knowledge that the tale she tells, of Elisabet as mother, is her tale, too, and a cautionary one for all who think motherhood will complete them. This a truth universally acknowledged, with one's goodness thereby confirmed in the eyes of the big Other.

Over against all that, and in the coldness and cruelty of an unsparing consciousness, Alma offers one of the most psychologically terrifying pictures of motherhood released into words. From fear the child will tie you down to a single role that will drain you dry; to resentment so great you'd be rid of this thing if you could; abortion desired or achieved, becoming hatred; magnified by the helpless infant sucking at you, the milk of human kindness becoming gall in disgust with this shitting, puking, pissing, and hideous blob of nauseating flesh; a desire for its death the only defense against what's truly unbearable – the desperate clinging of this child's love for you; and with each rejection, each flowering of your hatred, a greater love, tearing away at whatever's left of your soul, in this dying within called motherhood. To Lacan's most scandalous proposition, Alma provides the corollary: there is no maternal relationship. Motherhood: either the sacrifice of one's being to another or a murderous projection of one's conflicts and desires into one forced to serve them in Kafkaesque self-delusion.

No need for Elisabet to look for that photo of the son in the rubble of her heart. It has now been torn to shreds – in another instance of the power of words. And through them a realization of what can't be seen: an Artaudian image of the Unconscious made manifest, as if emerging out of her words what Alma must deny, in furious and futile assertion of the "I, I, I ..." of an ego insisting "I am not you," to negate the merged psyche forged by cruelty, any countervailing possibilities the desperate plunge of sentences one will be unable to complete: "I love ... I haven't ..."

The Grimace of the Real

Suffering may have no limits, but cruelty does. What's behind, beneath, within all Personae. In Lacanese, the Gaze of the Real. *Das Ding*: that extimate excluded interior, what the psyche refuses to know about itself, what it can't bear to face, here made visible.[16] A face no one has ever seen, composed of two faces mashed together. Two women of great beauty rendered inhuman. A face neither can see. This confirmed by the reaction of both actresses when separately shown this face by Bergman. Each saw in it the face of the other actress – on a bad day. That a cruel irony at the expense of art: the inability to recognize oneself in the traumatic image your work has brought into being. Disavowal as the only possible response to this effacement of the face.[17] All those expressive features, gestures signifying the humanity we seek in the faces that we meet, turned inside out (again as at autopsy) – all symmetry of features, all grace disintegrating in an agony, denied any possible mediation. The cruel psyche thus offers a view of itself from within. A grimace – not of the *en soi* but of the *pour-soi* reified in negation of the freedom claimed for it. That dream extinguished in an image that marks one's annihilation as a subject. The Gaze – what our fascination with the face enables us to deny, here realized, made visible – as what is looking at us (like Picasso's *Demoiselles d'Avignon*) eradicates that voyeuristic rot in the psyche, offering a hiding place in Plato's Cave and a breast to suck whenever we go to the movies,[18] here given a violent weaning. In the gaze of the two faces merged, we see ourselves the way Picasso's women see us. What we hoped to enjoy in the anonymous darkness of the cinema: the chance for an hour of so to get inside a sexy woman's psyche – okay, two – transformed to Anxiety of which we can't bear to look. The appropriating (male) look delivered over to the gaze. Woman as masquerade, stripped bare. The film proclaiming its most radical reach: "You aren't looking at me. I'm looking at you."

For the boy dreamer and adult filmmaker, an ultimate terror: the mother's face not the purpose of the poem[19] but its un-signifying other. The splitting that gave birth to the work – in an attempt to separate the good mother from the bad – here "healed." The picture torn within you now glued back together. In the death of every dream of love, of inter-subjectivity as merger, fusion, inter-inanimation of two souls thereby finding completion, and through the other a healing process, here delivered over to the Sartrean truth: Hell is other people.

The Sado-Masochist Sublime: Self-Laceration and Vampirism

One more step and we shall have attained the limit of suffering. Alma, back in her nurse's uniform, in the strictures and pose of the ego, reasserts control through the most reductive interpretation of what's happened:[20] "I've learned a lot from you." Empty words, collapsing with their assertion, and with that the claim of the ego's ability to develop and grow by mastering disruptive experiences negated by the force of irreversible inner change. In panic to deny it, fists pounding on the table as language collapses, psychotic regression revealing the justice of human relationships. We become what we do, *die Rechnung* here a monologue reminiscent of Beckett's "Not I" by way of Lady Macbeth's hand-washing scene. Alma – a psyche persecuted by the return of the projections. That's how we get our just desserts. Our deeds eradicating whatever within fails to correspond with them. That judgment, in the psychological stages of self-undoing, here rendered with meticulous care.

> "Say nothing … cut a candle … not now. No, no …" – silence, prayer, vain/ hopeless pleas against what can no longer be delayed.
> Regrets, recrimination, rationalization … powerless, mitigation meaningless … "Warning and timeless … unforeseen … when it had to happen it didn't, so … failure …"
> "You stand there, but I … should be" – "not inward … not close …" ego and superego together "say … and advise others …" powerless to beat back this torment of inwardness –
> A fitful I – "I take… yes…" dissolving in dread before what is closest (most intimate, extimate, within) –
> "But what is the closest?… What is it called?" –
> What you'd deny if you could… "No no no no…" but with no pronoun left –
> "…us, we, me, I…" evanescent, fading non-signifiers…
> Powerless… "many words and disgust…" to prevent unbearable pain.
> "The nausea…" and in it the aphanisis of the I completed; what was before imaged in the gaze, here realized within through words.

What's thereby dramatized, here summarized in concepts:

(1) The attempt by the ego to deny, delay.
(2) To claim ignorance as an excuse.
(3) The super-ego invoked, one's ethical identity the last line of delusional defense.
(4) The denial of inwardness …
(5) … as now no more than a desperate self-cancelling assertion, powerless to exorcise.
(6) The inability to name what is closest, what abides in the innermost privacy of the psyche: as nameless dread.
(7) Negation negated, annihilated – all pronouns interchangeable, empty.
(8) Psyche delivered over to the final affect – a fusion of self-contempt, suffering and nausea.

Spoken it can now be imaged. The sado-masochist sublime – to lacerate one's own flesh, offering one's blood to its greedy consumption by an insatiable other. Elisabet sucking, held there by Alma's hand entangled in her hair, while with the other hand Alma strikes Elisabet again and again, unable to stop – ever – this the act one can never complete, aggression now one with Munch's scream.

Act Five: The Drama of Nothingness

Catechism: The Word Made Flesh

Panther eyes gleaming in the darkness usher us into the scene. Eyes of an animal on the hunt, savage, predatory, and unforgiving. Eyes that in slow illumination we now see as Alma's, her face emerging in readiness for the one duty that remains – to give birth to the Word, as catechism, in a return to the beginning (as if to dream backward, finding what was already there had you the wit to see it). Sister Alma re-entering the room where her now catatonic patient lies; lifting her up – Pieta like – not into maternal babble of comfort, but into the arms of necessity. The one word demanded, repeated until Elisabet says it too – "Nothing" – her face recording the pain of it; Alma's in cold, impassive, dismissive reply, "It'll be alright. That's how it must be." For nothing can come of nothing. No action. No drama. Only repetition. Death-in-life. But before we pass to the imagining of that end, we must pause to constitute the meaning of this Nothing. In Hegelese – *die an und für sich selbst* of it – in and for the psyche.

Nothingness

Experienced through *Persona* as a black hole that sucks all meaning into a void from which nothing can re-emerge. Subjectivity through cruelty, an abyss of self-dissolution; a death-in-life into which one sinks without the possibility of any reversal. Sartrean absolute freedom actualized in self-reification. Nothingness experienced as far deeper than meaninglessness; the chuckle at its pretensions to conceptualize what's only known in its deadening power when experienced from within.

Repetition: as Death-in-Life

Persona, in rounding back toward its beginning, stays true to its scorched earth policy – Alma and Elisabet abandoned to what drama has made of them.

Alma – looking worn, much older – before a mirror, in a business suit with a tight fitting hat. The tic returned, but in its application, ever so briefly, a ghostly after-image of what's lost – that moment of singularity in her first dream, flickering, superimposed on her face, and with the two woman's hands now joined at her forehead. A fading memory extinguished by the hat pressed down to keep everything tightly composed. Then a bitter, chilling farewell. In final visitation of the beautiful image – its completion – what wasn't seen before, in a long close-up, not of the two women, but of Alma, now the one looking straight into the camera – at us – Elisabet's smile appropriated, rendered avaricious and cynical. And with eyes not erotically closing but wide open, as if to watch, as her hand slowly draws Elisabet's hair back across her face, that image seen in blurred focus and ever so briefly before, now crystal clear – in intimation of a secret Medusan knowledge.

The Artist Destroys His Work

A further cruelty is reserved for Elisabet. Back at work, but stripped of the Elektra mask, a face without makeup, filmed upside down (like the woman in the morgue), eyes wide open, as the filmmakers, Bergman and Nykvist, on a crane, swooping down on her like some gigantic bird of prey. Like Max Ernst's *The Angel of the House.*

Elisabet and Alma, two personae now trapped in roles they must repeat, under the male gaze, and as the film grinds toward a close, a long shot of a grainy earth after a bus passes over it – this, too, an image from the prologue – and through it the return of Bergman's dream to its source: the pubescent boy still reaching out to touch a face that now remains blurred, out of focus, in keeping with the futile persistence of an impossible desire.

And in this image the film dies: in art as death–work applied by the artist to his creation. All that the film has enabled the artist–dreamer to know about the mother who rejected him – and his own resulting inability to love – and in anxiety of irreparable loss, that hand still reaching out to touch that face … And then, in some violent recoil against that immortal desire, a violent closure. The apparatus breaking down, the film snapping, that fusion of arc, light, and rod that made its projection possible ruptured, the two thrust apart – as universal darkness covers all. And we the viewers plunged into that darkness, offered as final image – a black screen. Self-reflexive art for Bergman isn't a cute deconstructive game in service to some superior cynical, ironic posture, but a deadly process – the negation of everything that protects artist and audience from those psychological depths now beckoning to those who sit spellbound – in darkness – arrested and alone.

Coda: Dramatistic Conceptualization

Considerations of length confine us to a few heuristic conclusions on what would be required were internalizing a work of art to define our relationship to it. As it should, for art is a co-created inter-subjective trans-action in which the subjectivity of one subject intends and is intended by the subjectivity of another. And so I proffer these as aids to tragic reflection, and something to take along the next time you go to the movies.

Like Hegel's *Begriff*, existentializing concepts are one with their dramatistic development. Thus, thanks to *Persona,* the following developments of our initial formulations:

Inwardness in internalizing anxiety becomes a self-reference voided of everything but the psychoanalytic interrogation of those experiences that engage
one's deepest conflicts: who you are when assaulted by the self-division at
the core of the psyche becoming action within, as the only way to sustain a
self-mediation irreversibly at issue and at risk.

Subjectivity is the process whereby traumatic suffering becomes existentializing
self-knowledge.

Existence is not something given, but a self-reference attained. As process:
through the series of traumatic experiences a psyche must go through in order
to strip away all the personae of the ego and the We (the big Other). The goal:
the assumption of absolute responsibility for concrete engagement in actions
that advance and deepen the drama within.

Drama is the being of the existentializing psyche. Freud revealed the split of idea and
affect as the primary act in the psyche's constitution. Drama is what happens
when they come back together in a situation that is traumatic because it engages
everything you don't want to know about yourself. Core conflicts deeper than
desire (that cunning displacement) clash with countervailing possibilities that
can only be sustained by deracinating the hegemony of the other within.

Concrete example: the murderous super-ego forbidding you to love that other who
threatens the terms of the super-ego's control over you. Concretized: *Sexuality* as the
primary source of self-knowledge. It is the deepest, richest, truest drama. Spinoza
reclaimed. To cite the most pregnant example: sex as possibility of self-transforma-
tion exists when the anxiety of *jouissance* is sustained in defiance of the prohibitions
of the super-ego; when Eros triumphs over the assault of Thanatos in the body.
When two incarnate psyches pull for prime in the joy and terror of erotic intimacy,
a fundamental threat has been posed to all the ways we limit Eros in order to protect
mutually reifying self-images (i.e., masquerade and imposture joined in mirroring
the safety of a non-relation). In rebellion against that, psyche in sex engages again,
as drama, the conflicts of its origins: (1) The *impositions* whereby the m/other's
conscious and unconscious conflicts are made ours. (2) *Rejection*, their sustenance,
through love promised then withdrawn in order to guarantee the continued sacrifice of our desire to the other's. (3) *Abandonment*, the abiding threat of a loss so
shattering that a life becomes the failed quest to recover what we never had nor
can have – yet can't renounce. Such is the power of the super-ego, as death–work,
planted within. Three traumatic origins which, in concert or alone, create a psyche
in conflict with itself, driven by love and hate in the terrible toils of a fundamental
self-division. For we have only one choice with respect to our core conflicts: to be
crushed by them, as Alma and Elisabet are, or to begin again, with a new artwork,
found within by tunneling deeper into the disorders that define our psyche. That is
the labor and duty of art. Not resolution and return to some cleansed ego restored to
the securities of a self-deluding self-reference, but re-engagement in that risk that is
only creatively alive when Anxiety is the medium within which we live and move
and have our being. In *existential freedom*: deracinating reversal, sustained as the
only way to live out an ethical relationship to the conflicts that define you.

Notes

1 For pop existentialism read Norman Mailer, Rollo May, and with respect to *Persona*, Susan Sontag's now canonical essay: *"Persona*: The Film in Depth," in *Ingmar Bergman: Essays in Criticism,* edited by Stuart Kaminsky (London: Oxford University Press, 1975). An exceedingly abstract and formalistic analysis builds to this culminating insight: Bergman "has only a single subject: the depths in which consciousness drowns." An abstract existentialistic commonplace is thus substituted for an examination of character and action as psychological–existential drama.

2 For a formalistic examination of the film in terms of images of merger and division – and thus the repetition throughout the film of the initial action of the arc light and rod – see John Simon, *Ingmar Bergman Directs* (Harcourt Brace Jovanovich, Inc. 1972). Once again, unfortunately, formalism becomes a substitute for concrete interpretation, as meticulous attention to every image of merger and division in the film confines its action to an abstraction. What is merged, what divided, why and therefore, remain unaddressed questions.

3 See Chapter 4 in Walter A. Davis, *Inwardness and Existence* (University of Wisconsin Press, 1989); *Get the Guests* (University of Wisconsin Press, 1995); and *Deracination* (SUNY Press, 2001). I am indebted to conversations with Todd McGowan for the rapprochement here attempted between Lacan and my theory of the existential psyche.

4 Literalization of complex psychodynamics is the common error. For a representative example see Richard Corliss in *Film Quarterly* (Summer, 1967). For Corliss, it's a story about a vampiristic actress using another as a prop in her game. One need delve no deeper to resolve all problems posed by Bergman's cinematic art.

5 The idea of the deep dream adumbrated here has similarities to Kohut's theory of the self-state dream. Dreaming as an attempt to imagine the current inner condition and constitution of the psyche.

6 For a careful analysis of every image in the prologue, see Bruce Kawin, *Mindscreen: Bergman, Godard, and First-Person Film* (Princeton University Press, 1978).

7 Wright Wexman, V. & Ullmann, L. "An Interview with Liv Ullmann." *Cinema Journal*, 20.1, Special Issue on Film Acting (Autumn, 1980). Austin: University of Texas Press, pp. 68–78.

8 See Lacan, *Seminar XX: Encore,* and for a succinct and incisive discussion of feminine jouissance and the representation of women in cinema, see Jennifer Friedlander, *Feminine Look: Sexuation, Spectatorship, Subversion* (SUNY Press, 2008). And as background to exploring Voice as *objet a,* see Mladen Dolar, *A Voice and Nothing More* (MIT Press, 2006).

9 Artaud's definition of the goal of acting.

10 I hasten to add that my conception of an existential ethic contrasts sharply with the somewhat bizarre ethic of the drive that Slavoj Žižek derives from a reading of Lacan's essay "Kant avec Sade." Notice should also be given that my concepts of thanatos, death–work and soul murder have nothing to do with the ideas contained under the single most inappropriate word choice in Freud. If, that is, that term signifies what Žižek claims, as in the following representative statement from Žižek and Dolar in *Opera's Second Death* (Routledge, 2002, p. 107): "The paradox of the Freudian death drive is therefore that it is Freud's name for the very opposite of what the term would seem to signify, for the way *immortality* appears within psychoanalysis, for the uncanny excess of life, for an undead urge that persists beyond the [biological] cycle of life and death," etc. With that as the end of all our striving, we can all rest in the assurance of deliverance from our actual inner conflicts.

11 The classic text on this logic and Lacan's formulae of sexuation is Joan Copjec's stunning Kantian essay "Sex and the Euthanasia of Reason," in her book *Read My Desire* (MIT Press, 1994).

12 And as such something beyond the reductive assumptions of both Jungian and lesbian feminist readings. The first render mystical and inane what must be experienced in the body; the latter reduce the latter to only one possible incarnation. For a Jungian approach, see Donald L. Fredericksen *Persona and Shadow in Film* (Martinus Nijhoff, 1966); and for an example of the strictures of recent lesbian feminist readings see Gwendolyn Audrey Foster, "Feminist Theory and the Performance of Lesbian Desire in *Persona*," in *Ingmar Bergman's Persona*, edited by Lloyd Michaels (Cambridge University Press, 2000).

13 Or, through *Compassion* a radically different mode of affective self-mediation, but to mine it you must reject identification with the aggressor in favor of a deeper trauma of the psyche, humiliation sustained as the basis of an ethic of relationship and self-mediation based on making the wound at the heart and origin of the psyche the creative principle of one's opening to the other. When Gandhi spoke of a way out of hell, this is what he had in mind. But as a psychological process it is the most traumatic route a psyche can take in the attempt to mediate its defining conflicts. Cruelty and Compassion, the two ways in which the psyche lives out the wound that defines it as who/why. (I return to this theme at the end of the essay.)

14 Marilyn Johns Blackwell in her fine book *Persona The Transcendent Image* (University of Illinois Press, 1986) suggests that this entire sequence, "would seem to have been shot with a telephoto lens," creating thereby the lurching forward of the background and the flatness of the images, as if they exist on the same plane. Which, of course, they do in dream, the tangled roots and branches of setting mirroring the knot and impasse of human relationships.

15 As in the biological essentialism grounding the "psychoanalytic" theory of the bonds of love developed by the American ego relational psychologist Jessica Benjamin. In her attempt to posit, as if guaranteed, a myth of perfect mothering.

16 For as superb discussion of Das Ding and Anxiety in Lacan see Richard Boothby's magisterial *Freud as Philosopher: Metapsychology After Lacan* (Routledge, 2001).

17 For a brilliant paragraph on this face as the effacement of the face, see Gilles Deleuze *Cinema 1: The Movement-Image* (University of Minnesota Press, 1986), pp. 99–100.

18 Early psychoanalytic film theory was onto this dual dimension of the cinematic experience: my privileged position as one with the projector casting oneiric images onto a screen, offering us a good breast to feed on. *Persona* is one of the most radical realizations and de-familiarizations of this experience, but considerations of length required its omission in this essay.

19 This phrase from Wallace Stevens' *The Auroras of Autumn*.

20 As in relational psychoanalyst Barbara Young's *The Persona of Ingmar Bergman: Conquering Demons through Film* (Rowman & Littlefield, 2015) where at the end of their journey Alma and Elisabet both return – renewed – to their lives cleansed of demons; as was the Bergman of those late films so full of reconciliation and resolution and affirmation – as if that were the summit of his art and not its decline; as if the tragic were something to be overcome and cast aside, rather than endured as the highest formula of affirmation possible for an existing human being.

Bibliography

Shargel, R. (2007). *Ingmar Bergman: Interviews*. Jackson: The University Press of Mississippi.

Chapter 11

Beyond Silence

On the Absence of God in the Films of Ingmar Bergman

Pablo Lerner

I have nothing to add, nothing to say.

The scope of the literature on the demon director Ingmar Bergman speaks for itself. This essay concerns the work, not the man.

I have only nothing to add – to speak about – and about one of the disguises it wears in his films – the absence of God. I want to dwell upon its figurations in three of his masterpieces: *Det sjunde inseglet* (*The Seventh Seal*) from 1957, *Såsom i en spegel* (*Through a Glass Darkly*) from 1961, and *Nattvardsgästerna* (*Winter Light*) from 1963.

Ingmar Bergman was by no means the first director to stage the implications of the absence of the Christian God in the medium of film. Among his predecessors, especially Robert Bresson's *Journal d'un curé de champagne* (*Diary of a Country Priest*) from 1951 and Carl Theodor Dreyer's *Ordet* (*The Word*) from 1955 deserve to be mentioned. It must, however, not be overlooked that a vague yet distinguishable line of demarcation separates the works of Bergman from the above-mentioned ones, whose resolutions – despite the bleak tones of the films – perhaps lend themselves to be categorized as optimistic or apologetic: in the former, God's grace animates the agonized priest on his deathbed; in the latter, God imparts to the pleading family the Word in the redeeming instant of the miracle. The particularity of Ingmar Bergman's *mise-en-scène* consists in the avoidance of such denouements: doubt does not transition into conviction, absolution, atonement, salvation, miracle; nor does the world's indelible godlessness leave man in an irreversible state of dejected perdition. An irresolute and shifting disposition seems to be at hand – thus it is not inadequate to claim that Bergman's films accommodate a nebulous space of indecisiveness whose transitory signification is to be determined by the contingency of interpretation.

This essay consists of three sections. In the first one, I will account for the dawn of the thought on the absence of God in the Christian literature; in the second, I will analyze the staging of the absence of God in the films of Ingmar Bergman; lastly, I will let psychoanalysis guide me in the interpretation of this absence.

DOI: 10.4324/9781003200246-12

Deus Absconditus

Genesis: "And God said, 'Let there be light,' and there was light."[1] St John: "In the beginning was the Word, and the Word was with God, and the Word was God … In him was life, and that life was the light of all mankind. The light shines in darkness, and the darkness has not overcome it."[2]

God is λόγος, and this λόγος is φῶς, *lux*, which in turn is ζωή, *vita*. Where is the Word and the Light to be found in the world? The Word is not the words enunciated by mankind. The Light is not the light illuminating the field of vision. The Word stands outside the world of the word, rings outside its limits; the Light stands outside the worldly light, shines independently of the light radiated by the celestial bodies. An echoing silence is inscribed in the world of the word; an impenetrable darkness in the domain of the image – the absence of God in the world.

But we know as well that "the Word became flesh,"[3] and that God in the name of love suicided his own materialization – grace. We know that "whoever does not love does not know God, because God is love,"[4] and that this love is the trace left in humankind by the crucified. What of those abandoned by love?

In the Hebrew Bible, God does not show himself as man, as love – he discloses himself in the enigmatic moment of the revelation, as *Deus revelatus*. It is the God who speaks from the burning bush, from the storm. God does not show himself without the Occurrence – where is God when nothing happens?

In the Hebrew Bible we read: "*Vere tu es Deus absconditus*," "Truly you are a God who has been hiding himself."[5] The hidden one is not to be found on earth: "If only I knew where to find Him; if only I could go to his dwelling … But if I go to the east, he is not there; if I go to the west, I do not find him. When he is at work in the north, I do not see him; when he turns to the south, I catch no glimpse at him."[6] Like the tormented Son nailed to the cross, like Job who cursed his birth on the sickbed, the despairing man finds himself abandoned in his agony: "My God, my God, why have you forsaken me? Why are you so far from saving me, so far from my cries of anguish? My God, I cry out by day, but you do not answer; by night, but I find no rest"; "Listen to my prayer, O God, do not ignore my plea; hear me and answer me."[7] The lamentations of mankind die away in the ear-piercing silence of God.

Nicolas of Cusa was the first theologian of weight who explicitly dwelled upon the question of the hidden God. In *De Deo absconditio* (*On the Hidden God*) from 1444, he stages a dialogue between a Christian and a heathen;[8] the former declares he only adores the god he does not know, worships that which he cannot grasp. Everything he may understand is located within the sphere of the knowable, but God stands by necessity outside it. The Creator is for the created what the vision is for the visible: it stands outside the field it causes, and is thereby ungraspable on the basis of all of its effects. The Ultimate Cause is not inscribed, but hidden in the sphere of all its effects – hence God cannot be the object of knowledge, only of faith.

Nicholas of Cusa situates the question of *Deus absconditus* in the epistemolog-ical field; it concerns the transcendent God dwelling beyond the reach of thought. Martin Luther, on the other hand, lifts down the hiddenness of God on Earth, first in *Disputatio Heidelbergensis* (*Heidelberg Disputation*) from 1518, thereafter in *De servo arbitrio* (*The Bondage of the Will*) from 1525. Luther rejects the pos-sibility of theology to think of the transcendental attributes of God as if they were sensuous – theology may in the sensuous merely perceive God in a form standing in contradiction to the transcendental.[9] Consequently, philosophical contempla-tions of God are out of the question – we can only speak of a god who maintains his hiddenness in his revelation, of a contradictory unity of *Deus revelatus* and *Deus absconditus*. Luther speaks about God's *absconditum in passionibus*, about how he in opposition to his real attributes conceals himself in Christ's manifest weakness, suffering, humiliation, just as his mercifulness is hidden in his eternal wrath, his righteousness in apparent injustice. Hence, silence and darkness veil God's presence in their respective domains. I will take the liberty to conceive Luther's approach to God's absence–presence in the world as a disavowal of its manifest godlessness.

For Nicholas of Cusa, God lies hidden in the domain in thought; for Luther, in that of the world. In his posthumously published *Pensées* (*Thoughts*), Blaise Pascal imports the question of *Deus absconditus* in the human being; rather, in the human being in the world. Since "nature is corrupt" and "we are miserable, cor-rupt, separated from God,"[10] there is nothing in this world capable of convincing us of the existence of the concealed god. Man yearns for certainty, but falters in the face of every rational argument for His existence, all of them haunted by an inevitable insufficiency. Consequently, he who wishes to believe is prone to be tor-mented by doubt. Pascal contemplates the condition of the forsaken humankind:

> When I see the blindness and the wretchedness of man, when I regard the whole silent universe, and man without light, left to himself, and, as it were, lost in this corner of the universe, without knowing who has put him there, what he has come to do, what will become of him at death, and incapable of all knowledge, I become terrified, like a man who should be carried in his sleep to a dreadful desert island, and should awake without knowing where he is, and without means of escape.[11]

The abandoned man finds himself surrounded by the silence and the darkness which the god who does not reveal himself has left in the ruined world; he is, by the indifference of the endless emptiness, thrown into a horrifying uncertainty regarding his own fate. The human being trembles before his absence, before the possibility that nothing awaits him beyond extinguishment, before "this desertion in the horror of night," "the eternal silence of these infinite spaces."[12] He desper-ately searches for a way to break the silence, or at least replace it with an argument permitting faith to take root in the heart – but every ground slides away and leaves him disquieted and uncertain. Consequently, faith cannot find its base in reason

– God is truly not to be found in this world. Pascal's apologetic conclusion arises from the certainty that the life of the tormented and insignificant man is a nothing-ness – particularly in comparison with the eternity preached by the Scripture – and that the awareness of his own perdition implies that he has absolutely nothing to lose in believing. This reason is by itself sufficient for man to allow himself to terminate his own reason in favor of faith. Only the heart may reach him: "Where is God? Where you are not, and the kingdom of God is within you."[13]

Departing from the meditations of the Christian tradition on the relationship between man and *Deus absconditus*, his absence *for man* seems to take the form of silence and darkness – the former appears to be an absence in the field of words, the latter in the field of images. We must immediately note that darkness – to a much greater extent than silence – must be understood metaphorically, since the particularity of the creation myth of the Abrahamitic religions in relation to (many of) their polytheistic predecessors consists in an elliptical substitution, caused by the Word, of the material source of light–life–being for the transcendent one. The Light of God is not the light propagating through the endless spaces. We can perhaps speak of a specular metaphor internalizing the light in man in analogy with the sun's gift to the worldly darkness – a metaphor that is not without trans-formative effects on the meaning of the word. The mirror metaphor of Christianity interiorizes the light through an equation of word and light and life and love – the equivalences of St. John retroactively transforming the light in Genesis into love. He who loves is animated by light, sees clearly; the loveless one, on the other hand, descends into compact darkness.

The Absence of God in the Films of Ingmar Bergman

I will now compose an analysis of man's relation to the absence of God in *The Seventh Seal*, *Through a Glass Darkly*, and *Winter Light*. I will omit *Tystnaden* (*The Silence*) from 1963 (often regarded as the last film of Bergman's cinemathe-ologic triptych, which also includes *Through a Glass Darkly* and *Winter Light*), since the theme of the absence of God is but implicitly present in it; I will never-theless comment on it later on.

I will take the liberty to presume that the reader is acquainted with the films in question.

I

The Seventh Seal lets itself be understood as a staging of the indissoluble ten-sion between the questions of death and faith. It concerns an otherworldly *Deus absconditus* who remains undisclosed before the horror-struck man awaiting The Last Judgement, the extinction about to be realized on the wretched earth. The doubt of Antonius Block is about the reverse of life, life in the light of the opaque eternal blackness of death. The Reaper himself remains unknowing – he does not know God. An abyss disjoins death and the concealed God, an abyss reduplicated in the rift separating the faith of the heart from the doubt of thought – no encounter or conciliation comes to be. Reason does not allow the knight to extinguish the unease he bears, neither is he capable of disavowing the perdition of the surrounding world. Hence this by no means has to do with a Lutheran disposition which – like the film's ecclesiastical advocates – in the forthcoming end of the world sees *Dies irae* and in the day of wrath God's hidden love and righteousness. It rather concerns a surprisingly precise parallel with the relation between the human being and *Deus absconditus* drawn by Blaise Pascal: it is particularly his impending death that drives Antonius towards the necessity of faith, but he finds no argument enabling him to believe, nor a way to annihilate the vacillation of reason by a faith which independently of thought anchors within him.

Antonius expresses his perdition during his confession, unaware that Death sits on the other side of the grate:

> I want to confess as honestly as I can, but my heart is empty. And emptiness is a mirror turned to my own face. I see myself and am seized by disgust and fear. Through my indifference to people, I have been placed outside of their society. Now I live in a ghost world, enclosed in my dreams and imaginings.
>
> Is it so terribly inconceivable to comprehend God with one's senses? Why does He hide in a cloud of half-promises and unseen miracles? How can we believe in the faithful when we lack faith? What will happen to those of us who want to believe, but cannot? What about those who neither want to nor can believe? Why can't I kill God in me? Why does He live on in me in a humiliating way despite my wanting to evict Him from my heart? Why is He, despite all, a mocking reality I cannot be rid of? ... I want knowledge! Not faith, not assumption, but knowledge. I want God to stretch out His hand, uncover His face and speak to me.
>
> – But He remains silent.
> – I call out to Him in the darkness. But it is as if no one is there.
> – Perhaps there isn't anyone.
> – Then life is a preposterous horror. No man can live faced with Death, knowing everything's nothingness.

Antonius bears an echo, a shadow, a trace of a mute and veiled god, impossible to grasp or obliterate. The silence throws him into the darkness of inextinguishable doubt and desperation, leaving him unable to reconcile with the inevitable, reflecting a forlorn man awaiting an unbearable, frightful fate. Burned by the purgatory of disbelief, Antonius is driven away from mankind, towards a vain inner-worldly pursuit of the otherworldly god who does not reveal himself; his plaints echo in the silence of God, as he lapses down into an enfolding darkness populated by shadows of Light or of Nothing. The doubt inflames a longing inciting both wish and hatred, but the wish does not enable him to reach God nor does hatred liberate him from the agonies of lost faith.

The difference between Bergman and Pascal primarily consists in Antonius, in spite of his despair, finding an ephemeral moment of serenity on earth: in the encounter with the jester family who bear the piety he lacks, in the godly ungodly communion where wild strawberries and milk replace the body and blood of Christ. The jesters are animated by the love preached by the Scripture: they represent the presence of God in man – but without any reference to God. Piety without reason (Nicholas of Cusa), disavowal (Luther), perdition (Pascal).

We may discern a displacement of the divine from the otherworldly concealed towards inner-worldly love. In the words of Bergman: "if you peel off theology, the Holy remains."[14] Reason cannot lead man towards faith: the domain of the holy begins where that of thinking ends, and this insight cannot in itself convince man of God's existence – Antonius does not manage to follow the path of Nicholas of Cusa. Although Antonius obviously is seized by a conflict between faith and reason, this conflict is not to be understood as an essential one: the conflict only consists in Antonius' incapacity to leave the dimension of knowing, and this stands in contradiction to faith *only* in so far as faith is not to be found where he searches for it – the dimensions are separated rather than incompatible. If Antonius succeeds in leaving reason behind, the conditions of faith are at hand, and vice versa; if this is not the case, he will remain divided in faith as well as thought.

Thus the path from perdition towards faith remains obscure and enigmatic from the point of view of reason. This mysteriousness is far from absent in the film's penultimate scene, where the mute maidservant is animated by grace allowing her to break her silence and affirm death. It is not far-fetched to presume that she (apart from the obvious reference to the death of Christ) first and foremost represents the faith Antonius does not find – the one emanating from the heart, not reason.

II

In *Through a Glass Darkly*, the problematic of God from *The Seventh Seal* undergoes a radical transformation. In the latter, the jesters bear an inner-worldly holiness separated from the otherworldly one pursued by Antonius Block. In *Through a Glass Darkly* the displacement from the otherworldly in the direction of the inner-worldly reaches its culmination, is consolidated and becomes a complete substitution.[15] The conception of the transcendent God is abandoned.[16] The relation between Father and Son is replaced by that between father and son. The Word is replaced by the word, Love by love. *Deus absconditus* becomes *Pater, Verbum, Amor absconditus*. The division between the inner- and otherworldly is discarded and taken down on earth – all the family members live in split worlds consisting of inner-worldly worlds without interrelationships, finding themselves divided at the threshold of the divided worlds. Transcendent transcendence is replaced by immanent transcendence. The family is the shared world to which all of them have access, but they each have their own beyond. The mysterious tapestry is the limit of Karin's worlds.

Minus is about to take the leap from the world of the boy to that of the man. David finds himself divided between his roles as father and writer. Each protagonist stands before a choice of fate – they are forced to choose and to sacrifice.

Ingmar Bergman did not avoid religious connotations: it is not impossible that there is a reference to David's biblical namesake – the scald, the king of Israel – who neglected his son for his political commitments. Although David is not without guilt and anguish regarding his split, he neglects his children in favor of his writing: he is indifferent towards his son's approaches and establishes a parasitical relation to his daughter's insanity. His selfish mendacity marks the unmistakable absence hidden beyond his presence. In the film's epilogue, after acknowledging the irrevocable and disastrous consequences of his abysmal fatherhood, David shares his conception of God with his son, Minus:

- I can only give you an indication of my own hope. It is knowing that love exists for real in the human world …
- So love is the proof?
- I do not know whether love is the proof of God's existence, or if love is God.
- For you, love and God are the same?
- I rest my emptiness and dirty hopelessness in that thought … Suddenly the emptiness turns into abundance and hopelessness into life. It is like a reprieve, Minus … from a sentence of death.
- Dad … if it is as you say, then Karin is surrounded by God since we love her. Could that help her?
- I believe so.[17]

God is love, love is God – the chiasmus rings false, but is at the same time to be understood as an insightful confession arising from his guilt and his emptiness: he becomes aware of his perdition, that he lacks God within, and that his children have paid the price for his lovelessness, his silence, for their abandonment to a godless world, that is, to a world where the love of the father is absent.

Minus, the childish observer, is perhaps – like Alexander in Bergman's last masterpiece – the character who, due to the peripheral and passive role he occupies in relation to the central drama of the film, confers on the work its specific signification. He bears an innocent wish to approach his father: he idealizes, imitates, follows, listens to him, appeals to his presence, is possessed with expectations of an encounter and a dialogue – but like Antonius Block he meets only indifference and silence, whereas, unlike him, Minus' appeal has not yet become a lamentation. The title of the film is retrieved from the Bible:

When I was a child, I talked like a child, I thought like a child, I reasoned like a child. When I became a man, I put the ways of childhood behind me. For now we see only a reflection as in a mirror [in the King James Version: "For now we see through a glass, darkly"]; then we shall see face to face. Now I know in part; then I shall know fully, even as I am fully known.[18]

The reference is about the leap into the not-yet-known, the transformation of uncertainty into certainty, the transition which culminates in "conquered certainty."[19] This is valid for every protagonist, but especially for Minus' transition from boy to man. The father remains something of a riddle for Minus; the absence of the father's mediation destroys every bridge capable of leading Minus away from childhood, and he remains unable to transcend it towards the enigmatic world of the adult. We perceive his disorientation on the threshold of the passage. Speech and love are God's presence on earth – the father's absence, silence, lovelessness are Minus' *Pater, Verbum, Amor absconditus*, his inner-worldly *Deus absconditus*: "I wish I could talk to dad, just once, but he is so wrapped up in himself." The sporadic disavowal of the absence in the presence protects his infantile belief in the father he wishes to know in order to be able to find a path leading to manhood. Although we perceive some anticipatory manifestations, his expectation has not yet transformed into the disillusioned sorrow, disappointment, anger of the adult. Instead of the father's mediation, the leap is taken with the sister at the price of an irreversible perdition – the father speaks *post festum*.

Apart from the epilogue (and an earlier dialogue between David and Martin), there is only one manifest reference to God: Karin's relationship with the alluring world behind the arcane tapestry where the god about to descend to earth dwells. *Deus absconditus* promises to reveal himself. She finds herself divided between her loving husband's appeals and the imperatives of the voices; her faltering reflects the division of the god, a god with "two faces: the one shining of goodness, the other blinded by the fairest evil."[20] The good one lends safety, hope, enjoyment; the evil one is fearsome and repugnant and remains relatively hidden until the atrocious revelation. Her presence in the family becomes more and more perverted by the voices' impositions, her oscillations between the worlds becomes increasingly violent – she comes apart. She rejects the bond to the family in favor of the god at the cost of a crushing certainty regarding the impossibility to keep living in the shared world, and the destruction of her deepest longings in the encounter with the abominable monster, the spider god, the rape god.

Martin is also seized by a division – but between the divided parts there is no incompatibility or neurotic conflict. Once again, it concerns love and reason. Martin is a worldly man, rejects the divine, adopts a rational perspective on the world, not least in relation to the divided worlds of the other protagonists. In spite of Karin's incurable condition, he does not falter when it comes to his bond with her. His devotion remains unaffected by his certainty. He manages – unlike Antonius – to avoid every conflict between them. Once more – the rejection of the holy does not stand in contradiction to it.

III

In *The Seventh Seal*, Antonius Block's doubts concern the existence of the otherworldly god, in *Through a Glass Darkly* the holy descends to earth, becomes word and love. *Winter Light* lets itself be understood as a resolution of the conflict between these dispositions towards *Deus absconditus*.[21]

Once again a biblical reference – the doubting apostle. After his wife's passing, Tomas' fragile faith capsized, the betrayal of God having induced a wrath and left an emptiness within, annihilating the faith in the otherworldly God and in love as His presence in man. God died with her. His faith was already from the beginning erected on weak foundations, on a reciprocal love between him and the fatherly god who answered his prayers in accordance with his infantile wishes. When the reflections of the mirror god ceased, his faith disintegrated and was replaced by an untrue duteous occupational practice. His mechanical staging of the eucharist in the prologue reflects his incapacity to authentically bear his role as priest. He lost the capacity to love and be loved.[22] Faced with the contemplations of the suicidal Jonas, he stands perplexed and mute – at best. His self-centered, unrestrained confession before the man standing on the edge of death testifies to his impiety and to his life's catastrophic evolution:

> I refused to see what was going on. I refused to accept reality. My God and I resided in an organized world where everything made sense. You see, I am no good as a clergyman. I put my faith in an improbable image of a fatherly god. One who loved mankind, of course, but me most of all. Do you see, Jonas, what monstrous mistake I made? An ignorant, spoiled and anxious wretch makes a rotten clergyman. Picture my prayers to an echoing god who gave benign answers and reassuring blessings. Every time I confronted God with the realities I witnessed he turned into something ugly and revolting. A spider god, a monster. So I fled from the light, clutching my image to myself in the dark … If God does not exist, would it really make any difference? Life would become understandable. What a relief. And thus death would be a snuffing out of life. The dissolution of body and soul. Cruelty, loneliness, and fear … all these things would be straightforward and transparent. Suffering is incomprehensible, so it needs no explanation. There is no creator, No sustainer of life. No design.

The disavowal of the misery of the world shields a naïve conception of God at the price of an increasing latent pulverization of faith and of the growth of a split-off monster god; the collapse of the disavowal drags the self-centered and deceptively reciprocal love for God with it. The echo god dissociates from the wrath, disgust, and fear directed against the repulsive spider god, and veils the abandonment of *Deus absconditus* and its concomitant lovelessness. Tomas repeatedly complains about the excruciating silence of God, but unlike the silence in the face of the eternity of the impending extinction which horrifies Antonius Block and Blaise Pascal, it does not concern a silence with respect to the very existence of God, since the faith in a more profound sense is already obliterated – it rather concerns a silence to be understood as an absence of response to an appeal arising from his selfish wishes, a silence destroying the bond to love and pulling him deeper down into the darkness hiding beyond duty. He holds on to God in order not to perceive his own corruption emerging from his yearning for exemption from Him. His mendacity transforms the inexistence of God into a liberty to die without meaning, a liberty from the prison which the meaningful death becomes for the man forsaken by God.

Tomas appears to have a manifest non-relation to Jesus Christ. Märta points out that he seems to be unaffected by his suffering. It is not unreasonable to assume that his turning away from the crucified testifies to a jealousy based on the Father's love for the Son. His indifferent coldness towards Märta, his imposition of silence, his hate and disgust of her stigmata, frailty, suffering, love, forgiveness, devotion, reflect the negated relation to the crucified – Märta is not without connotations to Christ. Unlike the joyful holiness animating the jesters in *The Seventh Seal*, however authentic Märta's love and vocation may be, they also seem to be based on a divided relation to her martyrdom, her dolorous struggle for love – one could speak of the passion of Märta. Märta does not resign when confronted with the cold silence of Tomas: she wants to speak with him, wants him to tell her about his solitude and agony, wants to mediate her suffering, love, bleak hope; she wants to retrieve the meaning both of them have lost in love. It is not difficult to perceive Bergman's transformed view of the holy in Märta's striving for love and her rejection of the otherworldly: on the one hand, "God's silence, God will not talk ... God has never spoken because God does not exist. It is as simple as that"; on the other, "If only we could feel safe and dare show each other tenderness. If only we had some truth to believe in. If only we could believe ..."

Piety in its naïve purity is embodied in Algot, the innocent hunchback of Frostnäs' chapel, who pushes Tomas towards the awareness of the equation between his suffering and that of Christ:

When Jesus was nailed to the cross and hung there in torment, he cried out: "God, my God! Why hast thou forsaken me?" He cried as loud as he could. He thought that his heavenly father had abandoned him. He believed everything he had ever preached was a lie. The moments before he died, Christ was seized by doubt. Surely that must have been his greatest hardship? God's silence.

Tomas realizes his abandonment, his suffering, the lovelessness that the silence enveloping his worldly condition induces in him. He realizes that he has neglected the inner-worldly in favor of a concealed otherworldly God he no longer believes in. The redemption comes to be in the moment disavowal bursts – it regards a "penetrated certainty."[23] The displacement from the otherworldly from *The Seventh Seal* towards the inner-worldly in *Through a Glass Darkly* is in *Winter Light* staged as a passage realized by the shattering of faith in favor of the awareness of the lovelessness of the world; a passage reflecting the movement from the disavowal of Luther towards the perdition of Pascal. His insight implies that Märta's abandonment is his own, that he bears guilt for his lovelessness. Humankind is forsaken by the otherworldly *Deus absconditus*, and the place in man where love is absent is left in the hands of the loveless. God is the resurrection of love in the human being in the encounter with the human being. Lovelessness is the condition for God's existence in man.[24]

Perhaps the light reaches Tomas. He chooses to carry out the communion in the desolate church before no one but Märta. The epilogue is not without ambiguity: unlike the liturgy of the prologue, where an austere empty dead gaze arises from the twilight of faith, we may, in the face of the priest, discern conversion, resurrection, dawn.

IV

The films of Ingmar Bergman do not significantly deviate from the Christian tradition concerning the guise assumed by the absence of God. The God of Bergman in *The Seventh Seal* is an otherworldly *Deus absconditus*, in *Through a Glass Darkly* and *Winter Light* His absence is displaced towards the inner-worldly lovelessness. Bergman's central and recurrent metaphor for His absence is silence, the silence of God. The silence first and foremost concerns a lack of answer to man's prayer, appeal, lamentation. God remains mute, does not answer he who calls Him, pursues Him. The silence of God throws man into darkness, which primarily is to be understood as a metaphor for man's lovelessness and perdition. Silence is in the last instance a lack of words and knowledge, darkness a lack of love and faith.

Silence is the absence of the Word arriving from the beyond of words, permeating the abyss separating man from its transcendent residence. The silence of God is a void in language, a hole where the Word articulated by God is not. Consequently, silence initially functions as a metaphor for God's abandonment, for the otherworldly's (or beyond-inner-worldly's) absence in the world. Antonius Block, Minus (in an inner-worldly sense) and Tomas (before the moment of redemption) appeal to Him whose word is absent in the domain of words – they encounter the hidden one veiled by silence. The silence throws Antonius to damnation; Minus and Tomas preserve an infantile and frail – and, in the former's case, innocent – proximity to the fatherly love, partially by means of disavowal.

Darkness is the absence of love and faith in man, a lost capacity to love and to believe, a closedness in the encounter with the gift of love. Tomas and David realize their perdition through the awareness of having neglected those who love them; they have been loveless. The insight into darkness ignites the light, and the presence of the holy is enabled by the movement of the godlessness from silence towards darkness. Hence, Antonius and Tomas search God where he is not to be found – God seems to dwell beyond darkness rather than silence. The loving word must spring from the dark. Märta, Martin, and Minus keep the love alive although it is not requited; they bear an inner-worldly holiness. The Light descends on earth with the jesters. The difference between them is that the jesters tell us nothing of the passage towards the holy. Perhaps the jesters are to be understood as but a naïve and childish dream of the director.[25]

In *The Seventh Seal*, a complete separation between silence and darkness seems to be at hand: silence concerns the absence of the otherworldly Word, darkness the absence of the light in the human being. Antonius is seized by doubt and turns towards the absent Word, the separation between darkness and silence reflecting the gorge separating faith from knowing. The futility of his frenzied pursuit of the otherworldly (the holy beyond silence) in the inner-worldly (the holy beyond darkness) consists precisely in the unbridgeable nature of this very gap. The jester family, on the other hand, seems to bring down the pious love on earth without any connection to the locality where Antonius places the divine: a non-relation between Light and Word. The Word is so to speak subtracted from the domain of the holy.[26]

The leaps of the protagonists in *Through a Glass Darkly* can also be understood in terms of the relation between darkness and silence. Karin locates the residence of the Word beyond the tapestry and answers its appeals at the price of a breached bond of love with her husband. The Word resonates in the silence outside the world of love, and darkness is left within it – a non-relation between silence and darkness. David neglects his children in favor of his writing; his absent words, the words that remain to be articulated, are placed outside the family, and his words within it are emptied of love. Once more: silence beyond, darkness within – non-relation. Both David and Karin locate the word in the worlds outside the shared one, the family – that is, for Bergman, the world of love; thus, they, like Antonius Block, fail to surmount the rift between silence and darkness, their dissociation leading to a mutual nourishment. Only Minus stands on the threshold of the chasm of the holy: he longs for the father's articulation of the word with love, because of love – word *and* love or silence *and* darkness, an encounter between word and love in silence and darkness.[27] We assume this is not without reference to the Son. We assume that the catastrophes of the protagonists reflect Bergman's changed view of the holy, and that this is not without correlation to the equivalences of St. John.

Winter Light concerns the decomposition of the rift in favor of the possibility of convergence. Tomas is enveloped by darkness and summons the otherworldly *Deus absconditus* only to encounter his inexorable silence. Yet again: Tomas is seized by darkness and turns towards silence; like Antonius, his misdirected appeal implies – and presumes – the dissociation of darkness and silence. Silence beyond, darkness within – non-relation. The epilogue likely concerns Tomas' departure from his terminus, the transition from disavowal and ignorant damnation towards the insight that damnation is the precondition of the existence of love in man. The silence is no longer about the mute God, but the loveless answer of the human being confronted with the wish to love arising from lovelessness, the wish embodied by Märta. The insights of Tomas and David in the epilogues concern precisely the separation of silence and darkness, that is to say, the lovelessness in the articulation of the word.

Thus, Minus and Märta occupy a privileged position in the films. They search for the holy precisely where it is to be found: in the locality where darkness and silence converge. The opposite is the case for Antonius and Tomas, since they search for God where He is not, resulting in a widening of the gap between silence and darkness.

Hence, we may understand the evolution from *The Seventh Seal* to *Through a Glass Darkly* and *Winter Light*, on the one hand, as the displacement of the absence of God from otherworldly silence towards inner-worldly darkness, and, on the other hand – and this is undoubtedly much more precise – as a transformation of the relation between silence and darkness, a transition from total dissociation towards total unification.

Silence, Darkness, Emptiness

Well then! How can psychoanalysis help us understand the absence of God in the films of Ingmar Bergman?

I

For pedagogical reasons: the ABC of the French tradition of psychoanalysis – RSI. (The reader who is well acquainted with Lacan will not fail to perceive the moment when I begin to diverge from the metapsychological positions commonly attributed to him – note, however, that I never leave the space of possibilities consisting of all the innumerable variations of metapsychological dispositions on the combinatorics of the three orders.[28])

The symbolic order is a network consisting of signifiers whose meaning is overdetermined by their position within the structure, within language. The symbolic is the domicile of the word, the locality where the word is articulated, where the law is legislated and reigns. The symbolic is a domain which constitutes and inscribes the subject within itself, a field which does not belong to the subject it accommodates – the symbolic is the field of the Other.

The imaginary order is a dimension consisting of images whose consistency, totality, purity, unity cannot be attributed to anything outside its reach, but which every imaging nonetheless ascribes to its object. The beyond of the image is fragmented, incoherent, chaotic, violent – the imaginary veils and neutralizes the ungraspable; the recognition of the image misrecognizes the gap separating the picture from the pictured, the form from the formless.

The real order includes undifferentiated "elements" beyond word and image, ex-sisting outside the symbolic and the imaginary. The real is the unthinkable which is not word, not image, the dimension of the subjective experience which reality cannot interiorize, accommodate, neutralize. The real disturbs, distorts, demolishes image, word, reality.

The symbolic, the real, and the imaginary are three separate orders – there are no necessary interdimensional links. We can construct a topic – not to be confused with a topology (here I remain faithful to Freud rather than Lacan) – consisting of three separate orders, and we can think of the separation between them as voids. Where the orders do not converge, where the orders diverge – void. What takes place in these voids? On the one hand: nothing, since they are spaces where elements from the different orders by definition are not. On the other hand we are not afraid to occupy an Epicurean position: *encounters* between elements originating from different worlds – that is, different orders – falling in various directions independently of each other. Thus, every link between elements from different orders is to be understood as a result of a contingent (and not arbitrary) encounter taking place in the voids where the orders diverge.

Let us also postulate that these voids are not only at hand where the orders diverge, but that they also exist within the orders themselves – this is nothing else than claiming that each and every one of the three orders is haunted by an ineradicable incompleteness: "everything is riddled with emptiness."[29] Thus the three orders include *and* organize themselves around cavities impossible to saturate. Let us name these voids and elevate them to the status of concept: *silence* signifies each locality in the symbolic where the word is not, *darkness* each locality in the imaginary where the image is not, *emptiness* each locality in the real where nothing ex-sists. Each void inscribed in the symbolic, imaginary, real corresponds to the concepts silence, darkness, emptiness – the *trinity of void*. Thus, we can think of the voids in between the orders as follows: where the real and the symbolic diverge, emptiness and silence converge; where the real and the imaginary diverge, emptiness and darkness converge; where the symbolic and the imaginary diverge, silence, and darkness converge.

New categories: *void, encounter, divergence-convergence*; new concepts: *silence, darkness, emptiness*.

Let us immerse ourselves in the dynamic effects of the voids on the fields organized around them.

Silence – the signifier perpetually turns around the wordless abyss falling towards the unnameable. Silence is $\bar{A}$, a lack, a gap, a lacuna, a cavity, a hole in the field of the Other, in language. The rotation of the word around nothing creates nothing – *creatio ex nihilo*. Lacan never abandons this position: the signifier drills a hole in the real, creates an emptiness – let us designate this emptiness by $\varnothing$ – without which the signifier cannot oscillate, signify; it envelops a void in its own field ($\bar{A}$) descending towards a void outside of it ($\varnothing$). In other words: the symbolic evacuates an ex-sisting emptiness which it interiorizes. Thus, the word is not without a certain anorectic appetite: the signifier's creation of emptiness is identical with its devourment; the symbolic not only eats the real, it also engorges the emptiness it leaves behind in it.

What takes place in $\bar{A}$? Nothing and no-thing – silence is the place where object *petit a* arises and descends, the place of the ebb and flow of *jouissance*.

How may the signifier embank the real? By signifying $\bar{A}$, that is, creating an $S(\bar{A})$, a signifier for the lack in the Other, for the signifier lacking in the field of the Other. S(A̶) so to speak occupies the center around which the symbolic gravitates.[30]

What, then, is the symbolic order? A distribution of silences falling towards *a* and – if such a signifier is at hand – rising towards S(A̶), silences around which the words whirl and whirl.

But what is S(A̶)? In the artistic situation, the work of art; in the scientific situation, it finds itself foreclosed; in the religious (that is, Oedipal) situation, the signifier summoned in the space where language is empty – the Name(s)-of-the-Father. God is not His name, but the Name-of-the-Father nevertheless functions as the anchoring point of the words, alone able to prevent the disintegration of language, the transformation of silence into a gaping abyss, a black hole. The Name-of-the-Father is not an object of symbolic exchange between subject and the Other, it is the intangible addressee of prayer and lamentation, the lawmaker, the anchoring points of the signifiers repressing and throwing the signifiers into the depths of the vortex. There is no Other of the Other – that is, God – inscribed in the symbolic. The Name-of-the-Father nonetheless occupies the void left by the absent God, the sinkhole of the symbolic, the space where the Word is not, the reverberating silence falling towards the point of extinction of the word. S(A̶) keep vigil over the silence separating the symbolic from the real.

Darkness – the image veils that which is not image, reflects that which veils, synthesizes that which is reflected, superimposes that which is synthesized: consistencies reflecting and merging and superimposing consistencies. The realm of the image rises towards ideality, abstraction – and falls towards darkness. Darkness is the inner emptiness of the mirror, the absence of image, a hole in the synthetic consistency, a fissure running through the totality, an incongruence in the purity of the abstraction. The image reinforces S(A̶), intervenes where the word is not – fantasy, fetish, phobia, idol – but it also veils a void inscribed in its own field, in the field of the ego. The image shrouds the cavity where the image is absent, a hole hidden by mirrors reflecting outwards, by veils covering nothing. Darkness remains unreflected by every image – thus its mirror image is an empty image, the unimaginable mirror Image of the empty mirror. The empty mirror mirroring everything but itself is i(Ø); darkness is the mirror image of the empty mirror – i'(Ø). A rift shows itself in the reflecting shell, the images tumble through darkness towards the non-image, through emptiness permeated by shadow – melancholia – towards fragments and shards which perforate, demolish, pulverize. The mirror turns the image towards the image, its emptiness veils and reveals the nothing dwelling beyond it, the nothing falling towards the shattering, the real. i(Ø) keeps vigil over the darkness separating the imaginary from the real.

What takes place in the space where the symbolic and the imaginary diverge, the space where silence and darkness converge? The unity of the sign is broken. The field of the ego and that of the Other drift apart, a cleavage separates word from image, signifier from signified, law from narcissism, lack from consistency, difference from similarity. The signifier reaches out towards its absent signification, the image towards its absent anchor in the field of meaning: a non-relation between the locality where the gaze and the voice are placed in the Other and where the observed and addressed is localized in the imaginary. The disintegration of the sign destabilizes the effects of the signifier, of the gaze and voice of the Other on the ego – who am I? With the sign, the anchoring point of the ego in the Other slides away – the space where the symbolic and the imaginary diverge is located beyond the reach of the ego–ideal. The ego–ideal, I(A), keeps vigil over the internal fissure of the sign. Ego–ideal – guardian of the sign.

I will postpone my meditations on the phenomena related to *emptiness*.

Let us follow Lacan and localize the passions in the rifts separating the three orders from each other. The passions fuel, force the encounter between elements from the different orders in the voids separating them. Where the imaginary and the real diverge, where darkness and emptiness converge, in the void where the encounter between the image and the formless perforates the consistency of the image and causes its disintegration: hate. Where the symbolic and the real diverge, where silence and emptiness converge, in the void where the encounter between the word and the unnameable opens up a destabilizing hole in the domain of knowledge fueling the rotation of the signifier around it: ignorance. Where the symbolic and the imaginary diverge, where silence and darkness converge, in the void where the encounter between the word and the image – between the field of the ego and the Other – restores the unity of the breached sign, where the encounter takes place in the space where the melancholic darkness veiled beyond the ego and the silence dwelling beyond the words of the Other unify: love.

II

We are now ready to answer our question: Ingmar Bergman's staging of the absence of God takes place within the limits of the trinity of void. Antonius, David, Karin, and Tomas do *not* place silence in the void where the symbolic and the imaginary diverge – the space where love arises – but in the space where the symbolic and the real diverge, the residence of ignorance. In other words: each of them turns towards the silence in which S(A̶) oscillates, the silence where God by definition is not. Antonius and Tomas are seized by ignorance, they must know because they do not want to know, their lamentations are directed to S(A̶) – the Name-of-the-Father – the signifier localized in the place of *Deus absconditus* in the symbolic, the Hole where His Holiness hides; David turns away from love in favor of the production of the work of art, S(A̶); Karin awaits God – the real spider god – referent of S(A̶). What, then, of darkness? Ignorance triumphs over love: they seek to supplement the incomplete symbolic order with S(A̶), the subjects direct their speech towards the beyond of silence and neglect the bond of the word with the imaginary. The symbolic drifts away from the imaginary at the price of a loss of meaning. No encounter takes place in the space of love, the word does not seek its way through the darkness in the direction of the image. The ego immerses itself in its self-centered introversion, becomes increasingly curtained off from and independent of the shared world; the grip of the symbolic on the imaginary "object relation" weakens. Thus the incompleteness of the imaginary order is left without a stable anchorage in the symbolic at hand: the ego finds no supplement in the word and is abandoned to its drift towards Ø, that is through the void where the real and the imaginary diverge, the void where hatred burns. We comprehend the wrath of Antonius and Tomas, the self-hatred of David, the disintegration of the imaginary world of Karin: they seek to force the encounter with the real as a consequence of the neglect of the link between the imaginary and the symbolic. Let us not forget that the space where darkness and emptiness converge is left empty in melancholia: the ego bursts through darkness in pursuit of the lost object which has left a hole in the real. Antonius Block wishes to reflect himself on the visage of the absent god, David and Tomas are tormented by the loss of their wives, Tomas is anguished by the abandonment of the loving mirror god.

Minus wishes to orient himself in the void where i'(Ø) and A converge: the rift of love. The boy's forthcoming transition to man destabilizes the relation between ego–ideal and ideal ego. The transcendence of the gap between Minus', so to speak, boy and adult ego is in need of an anchoring point in I(A) – but Minus encounters only A, the silence of his father. The non-encounter between word and image in the gorge between them animates his longing for the loving articulation of the word. He wishes to reconstitute I(A) in his father, a guide in the symbolic. He seeks to supplement the inconsistency of the ego with the interpellated word – this hinders his fall towards Ø, the ego's descent into melancholia or disintegration. Märta's loving appeal to Tomas – which reflects that of Minus to David – is an attempt to bridge the very same void. She wishes to reach Tomas with words and love, to acquire a response proving that he is capable of receiving her love in order to regain lost meaning, restore the shattered sign. Yes, she gives what she does not have to someone who does not want it. Minus and Märta await the encounter with *not God*, making it possible for God to respawn in man. The insights of David and Tomas are precisely about the neglect of this void: hatred and ignorance at the price of love.

With Märta, the problematic of transcendence is obliterated; the distance she seeks to transcend is not that to the Other of the Other, but that between herself and the Other, Tomas. Martin is perhaps to be regarded as her predecessor. Minus also finds himself seized by the same question, in his case to complete the leap leading to adulthood. Their dramas first and foremost orbit around love *and* speech. The opposite is the case for Antonius, David, Karin, Tomas – a neglect of love in favor of its beyond.

Briefly concerning *The Silence*. The displacement from *The Seventh Seal* via *Through a Glass Darkly* to *Winter Light* is a relocation of the absence of God culminating in a substitution of the divergence for the convergence of silence and darkness. The transcendent Father–god in the beyond of silence–darkness may or may not abandon man, thereafter he may or may not resurrect as love in the union of silence and darkness. In *The Silence*, God has neither died nor resurrected; it is a temporal no-man's land where abandonment–resurrection is not even absent, where the holy is not even neglected. It is just not there. Christ is not even confined within the cave. Nobody searches for that which is nowhere to be found. Neither plea for the Name-of-the-Father (silence–emptiness) nor wish to love (silence–darkness). Neither S(Å) nor I(A). *The Silence* stages the untying – rather, not-tying – of the links of the symbolic to the other orders, letting the symbolic drift away from the fragile "unity" of the imaginary and the real; it is the farewell of the symbolic. What remains? Complete lovelessness and lack of meaning; melancholia and hatred; no law, no castration, no sublimation, only – as in the demise of Karin – emptiness overflowed by limitless *jouissance*. *The Silence* is the epitaph of the absent god in the works of Bergman, a mute, final inscription of the dispersed synchronous divergence–convergence of the voids – but it must not, of course, be overlooked that his later films are permeated by the fantasmatic presence of this absence.

The split absence of the Christian God in the films of Ingmar Bergman – on the one hand, His hiddenness beyond the dissociated silence and darkness, on the other, the non-event in the rift where silence and darkness converge – reflects the distribution of the voids in the subject: the human being either searches for the unnameable and finds – in the best of cases – nothing, or reconciles with the absence of God in the world as the precondition for His resurrection as love in the encounter between human beings. The absence of God is either to be understood as the separation of silence and darkness in unity with emptiness, or as a unity of silence and darkness without emptiness.

In the end, nothing remains other than these very chasms.

III

How shall we comprehend the absence of God in the films of Ingmar Bergman? On the one hand we could speak of the staging of this absence – the commentary above is such an attempt. But on the other hand we could speak of the absence in the staging of the absence – that is, what is actually absent in the very films. Let us take on the latter question.

An observation: except the case of Karin, nothing takes place in the space where darkness and emptiness converge. Karin's encounter with the spider god nonetheless remains invisible for the viewer. Nobody finds God, nobody meets God. The movement from separation to unity – which in some respect reflects the leap from the Hebrew Bible to the New Testament – is perhaps not solely a reconciliation with the non-existence (or eternal hiddenness) of the transcendent god, with love as the presence of the holy in the encounter between human beings. Perhaps it is also a disregard, or even a repression, of the phenomena pertaining to emptiness.

First and foremost: the sphere of phenomena of the real includes trauma, enjoyment, pain, anxiety – a presence without absence which destabilizes, knocks out, destroys word and image. It should be noted that none of the above-mentioned phenomena directly involve the real void. The presence of the real by definition implies that an absence of absence is at hand, that is, that emptiness is not "present." Perhaps this is a trace of the influence of Aristotle and Spinoza on Lacan, of their rejection of the thesis of the existence of the void in the world. It is, however, not inaccurate to argue that emptiness has no phenomena *of its own* in the works of Lacan. Let us immerse ourselves in this.

What is emptiness? Emptiness is perhaps the most unexplored non-concept of French psychoanalysis. We are acquainted with the position of Lacan on this question: only the signifier can create a hole in the real, there can be no emptiness without it. The real is by definition "full," without absence. The signifier creates and interiorizes emptiness within itself, transforms a region of this emptiness into the silence from which the symbolic surges – the symbolic is the dimension of the hole.

In addition to this perspective which Lacan reiterates on several occasions, he speaks only twice of the real void. In his fourth seminar: privation is a real lack of a symbolic object. In his sixth seminar: the loss leaves a void in the real, the work of mourning consists in its conquest by the signifier – the loss is strictly speaking the inverse of foreclosure. He never returns to these theses and their implications. Probably because they have not found their place in his metapsychology. Probably because they resist being incorporated into his metapsychology. Probably, emptiness lets itself function as object for a reading directed towards the conditions of the absence in the text, which thinks of the absence as a symptom of the theory in which it is excluded, that is, confined. This is not the place to make such an in-depth reading, nor to dwell upon the theoretical preconditions and implications of the ex-sistence of an independent emptiness. I will jump to the heart of the matter: I want to postulate that emptiness "ex-sists" in its own right. It presumes that the real in itself is not "full," that it contains a primordial emptiness which is not an effect of either word or image. Let us define it: *the non-effects of ex-sistence on the field of subjectivity.*

Lacan's affirmative meditations on emptiness concern the abyss separating the signifier from the real, the hole encircled by signifiers. Something remains to be said about the space where darkness and emptiness converge. What can take place in this locality? We could speak of the forced encounter: hate. We could speak of a non-forced encounter caused by the contingent emergence of a real object with demolishing effects on the image: trauma. We could speak of the non-event: melancholia. But we could also speak of a contingent emergence of an object arriving from the real *without* reaching the imaginary – an encounter at a distance, an encounter without encounter, an almost-encounter. How should we understand this? On the one hand, that the arriving object does not correspond to any image or signification that the subject carries. On the other hand, that the object does not reach and obliterate the image. It is an encounter without encounter with a real object where the non-encounter of the encounter implies a non-fragmentation, in the extreme scenario non-annihilation.

I would now like to draw the silhouette of the most disruptive subjective experience among all possible variations of the encounter which takes place in the void where the real and the imaginary diverge. If we meditate on the capacity that the state in question possesses to mark a human being for life, it is, to say the least, remarkable that so few psychoanalysts have dwelled upon it. It regards a state without which mysticism, nature, religion, and art remain shrouded in obscurity: *awe*.

Awe is a disposition bearing evidence of an encounter in a void completely outside the reach of the symbolic, an encounter in the void separating the imaginary from the real. In awe, the subject is overwhelmed by a feeling of *being but touched by an enigmatic, ungraspable Otherness which does not reflect him*. A real void separates the subject from the effects of the encounter with the object of awe, an ex-sisting object which the sphere of images and significations that he bears cannot mirror. Indeed, in many cases the absence of the real void in the encounter with the object of awe would have resulted in horror, trauma, extinction. Awe is an effect of an encounter with the real through two superposed voids, the one real and the other imaginary; an encounter which, due to the non-effects of the real void, petrifies the subject in a state of non-encounter, and, due to the non-effects of the imaginary void, in a state of *import without import*: he cannot yet discern the inapprehensible signification of the experience which in a double sense mirrors nothing. Perplexed by horrifying wonder before the unfathomable, the human being is thrown into a state of liberating, ethereal resignation, an incomparable humility, a serene yet redeeming gratitude, in the encounter with that which without annihilating him reduces him to nothingness. Awe is to be grasped as the human being's vertiginous encounter with the unthinkable objectivity of the subjective non-existence induced by an encounter in the void with the *nihilating ex-sistence of Otherness*.

In the singular, timeless event of awe, an-Other space opens up for man, outside language, beyond the real void and all the imprinting effects of the mirror image. Awe is in essence a mystical experience of being but tangent to a foreign dimension that suddenly becomes inscribed in the field of subjectivity. Thus, awe is to be understood as an encounter with the Other of the Other, who does not exist, but who precisely *can* ex-sist in the encounter in the void outside, and not within, the symbolic.

There is no relation between subject and object in pure awe. The object touches, but does not relate to the subject. Hence the overwhelming feeling of mercy in the nihilating event. The object of awe is, so to speak, unrelentingly autoerotic; its movement stands in relation only to itself. The enigmatic object of awe is an inwardly vaulted mirror, its hidden interior multiplies the ungraspable truth converging in its absent focus, in the event of awe open before the hypnotized gaze of man who, if only for an ephemeral second, discerns the contrapuntal movement of the unfathomable force in its own indifferent closedness.

Awe – the encounter with the mysterious in the void outside the reach of language – is the very phenomenological foundation of polytheism, animism. It is trivial to point out that the consolidation of monotheism superficially appears to be a sort of repression of the gods by the God – but not that the substitution in question is equivalent to a dislodging of the absence of the holy from a void outside language to a void within it. "The gods belong to the field of the real,"[31] only insofar as they have retreated from reality and return in the Event *through* their residual emptiness. Monotheism is a prosaic interiorization of the absence of divinity, a prosaic centralization of a symbolic disorder without center (in many ways not significantly different from the dispersed polyatheistic symbolic disorder of our times). The silence of the unnameable replaces the awe of the unimaginable: God is subtracted from the sphere of phenomena of the gods. Nowhere is this more apparent than in the *First Book of Kings*, where the absence of God is "present" in the encounter with the phenomena which in the animistic epoch were experienced as the gods; where the presence of God in the place of the gods is mediated by the voice arriving from the beyond of silence:

> A great and powerful wind tore the mountains apart and shattered the rocks before the Lord, but the Lord was not in the wind. After the wind there was an earthquake, but the Lord was not in the earthquake. After the earthquake came a fire, but the Lord was not in the fire. After the fire came a gentle whisper. When Elijah heard it, he pulled his cloak over his face and went out and stood at the mouth of the cave. Then a voice [i.e. the voice of the Lord] said to him ...[32]

The revelations of the gods are reduced to God's foreplay. The presence of the gods in the event is denied, the conception of the presence of the gods in the world in the occurrence of the encounter is repressed by the signifying element keeping vigil over the thunderous silence in the focus of the symbolic. Perhaps it is not inaccurate to claim that we can think of the absence of God in terms of silence and darkness, but we should not forget to note the imperceptible *emptiness* which is always–already there – the event's *non-occurrence* removing and alienating and liberating man from the nihilating enigmatic *poetic* effects of awe and horror.

IV

The staging of the absence of God in the films of Ingmar Bergman can be grasped as the disjunction and conjunction of silence and darkness; I would like to claim that the absence of God in the staging of the absence of God is first and foremost emptiness. When does the event take place? It is probably not inaccurate to claim – never. Neither in the above-mentioned films nor elsewhere. In other words: apart from the forced encounter – hate – *nothing occurs* in the void where the imaginary and the real diverge. Melancholia is the organ point of the films, its unmistakable ubiquity cannot be comprehended only as effects of silence and darkness: we must not forget the total *hiddenness* of emptiness – emptiness eludes attention for the simple reason that it never functions as a space where anything takes place.[33]

Hence the absence of God in the real in the films of Ingmar Bergman is *the absence of the gods*. Stated differently: *nature* – or its unimaginable equivalents – has been subtracted from the realities in which the films of Bergman take place, realities which could not have been constituted were it not for the imperceptible emptiness left behind by the complete foreclosure of their intrusive reverse. This is as true for the films of Bergman as for every purely intracultural or humanistic standpoint regarding the place of the human being in the world. Beyond the prevalent correlation between Bergman's framing of the absence of God and the theme of the death of God, we should not forget to discern its indiscernible undercurrent and repressed historical predecessor: *Great Pan is dead.*

God is stillborn. Nietzsche's proclamation but reaffirms the posthumous assassination of The Desurrected. The gods always return. *Vere vos estis di absconditi.*

Let us now hastily turn towards Ingmar Bergman:

> Creating films is a detailed, planned illusion, the reflection of a reality which I find more and more illusory.
>
> When film is not document it is dream. Thus Tarkovsky is the greatest of them all. He moves naturally in the room of dreams, he does not explain, and what is there really to explain? He is a watcher who has been able to stage his visions in the heaviest but also the most willing of mediums. I have all my life knocked on the door to the rooms where he moves so naturally. Only a handful of times have I managed to sneak in. Most of my conscious efforts have resulted in embarrassing failures.[34]

Bergman himself underlines his inability to stage the ungraspable, the dreamlike scenery where nothing needs to or lets itself be explained. I wish to propose that the dream is not only a rebus, an interpretable product of the distorting permutations and operations of the signifier. There is a beyond of the other scene within the dream: given that it has been evacuated, it is an empty not-yet-theater where the event can take place. We must invert Freud's metaphor from *The Interpretation of Dreams*: the gods arrive from the depths of the unknown through the inner vacuity of the navel. *The dream takes place in the void where the real, the symbolic and the imaginary diverge.* The dream is as much rebus as work of art – how do you decipher a painting by Rothko? The dimension of awe is not absent in the work of art, in the dream. There is doubtless something in the films of Andrei Tarkovsky which is hidden or missing in those of Ingmar Bergman which seldom, if ever, induce awe, vertigo, grace, or enigmatic and occasionally overwhelming redemption. This *something* which separates them resists every definition; it is nothing and no-thing, no-thing in nothing; it can vaguely be referred to by the definite plural noun *the gods* (think of the presence of nature in the poetic scenery in Tarkovsky's films). This lack which Bergman ascribes to himself should by no means be understood as a deficit in his works; perhaps its absence functions as one of the fundaments for the specificity of his staging of the absence of God, as well as in general; the hiddenness of emptiness contributes to the all-pervasive melancholic atmosphere of his films.

Why this difference between Tarkovsky and Bergman? Perhaps one of the keys is Bergman's *prosaic melancholia*, the above-mentioned documentation of an illusory reality:

I possess a vast arsenal of explanations for every feeling, every motion, every bodily disposition, why I use precisely these words. One nods understandingly, it must be precisely like that! Yet I fall head-long through the abyss of life, it sounds quite grand: I fall head-long through the abyss of life. But the abyss is a fact, it is furthermore bottomless, one does not even get crushed in a stony ravine or against a water mirror.[35]

The abyss of life – the fall through darkness towards the unimaginable; the fall through bottomless emptiness permeated by shadows of no-thing; the fall towards the absent image wrecked under the opaque surface of the specular water; the fall beyond the reach of the dream towards the demolishing gorge. Bergman's account is illuminating and exact (it must be precisely like that!): there is an unbridgeable gap between the void outside language – the empty space of melancholia, the space where the imaginary and the real diverge – and the field where prosaic speech is articulated. Neither explanation nor passion is capable of forcing distance between them. But how should we understand the inaccessibility of this abyss? Perhaps there was no open path enabling Bergman to wander between his melancholic residence and the domain of prosaic language, a passage which would, through the resonance of poetic speech in the void outside language, enable melancholia to pass over into mourning. The vacuity of melancholia remained a sealed asphyxiating timeless prison where nothing ever ceased to not occur:

> As a child I was an enthusiastic weeper. Mother saw through the tears and punished me. I stopped crying. Occasionally I perceive a lunatic howl deep down in the mine, only the echo reaches me, it gets to me without forewarning. A desperate howling child, trapped for eternity.[36]

Notes

1 1 Gen 1:3. The biblical citations throughout the text are retrieved from the New International Version (NIV).
2 John 1:1–5.
3 John 1:14.
4 1 John 4:8.
5 Isa 45:15.
6 Job 23:3–9.
7 Ps 22:1–2.
8 Nicholas of Cusa, "On the Hidden God (De Deo Abscondito)," in *A Miscellany on Nicholas of Cusa*, trans. Jasper Hopkins (Minneapolis: Arthur J. Banning Press, 1994), pp. 300–305.
9 "In order that there may be room for faith, it is necessary that everything which is believed should be hidden. It cannot, however, be more deeply hidden than under an object, perception, or experience which is contrary to it. Thus, when God makes alive, God does it by killing; when God justifies, God does it by making human beings guilty; when God exalts to heaven by bringing down to hell [...]. Thus God hides divine eternal goodness and mercy under eternal wrath, God's righteousness under iniquity." Martin Luther, *The Bondage of the Will* (Minneapolis: Fortress Press, 2016), p. 178,

also pp. 209–214. See particularly theses 20 and 21 in Martin Luther, *Heidelberg Disputation*, transl. Aaron T. Fenker (Holt: Higher Things, 2018).

10 Blaise Pascal, *Pascal's Pensées*, trans. W. F. Trotter (New York: Dutton, 1958), p. 155.
11 Pascal, *Pascal's Pensées*, p. 198.
12 Pascal, *Pascal's Pensées*, p. 61, 148.
13 Pascal, *Pascal's Pensées*, p. 186.
14 Ingmar Bergman, *Bilder* (*Images*) (Stockholm: Norstedts, 1990), p. 246.
15 "In that time I still bore some withered remains of a childish piety, an entirely naïve idea of what one could call an otherworldly salvation. At the same time, my current conviction had manifested itself. The human being bears his own Holiness and it is inner-worldly, it has no otherworldly explanations." Bergman, *Bilder* (*Images*), pp. 237–238.
16 "In *Through a Glass Darkly* the legacy from my childhood was obliterated." Bergman, *Bilder* (*Images*), p. 238.
17 "Somewhere it is written and often repeated that god is love but for me it becomes more serene and pure if I let myself say that love is god. Love is life and lovelessness is death, this I know from my own bitter experience. To live in love is to be enveloped in a god. We fall so easily outside the womb of this god since the dwelling in love requires the termination of every inborn primitive conception about self-preservation in a corporal as well as a spiritual sense. Now, love is a living reality and thus god is a living reality. The more I can merge with this reality the more natural words such as immortality, eternity and forgiveness become." Ingmar Bergman, *Arbetsboken 1955–1974* (*Workbook 1955–1974*) (Stockholm: Norstedts, 2018), p. 102.
18 1 Cor 13:11–12.
19 "These three films are about a reduction. *Through a Glass Darkly* – conquered certainty. *Winter Light* – penetrated certainty. *Silence* – the Silence of God – the negative imprint. Thus they constitute a trilogy." Ingmar Bergman, *Filmberättelser 1. Såsom i en spegel. Nattvardsgästerna. Tystnaden.* (*Film Stories 1. Through a Glass Darkly. Winter Light. The Silence.*) (Stockholm: Pan/Norstedts, 1973), p. 4.
20 "Every conception of god created by humans must be a monster." Bergman, *Bilder* (*Images*), p. 238.
21 "With *Winter Light* I end the religious debate and account for the result. This is less important for the viewer than for myself. The film is a tomb over a painful conflict which have run like a agonized lord through my conscious life. The images of the gods are crushed since my experience of man as bearer of a holy purpose has been annihilated. The operation is finally completed." Bergman, *Arbetsboken 1955–1974* (*Workbook 1955–1974*), p. 162.
22 "The Pastor is dying emotionally. He exists beyond love, in fact beyond all human relations. His hell, and he really lives in hell, is his insight in his situation. Together with his wife he maintained a kind of poem. The poem was called 'God is love and love is God.'" Bergman, *Bilder* (*Images*), p. 265.
23 See footnote 19.
24 Bergman summarizes the transition as follows: "First the image of god originating in upbringing, need for safety and general fear of the dark. The deity of self-suggestion. Then silence, turning away, emptiness, desolation, impuissance. Then the new faith which is a knowing. At least a trace or a glimpse of it. A something to start with. A leap or a spark. Onwards: Märta is seized by love. In this love grows the seed of rebirth of Tomas' image of god." Bergman, *Arbetsboken 1955–1974*, p. 120.
25 "If now the Knight is to die without delay and knows that these are his last hours which he has to fight for like a madman, then he suddenly finds that life bears an ungraspable beauty – a beauty which Mia communicates in their pastoral scene. [...]. Life is a treasure. Life is a treasure! What a bottomless banality. Come up with something better. If you can. Try to write this movie in such a way that it is consistent with your experience

but yet with new vomits. Try!" Bergman, *Arbetsboken 1955–1974* (*Workbook 1955–1974*), p. 24.

26 Formulated in terms of logical operators: the holy is the relative complement (difference) of Light and Word; the holy is Light \ Word, that is, Light *and* not Word.

27 The relative complement in *The Seventh Seal* is substituted by a logical conjunction: the holy is light ∧ word, love *and* speech.

28 This chapter was written in 2019. Some of the perspectives which I put forward here have since been modified.

29 Lucretius, *The Nature of Things* (London: Penguin Books, 2007), p. 13.

30 This symbol seems to have a somewhat fluid signification through Lacan's teaching. My utilization of it only partially overlaps with Lacan's, as I use it as a general term designating supplementary signifiers situated in the place where there are no signifiers which are related to the problematics of sublimation in general, that is, primarily, to religion, art, and science.

31 In Jacques Lacan, *The Seminar of Jacques Lacan Book XI*, trans. Alan Sheridan (New York: W. W. Norton & Company, 1998), p. 45.

32 1 King 19:11–13.

33 We must nevertheless note that the emptiness is referenced once in *The Seventh Seal*, even though it remains outside the field of vision of the viewer. When the crestfallen entourage witness the consummation by fire of the young witch, the despairing squire cries out: "Who will take care of that child? Is it the angels or God or Satan or just emptiness? Emptiness, Sire! … Look at her eyes. Her poor consciousness is perceiving something. Emptiness under the moon."

34 Bergman, *Lanterna Magica* (Stockholm, Norstedts, 1987), pp. 88–89.

35 Bergman, *Lanterna Magica*, p. 332.

36 Bergman, *Lanterna Magica*, p. 55.

Index

For Product Safety Concerns and Information please contact our EU
representative GPSR@taylorandfrancis.com
Taylor & Francis Verlag GmbH, Kaufingerstraße 24, 80331 München, Germany

www.ingramcontent.com/pod-product-compliance
Lightning Source LLC
Chambersburg PA
CBHW071413290326
41932CB00047B/2817